LATIN AMERICA AND THE MULTINATIONAL DRUG TRADE

INSTITUTE OF LATIN AMERICAN STUDIES SERIES

General Editor: Victor Bulmer-Thomas, Professor of Economics and Director, Institute of Latin American Studies, University of London

The Institute of Latin American Studies, a member of the School of Advanced Study of the University of London, was founded in 1965. The Institute is dedicated to research on Latin America in the social sciences and humanities. The purpose of this series is to disseminate to a wide audience the new work based on the research programmes and projects organised by academic staff and Associate Fellows of the Institute of Latin American Studies.

Victor Bulmer-Thomas (*editor*)
THE NEW ECONOMIC MODEL IN LATIN AMERICA AND ITS IMPACT ON INCOME DISTRIBUTION AND POVERTY

Victor Bulmer-Thomas, Nikki Craske and Mónica Serrano (*editors*)
MEXICO AND THE NORTH AMERICAN FREE TRADE AGREEMENT: WHO WILL BENEFIT?

Elizabeth Joyce and Carlos Malamud (*editors*)
LATIN AMERICA AND THE MULTINATIONAL DRUG TRADE

Walter Little and Eduardo Posada-Carbó (*editors*)
POLITICAL CORRUPTION IN EUROPE AND LATIN AMERICA

Eduardo Posada-Carbó (*editor*)
COLOMBIA: THE POLITICS OF REFORMING THE STATE
ELECTIONS BEFORE DEMOCRACY: THE HISTORY OF ELECTIONS IN EUROPE AND LATIN AMERICA

Rachel Sieder (*editor*)
CENTRAL AMERICA: FRAGILE TRANSITION

John Weeks (*editor*)
STRUCTURAL ADJUSTMENT AND THE AGRICULTURAL SECTOR IN LATIN AMERICA AND THE CARIBBEAN

Latin America and the Multinational Drug Trade

Edited by

Elizabeth Joyce
Fulbright Scholar and Visiting Researcher
Georgetown University
Washington, DC

and

Carlos Malamud
Director of the Contemporary Latin America Programme
Instituto Universitario Ortega y Gasset
Madrid

in association with
INSTITUTE OF LATIN AMERICAN STUDIES
UNIVERSITY OF LONDON

First published in Great Britain 1998 by
MACMILLAN PRESS LTD
Houndmills, Basingstoke, Hampshire RG21 6XS and London
Companies and representatives throughout the world

A catalogue record for this book is available from the British Library.

ISBN 0–333–71551–9

First published in the United States of America 1998 by
ST. MARTIN'S PRESS, INC.,
Scholarly and Reference Division,
175 Fifth Avenue, New York, N.Y. 10010

ISBN 0–312–17615–5

Library of Congress Cataloging-in-Publication Data
Latin America and the multinational drug trade / edited by Elizabeth
Joyce and Carlos Malamud.
p. cm. — (Institute of Latin American studies series)
Includes bibliographical references and index.
ISBN 0–312–17615–5 (cloth)
1. Drug traffic—Economic aspects—Latin America. 2. Drug
traffic—Government policy—Latin America. 3. Narcotics, Control
of—Latin America. 4. Political corruption—Latin America.
5. Money laundering—Latin America. 6. Latin America—Politics and
government. 7. Latin America—Foreign relations. I. Joyce,
Elizabeth, 1961– . II. Malamud, Carlos. III. Series.
HV5840.L3L37 1997
363.4'5'098—dc21   97–18828
                                                             CIP

This book is printed on paper suitable for recycling and made from fully managed and
sustained forest sources.

10   9   8   7   6   5   4   3   2   1
07   06   05   04   03   02   01   00   99   98

Printed and bound in Great Britain by
Antony Rowe Ltd, Chippenham, Wiltshire

CONTENTS

LIST OF CONTRIBUTORS

Andy Atkins is a Researcher at the Catholic Institute for International Relations, London.

Fernando Cepeda Ulloa is previous Minister of Government and Communication in Colombia, and previous Colombian Ambassador to London. He is currently the director of the magazine *Estrategia*.

Elizabeth Joyce is a Fulbright Senior Scholar at the Department of Government, Georgetown University, and the Center for International and Security Studies at the University of Maryland.

Roberto Lerner is Managing Director of Lerner and Lerner Psychological Services and Associate Professor at the Catholic University of Lima.

Anthony Maingot is Professor of Sociology at Florida International University and Senior Research Associate at the North-South Center of the University of Miami. His most recent book is *The United States and The Caribbean* (London, 1994).

Carlos Malamud is Professor of American History at the Universidad Nacional de Educación a Distancia and Director of the Contemporary Latin America Programme at the Instituto Universitario Ortega y Gasset, Madrid.

Jorge Orlando Melo is a Colombian Historian and currently Director of the Biblioteca Luis Angel Arango, Bogotá. He was Presidential Adviser for the development of Medellín during the Gaviria administration (1990-94).

Augusto Pérez Gómez is Professor of Psychology and Director of the 'La Casa' Programme at the Universidad de los Andes, Bogotá.

Peter Reuter is a Professor in the School of Public Affairs and the Department of Criminology at the University of Maryland.

María Celia Toro is Head of the Centro de Estudios Internacionales of El Colegio de México and author of *Mexico's "War" on Drugs* (New York, 1995).

LIST OF TABLES

LIST OF FIGURES

PREFACE

Elizabeth Joyce and Carlos Malamud

The contributions to this volume were presented in their original versions at a conference in Toledo, Spain, on 9 and 10 January 1995 entitled *El narcotráfico en Europa y América Latina: una industria multinacional* (Drug Trafficking in Europe and Latin America: A Multinational Industry). The conference was organised jointly by the Institute of Latin American Studies (ILAS) of the University of London, the Instituto Universitario Ortega y Gasset (IUOG), Madrid, and the Institute for European-Latin American Relations (IRELA), with the support of the British Council in Madrid, and the Spanish Ministry of Education and Culture (State Secretariat for Universities and Research).

The USA has long been concerned about illicit drugs cultivated in Latin America and in the last ten years has spent some $17 billion on international operations and programmes aimed at preventing these drugs penetrating its borders. Consequently, the USA's influence over Western Hemispheric drug control has ensured that the literature in English usually analyses the Latin American drug trade from the perspective of US foreign policy. The intention of the conference coordinators was to create the opportunity for a fresh approach. They brought together academics, analysts and policy-makers from Europe and Latin America (Anthony Maingot of Florida International University and Peter Reuter of the University of Maryland being the two distinguished US exceptions) who might together analyse the effects of illicit drug production, trafficking and consumption on the countries of Latin America and Europe, and the implications they have for domestic policies and international cooperation. In particular, they intended that the debate should include appropriate examination of the extent and consequences of the *demand* for illicit drugs in both regions, a feature of the multinational drug trade which is too readily neglected in discussion of policies designed to address the *supply* of drugs but which is necessarily an important determinant of policy.

The proceedings of the conference were enriched by the contributions made by María Emma Mejía, then Colombia's Ambassador to Spain, Aldo Lale-Demoz, of the United Nations Drug Control Programme in Vienna, Carlos López Riaño, representative of the Spanish government in the Plan Nacional contra la Droga, Alain Wallon, from L'Observatoire Géopolitique des Drogues in Paris, Alvaro Tirado Mejía, Colombian Ambassador to Switzerland, Andrew Crawley, Deputy Director of IRELA, and Javier Zaragoza, Teniente Fiscal at the Fiscalía Especial para la Prevención y Represión del Tráfico de Drogas in Madrid.

The conference coordinators, Eduardo Posada-Carbó of ILAS and Carlos Malamud of IUOG, would like to thank the British Council and the Spanish Ministry of Education and Culture for their generous support of the Toledo conference. Thanks are also due to the staff of the Fundación Ortega y Gasset's Centro de Estudios Internacionales 'San Juan de la Penitencia' in Toledo, where the conference was held. María Eugenia Marín of IRELA lent valuable assistance in planning, Montserrat Gutiérrez and Cayetana Mora of IUOG provided administrative skills which ensured the conference's success, and Emilio Lamo de Espinosa, Wolf Grabendorff and Victor Bulmer-Thomas, Directors of IUOG, IRELA and ILAS respectively, gave enthusiastic support before, during and after the event.

The editors of this volume would like to thank Pam Decho, Patricia Roberts and Simon Webb, who translated from Spanish several of the chapters reproduced here. The support provided to Elizabeth Joyce by the US-EU Fulbright Program in Brussels is gratefully acknowledged. She is also grateful for the institutional support offered during the final stages of the project by Eusebio Mujal-León, Chair of the Department of Government at Georgetown University, and Frances G. Burwell, Executive Director of the Center for International and Security Studies at the University of Maryland. Lastly, the editors acknowledge with thanks the expert administrative and editorial assistance of Tony Bell at ILAS.

INTRODUCTION*

Fernando Cepeda Ulloa

At a time when multilateral financial institutions and organisations are considering the problem of governability, it seems only appropriate to introduce a discussion of the Latin American drug trade with some reflections upon the serious threat that organised international crime poses for the state under the rule of law, that is for governability. This threat can be critical for developing countries but also affects industrialised countries. The corruption it encourages creates the scandals that destroy citizens' faith in politics and generate apathy and cynicism.

Factors Which Favour the Drug Barons

These include: the weakness of the legal system, a favourable environment, the reputation of power, and the lack of an effective international anti-drugs strategy. Let us briefly consider each of these points.

If one thing has become obvious during the fight against the drug cartels, it has been the weakness, if one wants to avoid calling it the incompetence, of the judicial and legal systems, both at national and international level. It can be stated with certainty that neither the penal code with its categorisation of offences, nor the system of evidence, nor the procedures for mutual legal assistance between countries, nor common jurisdiction, nor the traditional protection afforded lawyers and witnesses, have been sufficient to combat the criminal organisations linked to the drug trade. What is true of criminal jurisdiction is also true in other areas of the legal system: customs regulations, air and transport regulations, import and export regulations, the regulation of private security firms etc., are not always capable of resisting the drug cartels. Many aspects of legal systems around the world simply have not been designed to fight international organised crime, much less organisations of the size, wealth and brutality which characterise the modern drug cartels.

National systems have been inadequate, but the international legal system, admittedly less developed, has been even less capable of containing the threat. The measures which have been designed have still not borne any fruit and, in my humble opinion, are too complex and too difficult to apply. The international community is a long way from creating the appropriate mechanisms to counter the criminal capability of the international drug cartels. The cartels have been able to take advantage of legal systems which, because of their ineffectiveness, complexity and inadequacy, do not represent a threat to their business and, on occasions, even become allies of the drug cartels. In this way, the judicial systems, instead of being a deterrent to the criminal conduct of the cartels, are becoming a joke, or rather another resource of power or a factor which facilitates the use of the resources of power. Hardly ever, unless at a very high cost, do they act as a deterrent.

This explains the formidable effort which has been made in recent years, both on the international and the domestic front, to introduce new criminal legislation and even to adopt unorthodox methods of applying the law, alien to the traditions of some legal systems, such as the practice of using judges whose identity is protected in the Colombian case. This worthy task of creating new legal institutions is tantamount to a recognition that legal systems were inadequate to the task of counteracting this form of criminality. It remains to be seen just how effective these innovations prove to be. However, there are reasons for cautious optimism.

Things would be very different if the drug cartels encountered a world in which drug consumption was non-existent. Their work would not be as easy as it is now where there exists an insatiable demand. When demand subsides in one area, it emerges in another; when users tire of one drug, another becomes fashionable. But since the desire for consumption is joined by a drugs culture promoted by the media, endemic poverty and an excessive longing for easy enrichment, the ineffectiveness of the justice system and the tolerance of criminal conduct, the absence of public debate and the loss of traditional values, then we are faced with a scenario in which organised international crime and the drug barons count on a more than favourable climate for the growth, success and consolidation of their infamous business.

One of the main factors that has contributed to the expansion of the drugs business and the criminal conduct of its exploiters is the growing belief in the invincibility of the drug barons. The drug barons are becoming 'untouchable'. The international criminal organisations acquire legendary, almost mythical, characteristics. Their reputation for power becomes even greater to the extent that it goes in tandem with the state's reputation for impotence. Even the incarceration of leaders of the Cali cartel in Colombia has not destroyed their reputations in this regard. The trade continues to flourish. Sometimes the state appears less competent than it really is.

Successful operations must often be kept quiet to safeguard the lives of those involved. This may explain the conflicting versions reported in the media about the more successful operations: these are frequently trumpeted by those who run fewer risks, detracting from the just desserts that should be given to the national agents who prefer anonymity to a success which could prove mortal. This, then, is how the idea of the ineffectiveness and the impotence of the state and national society, and the reputation of the power of the cartels is reinforced, because in the eyes of the public it seems that the intervention of international law enforcement agencies is needed to achieve success (e.g. the outstanding actions of the British Special Air Service (SAS), the US Central Intelligence Agency (CIA), the US Drug Enforcement Administration (DEA) or INTERPOL). It is here that the domestic and the international media have a serious responsibility which they do not always exercise with due care.

I am convinced that there is not, and has not been, an effective anti-drugs strategy, or any strategy at all. The United Nations (UN) global action programme, the London declaration, the UN International Drug Control Programme (UNDCP), which is a reformulation of the previously existing UN organisations, do not constitute a convincing strategy against drugs. Not only does the organisation charged with executing the global programme of action lack the essential resources, but there exists no clear awareness in many countries of the scope of this agenda nor of the importance of its implementation. Any urgent demand that it should operate with the maximum human and financial resources available is absent. There is often a sense of urgency in bilateral rather than multilateral relations but, in my opinion, only when there exists a real multilateral strategy, that is, one equipped with appropriate economic and human resources operating within an adequate legal system, can one talk of an effective global strategy. In the absence of such an international effort and of an effective international response, the Latin American drug cartels – admittedly with some difficulties – manage the cultivation of coca, opium poppy or marijuana, the import of chemical agents, and the supply of consumers throughout the world with the desired merchandise. They ensure that the distributors receive the earnings they require, that the air routes allow them to reach distant markets in spite of radar and border controls, and that the huge profits their trade generates enter the international financial system and are always readily available in the quantities and type of currency appropriate to the circumstances. In other words, even with the odd setback, the international criminal drug organisations and the barons can rely on an international environment favourable to their monstrous activity.

Naturally, the cartels do not want information made available that is unfavourable to their image and, above all, they do not want the media to call for or to applaud government actions against them. Moreover, they want the media to collaborate in their public relations campaigns by misinforming the public. The cartels are also interested in maintaining their image of omnipotence, untouchability and invincibility, whilst the government, the police and judges continue to appear impotent, weak, wrong, antipatriotic or as instruments of US policy. And in the case of the judges, the alternatives are to submit, to disappear, not to act or to pay with their lives. Although in many cases it is clear who has run the risks, who has suffered, who has died, it is not always clear who has been in the service of the cartels. It is a story that still remains untold.

Public opinion is important for Latin American drug traffickers. The criminal organisations have sought to sway it in their favour or at least against the national or international anti-drugs policies. To this end, several key arguments are employed, for example the following:

- Nationalism; the drug problem 'is not ours'; the war against drugs is 'someone else's war';
- drugs help the economy and improve the well-being of the poor;
- the war against drugs is an impossible war to win (linked to the drug barons' legendary omnipotence and untouchability);
- the real enemy is the USA; and the USA is hostile to Latin America and pursues its drugs policy on that basis;
- confrontation aggravates the problem;
- the army should not participate in the fight against drugs; it must be protected from corruption and the militarisation of society must be prevented, thus avoiding the risk of coups, or greater interference by the military in the decision-making process.

The aim is to create a climate of despondency, of failure, which seeks to weaken the position of governments and, if possible, to delegitimise them. These and other arguments, used jointly or individually, depending on the circumstances, give the drug cartels the role of genuinely active agents in political life, with the advantage that the promotion of counter arguments, as already known, carries risks. I believe this to be one of the least considered dimensions of the action of the drug cartels when it comes to formulating a coherent international anti-drugs policy. I do not intend to suggest that the academics, politicians or public commentators who have produced serious and responsible studies on some of the aforementioned subjects are in the service of the cartels. It is precisely this grey area, one in which legitimate proposals and useful debates occur, that most suffers in being rejected by those who believe that a simplistic approach to the drugs problem is sufficient and who would like to dispense with further deliberation. A space for the free exchange of opinion is essential so that new approaches, new proposals and new solutions can be allowed to enrich the existing body of knowledge.

Political Consequences of the Drugs Trade

It should be pointed out that the drug traffickers have little regard for national sovereignty, yet those combating the traffickers must continue to be bound by these constraints. Borders, national judicial systems, police jurisdiction, air-space and maritime territorial sovereignty must all be respected in the international fight against drugs. Time and again they have been at risk, to say the least, in the laudable desire to achieve efficiency. Sanctions, or the threat of sanctions, by the developed countries, direct military operations, *de facto* extradition, and violations of air and maritime space are unjustified actions which strengthen the activity of the cartels and allow them to manipulate public opinion, if not in their favour, then at least against important international actors in this struggle, and also permit them to portray their governments as instruments or puppets of other countries. On the other hand, land borders frequently become veritable bazaars of unlawfulness and crime, exceeding the authorities' capacity for control: Free Crime Zones! It is a risk which must be anticipated and avoided as much as possible.

Second, the task of making elections clean and transparent; of ensuring that each candidate for elective office feels free to compete; of ensuring a total freedom of expression; and above all, of guaranteeing that the electoral contest is peaceful, civilised and intelligent, is jeopardised when the drug cartels decide to interfere in the process, to eliminate some election candidates, to finance others, to infiltrate some municipalities or regions directly, to discourage other candidates from standing by means of intimidation, to seek to impose a favourable position on their behalf, to intimidate the electorate in some regions, to corrupt them or to create, by means of terrorism, a climate which forces the postponement or cancellation of the electoral process. These are moments when attempts to destabilise and undermine democracy are felt most strongly.

In countries where marijuana, coca leaf and opium poppies are cultivated, the growing areas are subject to permanent interference by the cartels, resulting in a number of destabilising political consequences. An alliance is sought with the political and economic elite of the municipality or region that facilitates cultivation. The ensuing prosperity generates changes in the way of life and traditional relationships, and affects even the structure of the family. Soon, in one way or another, the police become implicated in the 'game'. Those who keep their distance are perceived as a danger because, by not sharing in the benefits, they do not enter into the chain of complicity and silence. They are seen as informants who endanger the business. These people are subject to intimidation, blackmail and harassment. Some opt to leave the area. The title of Albert Hirschman's well-known book *Exit, Voice and Loyalty* captures the alternatives available: to escape, to denounce or to be loyal, that is to say to be an accomplice of those who are dictating the rules of the game.

What I have just described as occurring at the municipal level is not as clearly manifest at the regional level. The complexity of regional society does not allow for the phenomenon to be so simple. The alliances exist as do the complicity and the intimidation. With the money come arms in both cases, and with them the spread of lawlessness and the 'might makes right' principle. Interference by the cartels, the production, distribution, sale and consumption of drugs and the colossal earnings that they generate at different levels – cultivation, processing, transport, export, distribution, money-laundering – radically change the system of values at all levels of society. Accelerated illicit enrichment then contaminates almost all sectors. Nobody in such a society wants to go through the slow process of working, saving, making profits, and investing wisely if alternatives exist. The urge for fast enrichment infects and takes possession of people who through their ambition or determination could achieve success, although less quickly, in other sectors. The world of drugs, or other criminal conduct, offers unrivalled opportunities. The use of violence, intimidation and blackmail becomes a form of conduct which affects even sectors not linked to drugs. Life is devalued. Honesty and hard work become virtues of the past. Entire families are criminalised. Public spirit and respect for law and authority deteriorate. New role models are created, as criminals appear as successful and internationally-recognised businessmen who have overcome countless national and international obstacles. They appear as excellent family men, good friends and generous citizens. It is a huge distortion of reality.

Cartel interference also seriously affects basic human rights. The right to life is especially threatened by their activity, as are the right to free expression and the right to participation in the political process. This crisis of human rights is not always fully identified by the international organisations charged with their promotion and defence. When human rights violations flagrantly committed by the drug cartels are ignored, they are condoned.

Violence, acts of selective or indiscriminate terrorism, the disturbance of the electoral process, limitations to the decision-making process, the perverse use of nationalist themes, the weakening of the system of values of a free and democratic law-abiding society, the human rights crisis, all create a situation of public order which can place a society on the verge of chaos. If other factors are added, such as guerrillas, the existence of economic and social problems, or corruption scandals (which may be linked to the drugs phenomenon) then one can speak of a crisis of public order. Not only are appropriate legal instruments required to overcome this problem, but also a firm decision not to resort merely to repressive instruments instead of a combination of measures which allow for the problem to be dealt with comprehensively, both on the national and the international level. In any other way, the crisis of public order would tend to become more serious and unmanageable. Citizens' confidence in the authorities, based on their credibility and their legitimacy, is fundamental in confronting any public order crisis. In sum, this crisis is normally accompanied by a crisis of credibility in authority fostered by the cartels' actions that prompts people to regard the authorities as individuals who are incompetent because they have been unable to control the phenomenon, or accomplices because they have allowed it to proliferate, or who are corrupt because their ineffectiveness together with the strength of the cartels is seen as the product of corruption. It is here that real successes in the struggle against the cartels are essential and that sensible choices in promulgating effective legislation and appropriate procedures are vital in order to maintain the credibility of the authorities who, for their part, should enjoy an impeccable reputation for integrity and honesty. If only a reputation for courage and determination accompanied this image! If that is not the case, it will prove very difficult to confront the crisis of public order and to stand up to the phenomenon.

The inadequacy of some judicial systems to fight drug-generated criminality (a difficulty which has to do with the international nature of this criminality and the systematic challenge to judges), on the other hand, leads to the emergence of vendettas and the creation of strategies that, applying the same methods as the mafia, assassinate selectively with the intention of inflicting on the cartel members and their *sicarios* (hired killers) the same feeling of intimidation and terror as they use themselves. It is a proliferation of violence. It is a dirty war in which decent society, the society which respects the law and obeys the rules, is caught between the two sides. This cruel form of private justice weakens the authority of the state because, by adding to the lack of trust in the judicial system and the forces of order, it appears to confirm that only violence can counter violence. Furthermore, it encourages rumours which compromise sectors of law enforcement agencies, insinuating collaboration or passive complicity. In this way distrust in the political system grows to become a new factor of destabilisation.

One of the perverse effects of the presence of the cartels in political life is that, sooner or later, the argument or rumour that a person (of course prominent) is allegedly in the service of the cartels is used to destroy political careers or to carry out vendettas against political opponents. It is a kind of 'kiss of death' which on occasions – how ironic – is used with the support of the mafia itself as an effective means to destroy people who hinder their objectives. When there are confrontations between cartels, a favoured recourse is to link the opposing cartel to an 'inconvenient' official. These accusations always cast a shadow of doubt that taints even people of undeniable integrity in their fight against drugs. Thus, in this all-out war of all against all, there are few people left in whom the citizens can believe. It is yet another way of eroding the political system. Disillusionment, mistrust, and then public contempt and apathy take possession of society.

Marijuana, coca and poppy plantations can mostly be found in remote areas, where the state's presence is weak, and where the presence of the cartels overshadows the presence of the state. It is even worse when there are alliances with the guerrillas in some of these regions. Thus the cartels gradually secure control of parts of the country, which they then consolidate by acquiring businesses and other property. This situation can become critical if forms of decentralisation exist which diminish the central state's capacity for control and which increase the cartels' potential for domination in the area.

Consumption or transit countries suffer a considerable number of the above-mentioned consequences, particularly in the regions and municipalities that are more exposed to the manipulations of the drug cartels. Crime, violence and insecurity increase; the future of young people is endangered; the work ethic suffers; the quality of urban life deteriorates as does that of neighbourhoods and municipalities. The vulnerability of the financial system to monetary manipulation by the cartels jeopardises the credibility of the institutions charged with the control of the financial system. The well-known BCCI case underlined this. The impact of the scandal was so great that it is still hard to believe that something like it could have occurred in one of the world's main financial centres, over such a long period of time, and with the involvement of personalities considered to be of great integrity.

This introduction could include innumerable pages of quotations taken from proposals by political leaders that sum up the impact of this combination of political consequences as a threat to democratic stability, a greater or lesser threat depending on the intensity and nature of the drugs problem experienced in their country. Presidents Reagan, Bush, Clinton, Barco, Gaviria, Samper, Paz Zamora, Sánchez de Lozada and Fujimori, former British Prime Minister Thatcher and the European Union have all, in their own way, said the same thing: drugs in their different manifestations constitute a grave threat to democratic stability. President Reagan went even further by stating that drugs constituted a threat to the United States. In reality, democracy is at risk if there is not an intelligent response soon, one that is appropriate to the nature of the danger which one seeks to thwart.

As the problem of drugs is an international one, it is inevitable that international relations should be affected. The international community cannot remain detached when confronted with a problem from which no one can declare themselves exempt. Only global and synchronised strategy can achieve real and lasting results which would mitigate or reduce the problem. But the crisis of credibility also affects the international organisations charged with fighting the drug trade. Administrative problems make the task more difficult. The lack of adequate budgets makes it a sham. The tentative application of new legal statutes does not help. And there is a lack of coordinated cooperation by agencies, such as the International Monetary Fund and the World Bank, at the global or regional level, such as has been requested by UNDCP Executive Director G. Giacomelli on several occasions. These are factors which affect the trust in the capacity of the UN system to confront this problem. This situation is lamentable since, in my opinion, the majority of countries prefer a multilateral focus because it is appropriate to the nature of the problem and because it makes the distribution of responsibilities more equitable and the fight against drugs, without doubt, more effective.

If the multilateral aspect is weak, something similar can be said of efforts on the other three levels of international cooperation, which coexist with the multilateral focus: (a) national borders; (b) subregional initiatives; and (c) bilateral relations. In all of these cases, it can be asserted that the cartels seek to poison relations between countries. Criminal incidents, border incidents and criminal activity in general introduce elements of tension into foreign relations. Consequently, this situation affects how other subjects on the bilateral or subregional agenda are addressed. Even worse, it 'narcoticises' a good part of the agenda. If, in addition, the subject is dealt with in purely domestic terms (for electoral reasons or short-sighted convenience), then the risks of confrontation are greater because it leads to apparently irrational behaviour by both sides. Matters deteriorate further if the media exaggerate or distort what is happening, and stir up public opinion against a particular country, thus making daily life difficult, if not disagreeable, and even humiliating for the citizens of countries unjustly labelled as weak in the fight against drugs. Trade and tourism suffer. These are not mere details. It is only natural that some countries should have found themselves compelled to engage international public relations agencies to help direct publicity campaigns and actions which would restore and, hopefully, improve their image. However, resentment and indifference because of unfair treatment and an attitude which 'sees the mote in somebody else's eye and not the beam in one's own' encourage chauvinist behaviour and, in some ways, weaken governments and strengthen drug cartels.

Although the activities of the drug cartels are capable of poisoning international relations, it is the duty of governments to prevent this from happening even in the most difficult circumstances. The media should also be clear about this so that they do not unintentionally play into the hands of the cartels. This is not to say that criticism should be tempered or that self-censorship should be applied; by no means. It is a question of preserving, even in the worst circumstances, the possibility of working cooperatively. It is a thorny subject if there are misunderstandings. The last thing I want is for these reflections to be misinterpreted as a desire to limit freedom of expression. What is required is a balanced and comprehensive focus of information, parallel to the comprehensive and balanced operations contemplated by the UN Global Action Plan against drugs. Parochialism and a lack of understanding of the realities of other countries are not good consultants in this fight.

Political Solutions to the Problem

How can a government fight the drug trade's threat to democracy, stability and the integrity of the state? The clear distinction between the drug trade and narcoterrorism (or drug-related violence) introduced by the Barco administration (1986-90) in Colombia was useful in responding to these questions. They mutually reinforce each other. The drug trade refers to the production, processing, export, distribution and consumption of drugs, and to the laundering of drug money. Narcoterrrorism refers not so much to the everyday use of forms of violence always present in the drugs business, but to the systematic use of violence to confront the state, to weaken and destabilise it with the objective of obstructing its action against the drug trade. Both the narcotics trade and narcoterrorism threaten democracy, assault the integrity of the state, corrupt, create problems of territorial control, affect national sovereignty, the electoral process, and human rights. Depending on the size and the intensity of the crisis, the likely political response will vary. Whether or not it is a question of extreme narcoterrorism, as occurred in Colombia at the end of the 1980s, a political response is necessary because the threat to democracy is always present. It can be even more dangerous when there is no narcoterrorism, because then the tendency to underestimate the threat can significantly damage the political system over time. In the case of narcoterrorism, the threat is so imminent that there is no other option than to confront it with determination.

The drug trade requires an international response endorsed by a national response, and not the other way around: a national response endorsed by an uncertain international one. In this introduction, I have referred mainly to the political dimension of this process. This should be multilateral in its conception and financing, and inter-regional, regional, subregional and national in its implementation. If this is unattainable, strategic coalitions that would perform the same functions should be created. The multilateral political response exists in writing, but is only modestly applied.

Narcoterrorism is a very different matter, because it affects specific countries at specific times. The country affected by it cannot allow itself the luxury of waiting for a multilateral political response. It has to confront the violence, ideally alone, with the greatest possible international solidarity. But it is a problem which does not permit delay, which cannot be transferred to others and which cannot be side-stepped. It has to be confronted decisively or its consequences will be suffered. In order for a democracy to confront narcoterrorism, there is only one alternative: the problems of a democracy are solved with more democracy and not less. Terrorism must be countered using the rule of law, with respect for human rights, for the electoral mechanisms, with persuasion and with the support of public opinion. However, there are not only democratic but also authoritarian and intermediate responses.

1. The Democratic Response

This is, without doubt, the most difficult response, but the one which offers more lasting and effective results. Narcoterrorism is terrorism. The experiences of the European countries which – particularly during the 1970s – had to confront this threat, are well known. They showed that the state cannot use terrorist methods in its fight against terrorism without the risk of losing its legitimacy in the process and, with it, the support of public opinion. Worst of all, the state's use of terrorism risks legitimising terrorism itself! The strength of the state lies in its respect for fundamental ethical values, the rule of law and human rights. Maintaining this respect in extreme circumstances is not an easy task, above all at the outset. In moments of particular anguish, public opinion often demands that the state resort to violence, that the law be bypassed, and that human rights be put on hold. The public calls for scorched earth, and influential groups support and encourage this attitude. There are groups in which the democratic position is seen as weakness, impotence and inaction, and there is no lack of those who equate it with complicity. A strong belief in democratic methods, a large dose of courage and a certain disdain for populism is required to remain steadfast in a political response which is often highly unpopular. The cartels encourage the rejection of a democratic response, and are the principal beneficiaries of its unpopularity. The democratic response is also unpopular when international support is precarious or non-existent or exhausts itself in words.

Colombia is an excellent example of how a country with almost two centuries of democratic tradition has – amidst indescribable sacrifices and with less effective international support than could have been expected – attempted to formulate a democratic political response to the formidable threat posed over the last decade by the drug cartels. It is admirable because, apart from the very problems of democracy in a developing country, Colombia also confronted the threat of several rural and urban, conventional and new-style guerrilla groups. This is not to say that there have not been excesses, abuses and violations of human rights; these have been well documented. Such transgressions not only demonstrate the weaknesses of the system but also the tremendous difficulties which the government has had to overcome. I particularly want to refer to the democratic political response offered with determination and profound conviction, in extremely difficult circumstances, by Presidents Virgilio Barco (1986-90) and César Gaviria (1990-94). I make special reference to these two administrations because there was a clear consistency in the strategies pursued by them with regard to the drug trade and narcoterrorism; a good number of those responsible for drug policy worked in both administrations. It is a rare example of continuity. Both administrations considered that the problems of democracy are solved by more democracy. Both were convinced that the cartels were a threat to democracy, a threat which became more imminent as a consequence of the complex interactions between the different guerrilla groups and the cartels – interactions which ranged anywhere between cooperation and total confrontation, to the extent that today the guerrillas are considered another cartel. Nevertheless, Barco and Gaviria effected a silent revolution in Colombia. Thanks to them and the Colombians' capacity for endurance, and a democratic tradition of almost 200 years, democracy was strengthened and today, more than ever, the government is equipped with the tools with which to confront the drug trade. It is doing so successfully. Paradoxical, but true. This is the reality. These have been two presidential periods in which radical changes in the legal, political and economic structures have been introduced. To explain them, or even just to describe them, would take another, perhaps more extensive, chapter.[1] I will limit myself to an incomplete sketch that will highlight the main characteristics of a democratic revolution which was the product of a bold political response to the attempt to destroy Colombian democracy. A more brutal assault has not been known, but nor has a more democratic response.

The state apparatus at all levels – as well as the political parties, the electoral system, the running of Congress, the role of congressmen and the code of ethics which should govern them – were subject to fundamental transformations, which undoubtedly improved governability in Colombia. Political society has been especially strengthened not only by the new and progressive Bill of Rights, but also by mechanisms for the protection of rights, such as the creation of the role of *Defensor del Pueblo* (or ombudsman) and the system of *tutela*. In addition, almost all forms of popular participation, such as the referendum, popular consultation, popular initiative, and the revocation of the mandate, have become practically inviolable. The concept of participation has also been incorporated into the running of businesses, universities and other organisations. The whole judicial system, fundamental to the orderly functioning of institutions, has been redesigned and strengthened not only by the introduction of an investigative system but also by the creation of the Constitutional Court. The need to exact accountability led to the establishment of norms and institutions that seek to guarantee efficient and honest financial administration. Hence the norms about transparency and the new and updated procedures of auditing and control which, while far from perfect, represent a considerable improvement on the old system. As a consequence of these transformations there occurred a redistribution of resources, functions and responsibilities between the central power, the regions and the municipalities and, with this, the direct and popular election of mayors and governors.

The conventional conception of the separation of powers was substituted by one which favours collaboration, convergence of aims and harmonisation between independent branches.   And as the new 1991 Constitution was intended to have the character of a peace treaty, indians, minorities and guerrilla groups receive preferential treatment.   Moreover, extradition, allegedly the cause of narcoterrorism, was prohibited, against the will of the government.

Unfortunately, these bold measures have been only partly successful in controlling two phenomena which elude conventional diagnosis: the drug trade and the guerrillas.   Both have been treated in ways that seek to preserve the rule of law, while offering generous incentives to overcome conflict and violence.   In the case of narcoterrorism, a compendium of measures aimed at stimulating the submission to justice of those involved in the illegal drug business has been adopted.   In the case of the guerrilla groups, not only was the successful peace process of the Barco administration consolidated, but new and more generous peace initiatives were implemented, which later led to the offer of a space for the guerrillas to participate in the formulation of a new constitution.   When this did not happen, the Constituent Assembly – which, like the government, conceived its task to be the elaboration of a peace treaty – included a whole catalogue of exceptional concessions to the guerrillas in the provisional articles of the new constitution.   Other initiatives, from the appointment of a Minister of Civil Defence to new peace proposals and new forms of negotiation, were adopted.

I have tried to draw attention here to the way in which the drug trade and organised crime affect governability in some parts of the world and, particularly, in the Andean region.   Yet, as before, the Colombian case is paradoxical: extreme legalism coexists with the spread of lawlessness; democracy with violence; a more than advanced constitutional architecture challenged by an armed criminal organisation more than bold in its methods and objectives; a public order force alongside armed and financially well-equipped bandit organisations.   And a well managed and prosperous economy in conditions which few consider auspicious for economic growth.

The Director of UNDCP was absolutely right when he began his recent report before the Third Commission of the United Nations with these cogent words:

> ...Drug abuse is indeed worldwide and in all its forms. Illicit production, trafficking and consumption, a factor of corruption, instability and violence which contributes heavily in making the world the rather unsafe place it has become.   In particular, countless armed conflicts, and

insurrections are being fed and financed by the illicit profits made by drug traffickers and organised crime.

2. The Authoritarian Response

The traditions and conditions that facilitate a democratic response to the crises that are generated by drug trafficking and narcoterrorism do not always exist. It is also not easy for a foreign observer to evaluate the internal conditions of a country. The magnitude of the threat, its geographical extent, the weakness of the anti-drugs agencies or their compromised position *vis-à-vis* the cartels, the weakness of the judiciary and other factors can lead to the decision to use authoritarian methods to overcome the crisis, in ways which might include:

- A *coup d'état* staged by a faction of the public order forces which, claiming to be 'untainted' and in alliance with other similar sectors, seeks a solution outside the conventional institutional channels.
- A request for military or judicial co-operation from a foreign power.
- Direct military or police intervention by a foreign power or by an international organisation (the UN Security Council, for example) which considers that a national situation affects its own or international security. This intervention can be a surgical strike, that is to say, a specific action such as the overthrow of a ruling individual or group, or it could assume the form of a prolonged intervention.

Similar options could present themselves in the case of a decision adopted by the UN Security Council. The difference would be that this would have greater international legitimacy.

The definition of the drugs problem as a *security* issue, with regard to one particular nation or with regard to the international community, can lead to the legitimisation of this type of intervention. Certain security-minded doctrines, such as that of *de facto* extradition resulting from the supposed right of a country to bring to justice criminals in any part of the world, create the rationale for such intervention. I am inclined to think that in all of these cases this kind of authoritarian response leads to local and temporary solutions that do not resolve the drug problem. Improvement can be achieved in the short-term, but in the medium- and long-term the problem can deteriorate and reappear in new or more subtle, but no less serious, forms.

3. The Intermediate Response

A third option is a response halfway between the democratic and the authoritarian. Rulers with access to extraordinary emergency powers would also adopt extraordinary measures, not so much to find democratic solutions to the crisis as to eradicate organisations which they considered to be involved with the cartels. They would also, nationally and internationally, argue for urgency in confronting the crisis and would present this option as the preferable lesser evil. As it is a question of an intermediate position by a democratically elected government, they would take care to assure the temporary nature of the decisions, and the re-establishment of democratic institutions and procedures. They would, of course, request international understanding and support. This option creates high risks of internal and international dissent; it is likely, therefore, that in providing more space for domestic and external pressure, this intermediate response lies closer to the democratic than to the authoritarian option.

What is important in evaluating these responses is their objective: to control the destabilising effects of the drug trade and narcoterrorism; and to control the threat to democracy. It is essential that the medicine should not turn out to be worse than the illness. It is a question of preserving democracy and not destroying it.

Political Risks

The greatest political danger that the drug trade can pose is the influence that can inspire a country's gradual evolution into a *narcocracy* – characterised by low levels of narcoterrorism and a high penetration by the cartels of the state apparatus and key sectors of the private sector and political parties.

The resources of power, a climate favourable to the illegal activities of the cartels, the tools they use, and the targets they attack, violently or subtly, can create the conditions for the emergence of a political regime controlled by the drug cartels. Outwardly, there would appear to be a problem, even a serious one, generated by drugs, but also a state capable of autonomously confronting the situation, while maintaining democratic expression. This, perhaps, is the worst of all situations, because the appearance of a healthy, democratic response would weaken the capacity to respond to the problem. In the process, there will be many individuals who, in order to save their undeserved good name, will do everything in their power to diminish the seriousness of the problem, to discourage effective action and to discredit people who, because of their integrity, could constitute an obstacle or a threat. Or if they are more audacious, these individuals will encourage measures which appear strong, but which only generate new frustrations and postpone real and effective solutions to the problem. Societies which fall into 'narcocracy' will be in crisis at some point, and that will be the moment to choose from one of the aforementioned political responses.

In comparison with 'narcocracy', which implies a subtle and growing means of controlling the political system, 'narco-fascism' is a brutal and blatant form of controlling the political system. 'Narco-fascism' does not hide its identity nor does it disguise the way it operates. It lacks subtlety. It imposes itself by force of violence, by the seductive power of money and by the complete lack of ethical values, even those which help to keep up appearances. In order for it to be threatened seriously, significant fragmentations, serious divisions or an external challenge are necessary.

The drug cartels are not interested in the existence of a transparent and effective democracy. They prefer a democracy that they can manipulate for their benefit; one that they can corrupt, make ineffective in dealing with their criminal conduct and their whims; a society with powerless judges, who do not make life difficult for them, but who legalise their behaviour, or who remain out of sight. A society with politicians submissive to the demands of the cartels. A government that sees no evil and hears no evil, and therefore does not act – and if it does act, then in appearance only. An accommodating society, which does not worry about the abuses, which is not surprised by lawlessness and remains apathetic, or at least cynical, towards the drugs problem. But in no way is this democracy. This is, at best, a caricature of democracy. Where there exists democracy, even if weakened and penetrated, there exists a capacity for responding democratically to the drugs problem. Where there is a mask, a caricature of democracy this capacity does not exist. The difficulty lies in being able to tell the difference between the two.

The criminal conduct of those involved in the drugs problem, the complicity and weakness that this conduct generates and the international factors which encourage and support this criminal conduct put governability in danger as much in countries with a democratic tradition as in those with an authoritarian tradition. If governability is weakened, political stability and the future of democracy, and with it the preservation of rights, are put at risk. Intimidation, blackmail, violence and corruption seek to replace liberty, harmony and transparency. The rule of law can succumb to the rule of 'might makes right'.

Notes

*   Translated by Pam Decho
1.   See, however, Posada (1997) for a detailed account of changes in
     Colombia under the Gaviria administration.

PART I

CONSUMPTION PATTERNS IN EUROPE AND LATIN AMERICA

CHAPTER 1

FOREIGN DEMAND FOR LATIN AMERICAN DRUGS: THE USA AND EUROPE

Peter Reuter*

Introduction

Although the United States customarily assigns to the Latin American nations, or at least the Andean cocaine-producing countries, a major portion of the responsibility for US drug problems, it appears that epistemologically the opposite is true. Demand for cocaine in the USA and Western Europe, and for heroin in the USA, are probably the principal determinants of Latin America's drug production problems. This chapter examines the available evidence on drug use in the USA and Western Europe to assess whether consumption is increasing.

The chapter is divided into three sections. The first examines the evolution of US drug consumption since 1980. In addition to presenting the standard data, it attempts to provide a coherent description of the dynamics of drug use that may explain these patterns, cautiously concluding that demand for cocaine is likely to decline. It also presents rough estimates of total US expenditure on cocaine, heroin and marijuana. This section also gives some consideration to heroin because about one quarter of US heroin comes from Mexico and Colombia. Supply side shifts, which go beyond the scope of this chapter, are much more important for the heroin market, since other regions more distant from the USA are major competitors with the Latin American producers. Marijuana, which presents a smaller problem in Latin America, being less associated with violence and political instability, is also considered.

The second section describes trends in Western Europe. The available data are skimpy and for some major nations (e.g. France and Italy) they are simply negligible. Moreover, the variation among nations is substantial, so that a description of 'Western Europe' is misleading in some important dimensions. Since Europe imports only cocaine from Latin America, acquiring heroin from Asia and marijuana from North Africa, these drugs are considered only to the extend that this contributes to our understanding of cocaine consumption. An effort is made to compare US and Western European consumption patterns.

The final section briefly considers the future of drug consumption in the United States. It argues that, notwithstanding recent upturns in marijuana use among adolescents, export demand has probably reached its peak and that the most likely future pattern is of slow decline, although confidence in these predictions has to be tempered by observation of how little is understood about the origins of drug epidemics.

Patterns of Drug Use in the United States[1]

For most of the last decade, the available indicators on drug use and abuse have been telling a confusing story. On the one hand, general population surveys showed declining numbers of people reporting use of illicit drugs; on the other hand, measures of problems related to drug use were increasing. Many observers have argued that the surveys are in error and that we should focus only on the indicators that are continuing to·worsen, such as the number of drug-related deaths and Emergency Room admissions. However the indicators, all of which are flawed, can be reconciled fairly simply to provide a consistent account. An important change in patterns of drug use and abuse has indeed taken place since about 1987. Overall use is down substantially and even frequent use of drugs has probably declined. The severity of problems caused by drugs has not declined, however, because those who use drugs most heavily and experience the most severe health and behavioural consequences have continued to take narcotics; the problems they cause themselves and the rest of society change, but do not abate, as their drug use careers lengthen.

Initiation into the use of drugs (as measured by the broadest population survey) rose through the later 1970s and perhaps into the early 1980s, but began to decline by the mid 1980s (Gfroerer and Brodsky, 1992). The total number of current users (including those who began earlier and continued to use) may have continued to rise a little longer, but was almost certainly in decline by 1987. Not unexpectedly the number of drug *abusers* – those persons whose drug use causes them significant problems – continued to rise even as intiation and use rates declined. That number probably flattened out at the end of the 1980s, but has still not yet declined significantly. Those who continue to abuse may, on average, cause more harm than in previous years.[2]

Thus, the composition of the drug using population has changed in important ways over the last decade. First, a higher fraction of all users are problematic users, increasing the association between drug abuse and crime in particular. Second, the decline in drug use, though occurring across all demographic groups, has been notably sharper among the more educated, probably reflecting a greater sensitivity to health concerns.

Surveys

The basic data are provided in Figures 1-3 and Table 1. Figure 1 shows self-reported use (at least once in the past 30 days) since 1975 among high school seniors in the annual survey known as *Monitoring the Future* (Johnston, Bachman and O'Malley, annual). In the first three years drug use was increasing and the figures were alarmingly high; almost one in nine seniors reported daily use of marijuana. Then the figures started to decline sharply, a decline that continued throughout the 1980s, flattening out at much lower figures (13.8% for marijuana in the last 30 days in 1991) in the early 1990s. For cocaine, the story differs only in the timing of the downturn (1986) and the much lower peak (6.8% in 1985). We leave to a later section analysis of the upturn that started in 1992. A similar pattern is reported in Figure 2, presenting data from the National Household Survey on Drug Abuse (NHSDA) (US Dept. of Health and Human Services, annual) for the age group 18-25.

Figure 1:
High School Senior Prevalence Rates, 1975-93

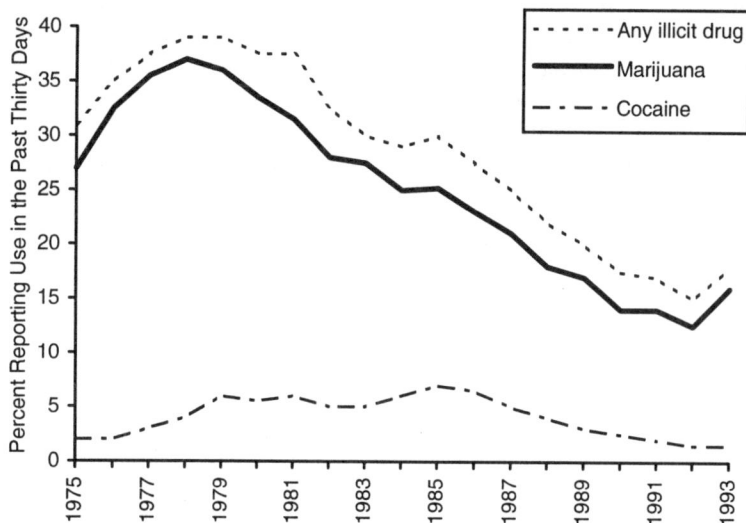

Figure 2:
National Household Survey, 30-day Prevalence Rates for 18-20 Year Olds

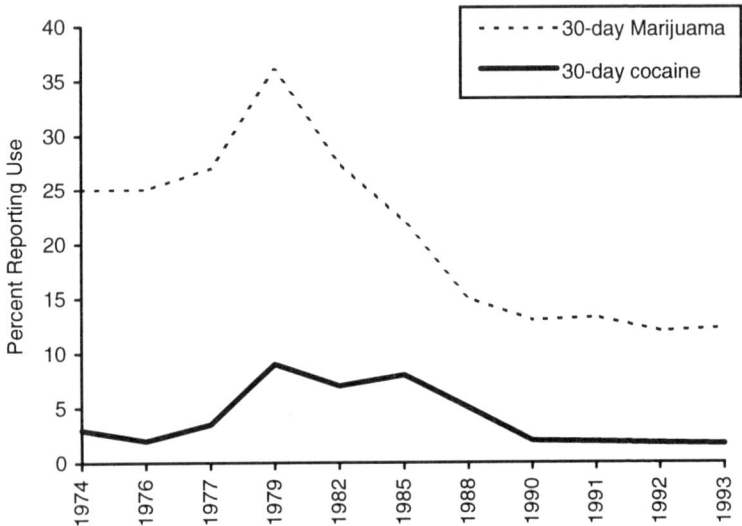

The NHSDA also permits analysis of changing patterns of association between drug use and education from 1985 to 1993. Although there were very substantial declines for all educational groups, the largest declines (as a fraction of prevalence in the base year) were among those who had completed high school. This is consistent with the theory that the primary influence for reduced initiation was consciousness of the health hazards associated with drug use, since health behaviour messages have greater impact on more educated persons.

Availability certainly played no role in the decline in prevalence. *Monitoring the Future* has included a question on availability since its inception: throughout the 1980s the figure for marijuana remained essentially unchanged with 80-85% reporting that the drug was available or readily available. For cocaine, reported availability went up until the end of the decade. Marijuana prices rose, but cocaine prices fell throughout the decade.

Arrests
If use in the general population was decreasing, were there any substantial sub-populations in which use was increasing? As it turns out, there was evidence of a rapid rise in the prevalence of drugs among those arrested, an uncomfortably large share of the young male population. The evidence

came from urinalysis of arrestees in various cities, which showed very high rates of involvement, particularly with cocaine.

The best data came from Washington DC, which is the only jurisdiction to have had a universal testing programme for all arrests over a number of years. Since March 1984, every adult arrestee has been asked to provide a urine specimen for testing in connection with determination of pretrial status. Figure 3 plots the percentage testing positive for cocaine, heroin and the hallucinogen Phencyclidine (PCP). When the testing started, cocaine ranked third among the three drugs, at about 15%. The percentage testing positive for cocaine started rising immediately, but so did the percentage using the other drugs. Only in 1987, when crack became available, did the figures for heroin and PCP start to decline. The cocaine rates have now declined from their 1988-89 peaks of 60%, but still remain consistently above 40%.

Figure 3:
Percentage of Washington, D.C. Arrestees Testing Positive

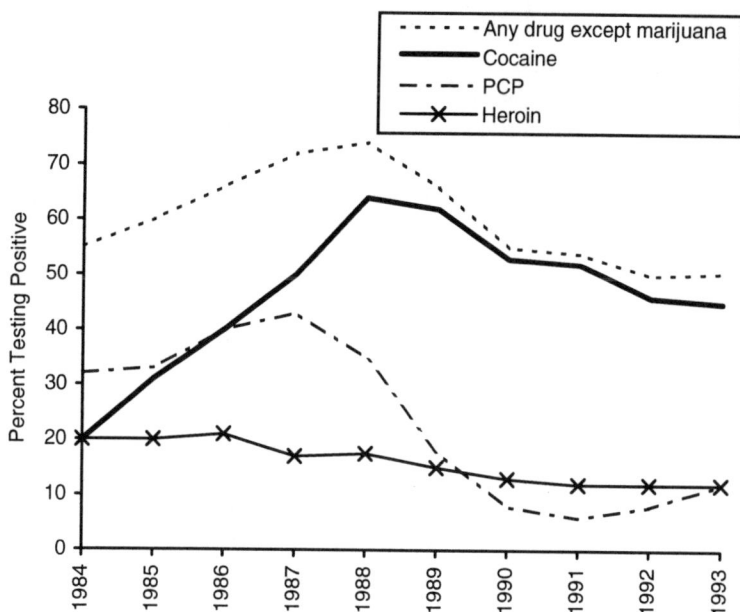

Such high rates are found in most cities included in the Drug Use Forecasting (DUF) programme (National Institute of Justice, annual). Table 1 shows rates for four cities.

Table 1:
Arrestees Testing Positive for Illicit Drugs (Percentage)

City		Any Illicit Drug		Cocaine	
		1988 (Q1)	1993	1988 (Q1)	1993
Los Angeles	Males	74	66	58	48
	Females	79	77	66	59
New Orleans	Males	58	62	32	48
	Females	60	47	37	37
Portland	Males	75	63	38	33
	Females	79	74	47	47
Washington DC	Males	67	60	59	37
	Females	76	71	73	62

Source: National Institute of Justice (1993)

In most cities the 1993 rates are below their highest levels, but still show very high rates of cocaine use. Data for three cities (in addition to Washington for comparison) are provided in Table 1. In 1993, 50% or more of males tested positive for cocaine in seven of 24 cities. The arrested population is now, and always has been, predominantly male.[3]

What can we learn from these results? Obviously they suggest a strong relation between drug use and crime, a notion that has been folk wisdom for centuries and in the research literature for decades. For policy purposes, the results focus attention on the desirability of controlling drug use among those on probation, parole or pretrial release in order to reduce their recidivism rate. Given that the tests pick up cocaine and heroin use only within the past 48 hours and using information from some interviews conducted along with the urinalysis tests, it is likely that those testing positive are frequent users of cocaine and heroin.

In addition, the results show that there is considerable variation among different segments of the population. In particular, the criminally active show vastly higher drug-use rates than their peers in the general population. This is a significant finding because the number of criminally active young males is quite high; in Washington DC, approximately 32,000 residents were charged with criminal offences in the three year period 1985-87 (Reuter, MacCoun and Murphy, 1990), compared with a population aged 15-45 of about 300,000 in 1987. Moreover, it does not appear that drug use in this high rate group has fallen nearly as rapidly as have rates in the general population, so that it is unlikely that the prevalence of frequent cocaine use overall has declined very substantially.

Systematically integrating the DUF data with that from the broader surveys is difficult. Most of those who are arrested are at least eligible to be in the household population sampled by the NHSDA, but we do not know whether their response rate is lower than that of other parts of the young male population. Estimates of the overlap between the two populations is largely guesswork.[4]

Hospital and Coroner Reports

The most direct measure of the extent of serious drug problems comes from the DAWN (Drug Abuse Warning Network) system, which collects information from a sample of Emergency Rooms and Medical Examiner offices in 22 major metropolitan areas (US Dept. of Health and Human Services, annual). The sample permits more refined analyses of the demographic characteristics of those showing up in emergency rooms. The remainder of this section analyses DAWN data looking both at trends and at prevalence rates across population groups.

It is common to think of an Emergency Room episode involving a drug as reflecting an overdose with that drug. In fact, individuals come to the Emergency Room for numerous reasons; since 1987, DAWN has coded six major reasons, such as 'seeking detoxification' or experiencing 'withdrawal' symptoms. Thus, Emergency Room episodes might increase if more people were trying to quit heroin and were experiencing trouble with withdrawal; indeed, withdrawal accounts for about 12% of those showing up at Emergency Rooms with heroin-related problems, although this motive accounts for less than 2% of cocaine mentions.[5]

What does DAWN add to our knowledge of the prevalence of drug use and abuse? The implicit interpretation has been that it provides data about the numbers of those most heavily involved with illicit drugs. That is, an increase in the number of Emergency Room admissions or Medical Examiner cases involving cocaine is indicative of an increase in the number of persons who are heavy users of cocaine. That is clearly a simplistic view, given the variety of paths by which an individual can come into the DAWN system. A first-time user who had an unexpected reaction from the drug could become a DAWN mention. Or a steady number of users could make more frequent use of Emergency Rooms over time as their continued use of drugs increases their vulnerability to various health problems. DAWN data on reasons for going to Emergency Rooms and motives for using the drug suggest that cocaine episodes involve mostly dependent users suffering chronic effects of drug use or withdrawal. Mortality rates (per use episode) are likely to be higher for people later in their careers after they have incurred extensive harm from chronic use. The Medical

Examiner data are also probably dominated by the number and behaviour of long-term users. For the purpose of this analysis, we adopt the conventional view that DAWN provides information about the tail of the distribution of drug use. Though DAWN may also pick up accident and injury victims and recreational drug users, they are less likely to appear with symptoms indicating drug use and therefore are less likely to be registered in DAWN.

Through most of the 1980s, the DAWN series showed a dramatic increase in the number of Emergency Room visits and deaths related to cocaine and heroin, with not much of a decrease for other illicit drugs; only at the very end of the decade, in late 1989, did the DAWN Emergency Room figures start to turn down for cocaine, and then only to increase again in 1991 and 1992. Figure 4 presents data on cocaine and heroin for the period 1982-1993; the number of cocaine Emergency Room admissions went up about tenfold over the decade.

Figure 4:
Emergency Room (ER) Mentions ('000s)

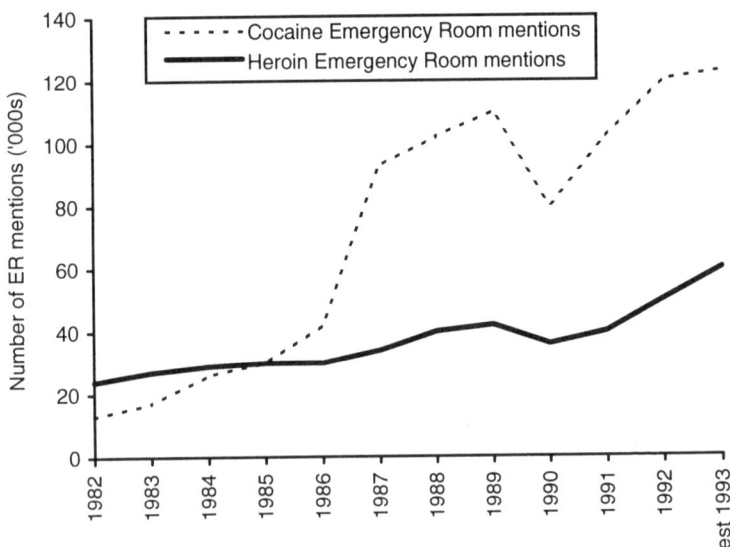

The number of Medical Examiner cocaine mentions paralleled the Emergency Room data for most of that time. Only after 1988 did the Medical Examiner data begin to diverge from the Emergency Room data, continuing to show increases. We discuss this matter below.

The demographic composition of those dying from cocaine use has also changed sharply. In 1982, about 23% of those dying were black; by 1989, that figure had risen to 46%. Somewhat more surprisingly, there was also a sharp increase in the age of decedents. In 1982, almost half were over the age of 30; by 1989 that proportion had risen to 76%; correspondingly, the percentage aged 18-24 fell from 23 to 14%. The Emergency Room data show very much the same trends in age and race composition.[6]

We will focus here on recent patterns in Emergency Room mentions of cocaine. The decrease starting in the last quarter of 1989 and extending through 1990 is quite striking; in the fourth quarter of 1989, the total number fell from 29,900 to 22,600, a decrease of 25 per cent. That decrease came after a three quarters-long plateau, reflecting the only recent period of price increases (Hyatt and Rhodes, 1992), and was then followed by another three quarters of steady and more modest decline. Then, beginning with the first quarter of 1991, the pattern changed. DAWN episodes began to increase and have continued to increase nearly every quarter to a figure more than 60% higher than the fourth quarter of 1990.

Figure 5:
Cocaine-Related Emergency Room (ER) Episodes by Facility Location,
1988-93

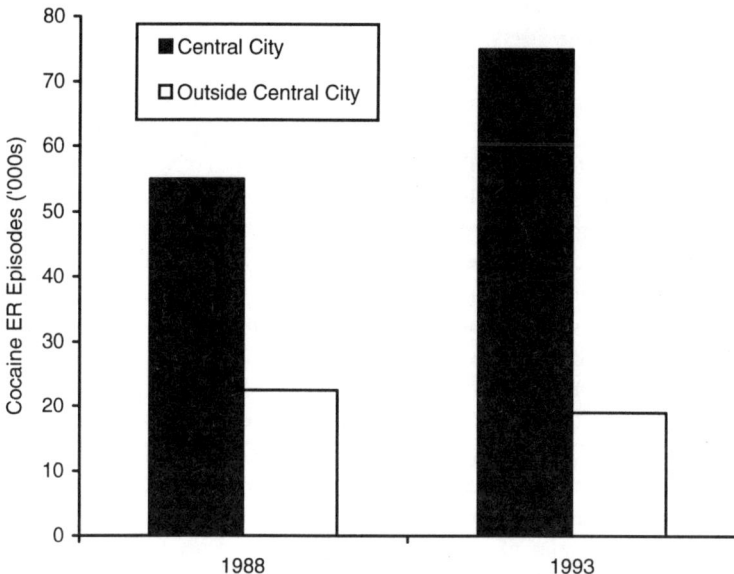

The sharp one-year decline is very puzzling in that most DAWN cocaine incidents involve persons who have been using cocaine heavily for some time. Almost 60% of the DAWN cocaine records indicate dependency as the motive for taking the drug. This is a population that is likely to find it difficult to quit in a short period of time. Nonetheless, there is credible evidence of a sharp one-year reduction in cocaine use; interestingly, there was also a substantial, though smaller, reduction in heroin-related Emergency Room mentions.

The data also permit examination of variation within metropolitan areas. Figure 5 cumulates the number of cocaine episodes for all DAWN metropolitan areas and separates those in centre cities from those outside the centre cities for 1988 and 1993. As can be seen, a large and rising share are found in central city Emergency Rooms.

Integrating the Indicators

The data sets described above were not developed through an integrated scheme intended to describe patterns of drug use and abuse in the nation. Each series was generated by a particular institutional interest or need. As one might expect, it is not easy to put the pieces together to describe the whole picture. The focus here is on the long-term changes.

It should already be apparent that the various indicators need careful reconciliation. The stability of the household and high school senior survey figures, showing a slow increase between 1979 and 1985 in the total number of cocaine users, contrasts with the dramatic increase in total numbers of Medical Examiner reported deaths and Emergency Room admissions that occurred even before crack had become widely available in most cities. The downturn in the survey figures between 1985 and 1992 appears inconsistent with the sharp growth in DAWN. Sceptics have suggested that this invalidates the self-report surveys. Instead, it points to a need for an understanding of drug use as a career rather than as an event; we continue to focus here on cocaine.

During the late 1970s and early 1980s, many individuals (mostly young adults) experimented with cocaine. Some became regular, but occasional, users; a smaller group went on to become regular and frequent users. By the mid-1980s, the flow of initiates had slowed down substantially. But the total stock of drug users did not begin to decline because so many of the earlier initiates were still using. As the dangers (medical rather than legal) of cocaine use became much more prominent, regular users who were not dependent (generally less frequent users) became increasingly likely to quit. The overdose deaths of prominent athletes Len Bias and Don Rogers, young men in excellent physical condition, may have had a pronounced effect; that is certainly one plausible explanation for the sudden drop in the high school senior rate in 1986. The better educated, occasional users were more likely to be influenced by the health messages than their less educated counterparts.

Thus, there was a marked change in the composition of the cocaine-using population. As cocaine became cheaper (and more addictive), those who used it became more likely to use it more heavily; and poorer people, whose use has more serious effects both for themselves and for society, may now constitute a larger share of the total user population. As a result, there is now a stronger association between cocaine use and health problems (thus the DAWN rise) and a strong association between cocaine use and crime.

The failure of the Medical Examiner figures to turn down in 1989, when the Emergency Room figures dropped sharply, is consistent with this story. Death from cocaine-related causes comes later in drug-using careers than does appearance at Emergency Rooms. We mean something more than the tautology that death is the last event; death is more likely later in a drug user's career than earlier. Thus, even as the population of users or heavy users declines, the total mortality of the user population may rise, with a higher share of them in their fifth or later year of regular use.

Quantities and Expenditures

For the purpose of understanding how Latin American nations will be affected by patterns of US consumption it is necessary to go beyond prevalence and consider quantities and expenditures. Although tolerable price data are available, quantity estimates are quite weak.[7] Tables 2 and 3 show recent official estimates of consumption and expenditure for cocaine, heroin and marijuana.

Table 2:
Total US Consumption of Illicit Drugs, 1988-1991 (in metric tons)

Drug		1988	1989	1990	1991
Cocaine	High	269	292	199	254
	Low	188	210	142	182
Heroin	High	12	14	11	13
	Low	8	8	6	7
Marijuana		1,750	1,190	1,025	

Source: What America's Users Spend on Illegal Drugs, Abt Associates Inc., 1988-91

Table 3:
Total US Expenditures on Illicit Drugs, 1988-1993 (in $ billions)

Drug	1988	1989	1990	1991	1992	1993
Cocaine	41.9	43.2	39.5	35.8	33.7	31.9
Heroin	11.7	12.0	10.8	8.6	7.3	7.4
Marijuana	8.9	9.0	9.6	9.0	10.1	9.0
Total	62.5	64.2	59.9	53.4	51.1	48.3

Source: What America's Users Spend on Illegal Drugs, Abt Associates Inc., 1988-93

These estimates are all drawn from calculations of domestic consumption and turn out to be difficult to reconcile with figures from supply-side sources. The estimation problem on the consumption side lies in the need to obtain information about the quantities typically consumed by the small and often difficult-to-reach population of heavy users. A variety of studies show that consumption of cocaine and marijuana is highly concentrated; i.e., a high percentage of the total is consumed by a modest fraction of all users. For example, Everingham and Rydell estimated that 22% of all cocaine users, those who use at least once per week, account for 70% of total consumption (Everingham and Rydell, 1994). This very thorough study started with the official estimate of total quantity because of the difficulty of developing an independent estimate with the available data. The concentration among a small share of all users is a reminder of why changes in the total number of users have only a modest effect (at least contemporaneously) on the severity of problems related to a specific drug.

Official estimates of consumption have to be pieced together from estimates for particular user groups. The totals are given in Table 2 for the years 1988-91, the only ones available.[8] The cocaine figure has been fairly constant for the period since 1988, except for a drop in 1990 usually attributed to the law enforcement crackdown in Colombia following the assassination of presidential candidate Luis Carlos Galán in September 1989. The official expenditure estimates (see Table 3) show a steady decline since 1989. In current dollars the total fell from $64 billion in 1989 to $48 billion in 1993 (approximately 25%). Cocaine accounts for about two-thirds of the total in both years.

The share of this to be attributed to the producer nations is difficult to estimate for conceptual as well as empirical reasons. While processing and growing income is clearly attributable to the producer nations, payments for smuggling activities may include substantial amounts to transhipment country nationals, US nationals or Latin American natives resident in the USA. Nor is it clear how far down the distribution chain the source country nationals continue to participate and hence what share of total US sales revenues should be attributed to them. These are critical issues because the export price of drugs is such a small share of the retail price. Cocaine sells at less than $5,000 per kilogram at export, compared to $150,000 per kilogram at retail ($100 per gram for a 67% pure gram). Figures from production side estimates tell a very different story. Typically, the figures are much higher; for cocaine the production-based figures are about 50% higher than those developed from consumption sources. For marijuana, the differences are dramatic; the official estimate of Mexican marijuana production, almost all intended for the US market, is always at least three times that of total US consumption.[9]

Western Europe[10]

The Prevalence of Drug Use
It is difficult to make meaningful cross-national comparisons of the prevalence of drug use in the general population. Few European nations conduct regular surveys; indeed some have conducted none at all, in itself an interesting indication of differences in attitudes towards drug use.[11] Moreover, the surveys often have important differences in their population coverage and the questions asked. Coverage is a particularly vexing problem; for some adult surveys the sampling frame is all those above a particular age, while others have an upper bound. Given that drug use was rare behaviour for those coming to adulthood prior to 1965, rates for all those over the age of 18 are likely to be much lower than for those between 18 and 45.

The surveys support a few conclusions about prevalence across nations and over time. We conclude that throughout the 1980s, marijuana was used by a moderate to high fraction of youth in most Western European nations; the figures do not generally show any strong time trends in the decade. US rates, although declining rapidly throughout the decade, were much higher than those in Europe. Every nation in our sample, except perhaps Sweden, suffered at least a moderate heroin epidemic in the last 20 years; Italy, Spain and Switzerland, all relative late starters, have been particularly badly affected and Scandinavia has generally been least affected. Cocaine has still not had a major impact on Europe, notwithstanding large and growing seizures. Amphetamines are at least as serious a problem as cocaine in most of Europe. Table 4 represents our best effort to take account of the differences and present the basic data on prevalence of illicit drugs among the twelve nations in our data base.

Table 4:
Prevalence of Marijuana Use Among Juveniles (circa 1990)

Nation	Year	Age Range	Prevalence* Approx. Age 15	Prevalence* Teenage Range	Prevalence* Approx. Age 18
Denmark	1990	15	17%		
	1990	16-19		20%	
Copenhagen	1990	15	25%		
		18			52%
France	1988	18			20%
Germany	1990	14-25		15%	
Hamburg	1990-91	12-24		21%	
Italy					
Netherlands	1991	14-21		24%	
	1990	10-18		4%	
	1988-89	15-16	11%		
		17-18			18%
Amsterdam	1990	15-16	15%		
		17-18			36%
Norway	1991	15-20		8%	
Oslo	1991	15-20		16%	
Spain	1991	High School			17%
Catalonia	1990	12-14	3%		
		15-29		20%	
Sweden	1990	9th Graders	8%		
	1989	16	6%		
Stockholm	1990	15	8%		
Switzerland	1990	15-16	10%		
UK**	1991	14	10%		
USA	1991	12-17	13%		
	1990	High School Seniors			41%
	1991	High School Seniors			37%

* Prevalence columns reflect roughly comparable age groups.
** Prevalence of use of any illicit drug, not just cannabis.

Surveys of the juvenile population were used because they are more comparable in terms of the ages covered; they are also less affected by differences in when drugs first became readily available in the nation.[12] Emphasis is on comparisons with the USA. Table 4 presents two figures for each nation for which the data are available: the percentage of the 'juvenile' population reporting at least one experience of using an illicit psychoactive drug in their lifetime and the percentage reporting use of such a drug within the past year. The table also shows the age group covered by the data and the year of the survey.

It is worth noting what we shall see in all measures of problem severity, namely that the USA stands out as an extreme case. A higher percentage of the US population has tried some illicit drug, more of them have gone on to use such drugs on a regular basis for an extended period of time (at least some months) and more of them turn out to have suffered serious harm as a result, at least as reflected in the number that are classified as dependent. Yet experience with marijuana and other drugs is by no means a rarity for younger cohorts in most nations. For example, in 1988, 20% of French 18-year olds reported use of an illicit drug at some time in their life.

Prevalence varies among communities within a nation. As might be expected, drug use tends to be more prevalent in large cities. In Norway, a national survey in 1987 estimated prevalence of 8.2% among 15-20 year olds, while the figure for Oslo in the same year was almost exactly double that, 16.3% (Hauge, 1985).

Many European nations report clear declines in the prevalence of drug use since at least the late 1970s. In some cases, e.g. Sweden, the decline started even earlier: whereas at the beginning of the 1970s, 5% of conscripts reported use of an illicit drug in the last month, that figure had fallen to only 1% in 1988 (Swedish National Institute of Public Health, 1993, p.13), a result consistent with surveys of high school students.

As in the USA, a sharp decline in drug use among the general population in Western Europe does not necessarily generate a decline in the extent of drug dependence and related problems (Reuter, Ebener and McCaffrey, 1994). Those who were drug dependent in the early 1990s consist mostly of persons who became dependent in the distant past. The prevalence of drug use among the general population determines the flow of new users into the dependent category, so that the decline in that prevalence simply lowered or ended the growth in drug dependence. That is best indicated by the increasing age of the heroin-dependent in Western Europe. In Sweden, a study in 1992 found that only 10% of heavy drug abusers were under 25 years old, compared to 37% in 1979 (Swedish Council for Information on Alcohol and Other Drugs, 1993).

'Hard drug' use almost entirely involves heroin. That is certainly the case for treatment populations and overdose figures; typically heroin (or other opiates, including methadone) accounts for 90% of all European deaths recorded as drug-related. The figures on cocaine suggest that it is neither widely used nor heavily used by those who do consume it (Bieleman, Diaz, Merlo and Kaplan, 1993). In no country were we able to find evidence that for more than 5% of treatment admissions cocaine was the primary drug of abuse. In a few nations, notably Spain and Italy, it showed up as the secondary drug of abuse for about one quarter of the total. There are some indications of local problems in certain cities. Zurich has seen a major increase in cocaine use associated with the development of the Platzspitz in the centre of the city. In Britain, Home Office notifications of cocaine addicts rose from 1,085 in 1990 to 2,463 in 1993. Nonetheless, cocaine still accounts for barely 10% of all Home Office notifications.

Seizure data for cocaine rose rapidly in the mid-1980s in Western Europe; indeed, the figures for Western Europe from 1984-90 were almost identical to those for federal seizures in the United States from 1978 to 1984. However, the figures stagnated from 1990 to 1993 at about 17 tons per annum, compared to over 100 tons for the USA; in 1994, the figure jumped to 28 tons, still only one quarter of US levels.[13]

The data pointing to low levels of heavy use of cocaine suggest that Western Europe still accounts for a small share of South American drug production. That certainly is the best interpretation of the scraps of survey and treatment data and is consistent with data on border seizures. Seizure figures are difficult to interpret, but the USA is much more accessible to smugglers than is Western Europe; there is no equivalent of the Mexican land border providing low-risk opportunities for both small and large-scale smuggling. Although Europe may devote fewer resources to interdiction than the USA, it is likely that the interdiction rate in Western Europe is higher. If that is the case, then the recent seizure figures (less than 30 tons, compared to over 100 tons in the USA) suggest that the European market is much smaller.

The Future

Projecting the future of drug problems is hazardous even when a good deal of data is available; the epidemic of crack-cocaine still seems to be the result of an unpredictable marketing innovation rather than changes in the characteristics of demand. In Western Europe, the data are too poor for any but the most speculative projections, which I shall avoid in this chapter.

After a long period of decline, the general population surveys in the USA showed some increases in prevalence in 1993 and 1994. Youthful marijuana use has shown a large rise over that two-year period, particularly in *Monitoring the Future* (Johnston, Bachman and O'Malley, annual). Statements from senior officials as well as the principal investigator of that study predict that, unless firm action is taken promptly, we are likely to see a new epidemic of use of more expensive and harmful drugs. The call to arms has been reinforced by claims that heroin use among young adults in the USA has already started to expand as the price of heroin has plummeted and purity has risen. Both claims should be looked at with considerable scepticism: a rise in marijuana use is not a particularly plausible predictor of cocaine and heroin use, while the indicators of current heroin use show a surprising lack of evidence of new use, as opposed to more frequent use by current addicts. On the other hand, it is interesting to note that increasing incarceration rates may be the most significant source of demand reduction for cocaine and heroin in the past decade.

Marijuana Today, Cocaine Tomorrow?
Since 1992 the percentage of high school seniors reporting use of marijuana has risen sharply; for the last-30-days measure, the figure has risen from 11.9% to 19.0%. In 1993, the NHSDA prevalence figure for the age group 11-17 increased moderately. Since the probability that a non-marijuana user becomes a cocaine user later is dramatically smaller than the probability for a marijuana user, it is argued that this implies a cocaine epidemic is on its way.

The logic is not unshakeable. First, it does not distinguish between the 'average' and 'marginal' marijuana users. It may well be that, on average, marijuana users are much more likely to become cocaine users, but the tail of the marijuana user population (arrayed notionally in terms of the commitments to the drug) may not be at such high risk. In effect, some non-users who are at high risk of becoming cocaine users may tip over into marijuana use as the drug becomes cheaper, more accessible or less disapproved of. Second, only a modest fraction of cocaine users use that drug intensively and experience problems. The marginal marijuana users are likely to include many who will, at most, experiment with cocaine. The upturn in marijuana use may not generate any substantial increase in cocaine use in the next few years.

Heroin
Since about 1992, there has been concern that a decline in heroin prices, particularly in New York, and a rise in purity that allows snorting or

smoking of heroin, has generated a new heroin epidemic (BOTEC, 1993). The most recent *National Drug Control Strategy* (NDCS) states that 'data collected in hospital emergency rooms, police departments, criminal courts, public assistance programs, schools and on the streets show that heroin consumption in the United States is increasing' (Office of National Drug Control Policy, 1995, p.103). Yet most of the statistical evidence presented in the same report contradicts this. The exception is the number of Emergency Room admissions, which, as was argued above, is driven primarily by the number of long-term addicts.

Estimates from the National Household Survey on Drug Abuse show no increase in the estimated number who report use of heroin at least once in their life. The 1993 estimate of 2.3 million is up from the 1.8 million in 1992 but down from the 2.7 million in 1991 (*NDCS* Table B-3) and only moderately higher than the 2.0 million in 1985.[14] The official estimates of current heroin users show a downward trend among those using less than weekly; the 1993 figure of 229,000 compares with the 1988 estimate of 539,000. Finally, the DUF figures for heroin in recent years show essentially flat rates for all cities except Chicago.

It is true that prices are down substantially from levels that had prevailed from the mid-1970s. The official estimate is that retail prices for a pure gram of heroin (sold diluted in packages containing about 25 pure milligrams) in 1993 were between $837 and $2,553, compared to $1,612-$3,007 in 1988. Similarly, purity has risen, although the extent of that increase varies a great deal among cities; the fraction of users in various surveys reporting that they snort heroin has increased substantially in recent years.

The most plausible, though scarcely unassailable, interpretation of these data is that the lower price and higher purity have led to higher consumption levels by experienced heroin users and to some initiation into heroin use among experienced cocaine users. The urinalysis data suggest that even the latter effect is quite modest, since experienced cocaine users are at high risk of arrest and yet the rates of heroin positives among arrestees has remained quite stable.

Newspapers continue to provide a stream of stories about middle class heroin users – including some about quite young users – dying of overdoses. The surveillance systems are not well structured for capturing that type of problem, but it is at least surprising that those systems have picked up so little evidence of increased use in otherwise high-risk populations.

Prisons

An important factor influencing indicators of problematic drug use, such as the urinalysis and DAWN figures, may be the increasing population of persons incarcerated. Between the end of 1985 and the end of 1993, the US prison population increased from about 775,000 (including federal, state and local correctional facilities) to about 1,410,000. Moreover, there is reason to believe that the incarcerated population became richer in drug users over that time; for example, in 1990 (the most recent year for which the data are available), one-third of those sent to state prison were convicted of drug offences, compared to only 16% in 1986. Taking account of high-use rates among those charged with non-drug offences as well, perhaps a total of 600,000 additional drug users were removed from the population that might be captured in the DAWN system.

It is also important to note that the populations under supervision of probation and parole agencies have risen substantially in recent years – from 2.9 million in 1985 to 3.5 million in 1993. These programmes are giving increasing emphasis to monitoring and punishing drug use in these populations. This may also contribute to declines in the extent of frequent drug use.

The declines in most drug indicators may thus be something of an artefact. Rather than fewer drug users in the USA, it may simply be that more of them are currently incarcerated or under correctional supervision. This lowers the evidence of damage that drug use does to the rest of the community, while also reducing the harm that the incarcerated drug users do to themselves. But it also changes the interpretation of declines in DUF and DAWN data. Enforcement may not so much have changed the behaviour of drug users as, rather, have changed their circumstances. If incarceration and supervision do not reduce the propensity to use drugs (and few observers believe that current correctional programmes offer much hope in that respect), then unless the nation is willing to maintain its currently extraordinarily high correctional population, the drug indicators may worsen again. For better or for worse, it appears that the USA is indeed willing to maintain, if not expand, the size of its incarcerated population, whether through measures such as the California 'Three Strikes' law, passed by a popular referendum in 1993, or by the abolition of parole, as instituted by the state of Virginia in 1994, or in other ways.

The most plausible projection is of a slowly declining demand for the expensive drugs, cocaine and heroin. AIDS and other disease will surely make substantial inroads into an ageing heroin population. The Latin American share of this declining market will depend on the relative efficiency of Asian and Latin American smugglers; it is hard to make any projections on that matter. For cocaine, the decline should be slower, because the epidemic of new use was more recent and the current users are younger. With Western Europe still a relatively small market for cocaine, the boom period for the Latin American cocaine industry is probably over.

Notes

*   This chapter is based on research supported by grants from the Ford and Alfred Sloan Foundations to RAND's Drug Policy Research Center. I would like to acknowledge research assistance from Gina Hilger.

1.   This section draws heavily on Reuter, Ebener and McCaffrey (1994).

2.   A systematic model of this dynamic for cocaine is provided in Everingham and Rydell (1994).

3.   The DUF data also point to an interesting aspect of drug use, namely its variation among cities. In San Diego, amphetamines are detected in about 25% of adult male arrestees, whereas in most cities the corresponding figure is less than 5%. Heroin is detected in 19% of Chicago adult male arrestees, but less than 2% in Miami.

4.   Wish used DUF data to estimate the total number of current cocaine users at about 2 million in 1988 (Wish, 1990-91).

5.   DAWN is dependent on information registered in medical records, not on direct patient reports. The system is vulnerable to changes in record-keeping procedures and in the extent to which doctors ask their patients about specific drugs or order tests. It is hard to assess how these factors have changed in recent years.

6.   The DAWN data, like those from the Drug Use Forecasting system, also point to the great local variation in use of particular drugs. For example, in 1989, 35% of San Diego arrestees tested positive for amphetamine use, while in nine other cities less than 5% tested positive for that drug. In 1988, San Diego accounted for 20% of all the DAWN amphetamine Emergency Room incidents. In the District of Columbia, where PCP dominated urinalysis figures until 1988, there were more Emergency Room episodes in 1986 involving PCP than cocaine; in Philadelphia, PCP episodes were only one-fifteenth as frequent as cocaine episodes.

7.   It is interesting to note that quantity plays almost no role in policy discussions, though it is an important indicator of the severity of drug problems and potentially useful for programme evaluation.

8.   It is interesting to note that the federal government in its first *National*

Drug Control Strategy listed quantities of drugs as an indicator to be used for assessing progress in drug control, but then had to drop the measure because no reliable figures could be found.

9. For more detail on the absurdity of the Mexican marijuana estimates, see Reuter and Ronfeldt (1992).

10. This section draws on work done in collaboration with Robert MacCoun. The countries included in our work are Great Britain, Denmark, France, Germany, Italy, the Netherlands, Norway, Spain, Sweden and Switzerland.

11. The USA, with its emphasis on reducing the number of drug users rather than lowering the harms associated with drug use, has given much more attention to measuring general prevalence than to the extent of addiction or related problems. Great Britain, with a policy that almost explicitly rejects occasional use of drugs as a major concern of policy, has almost no prevalence data; a few questions in the Britain Crime Surveys of 1981 and 1992 so far constitute the only source of data on national prevalence in Britain (Mott and Mirrlees-Black, 1993).

12. For example, most of Western Europe experienced a sharp increase in marijuana use in the late 1960s, whereas Spain had low rates until the death of Franco in 1975. Thus, those aged 45 in 1990 in Spain were much less exposed than their counterparts in Sweden or Germany to marijuana use during their high risk years.

13. Seizure data provided by Interpol.

14. Lifetime use in a national cross-sectional sample – given that heroin use was very rare before 1965, was started by young persons in the late 1960s and 1970s and is not associated (for occasional users) with very high mortality rates – should rise slowly with a constant number of experimenters each year. However, there is a downward bias arising from the tendency of infrequent users not to recall use when asked about it many years later.

CHAPTER 2

DRUG CONSUMPTION IN LATIN AMERICA*

Augusto Pérez Gómez

To the attentive observer, it is obvious that illicit drugs are being consumed in most of Latin America, but the nature of the problem varies from country to country. Different degrees of consumption can be observed in various parts of Latin America, although some countries, such as Brazil, display a wide range of consumption patterns. This chapter divides the countries of Latin America into three groups in descending order, according to the data available about their relative rates of illicit drug consumption:

1. The Andean countries, Panama and the east coast of Brazil. These appear to have the highest rates of illicit drug consumption. ·
2. Central America and Mexico.
3. The four countries of the Southern Cone: Argentina, Chile, Uruguay and Paraguay.

This classification is based on reports presented by representatives of these countries in international fora, but any errors contained herein are mine.[1] There are few serious and systematic studies on the consumption of psychoactive substances, and in many of those that exist the quality of information leaves much to be desired. I have selected some of the best studies, which illustrate the existence of the problem adequately; some documents were omitted because they referred to very small samples or geographical areas, or used only inhabitants treated by health services (De La Quintana, 1992; Alcalá Afanador, 1990), or where they suffered from serious methodological limitations, or were more than six years old. In any case, the following general observations about the studies analysed in this chapter should be taken into account:

a. All the reports are household surveys, which implies that marginal sectors of the population (homeless adults, people resident in hotels, children and 'street urchins', prostitutes, prisoners) and soldiers, police or civil guards living in camps, were omitted from the samples. According to preliminary data, drug consumption in these groups is higher than among the general population.

b. The results of the surveys are not consistent with the clinical data:

medical records tend to indicate that the surveys considerably underestimate the consumption of illegal substances.

c. Household surveys in many Latin American countries (Peru, Haiti, Panama, Ecuador, Bolivia) indicate a high degree of falsehood and concealment amongst the inhabitants. Even in those cases where measures are taken to ensure confidentiality, the subjects appear suspicious; owing to the fact that they are being questioned at home, they believe that identification is always possible.[2]

We shall now examine the chief studies available, in a certain amount of detail.

Colombia and Peru

Consumption of a variety of illicit drugs is higher in Colombia and Peru than elsewhere in the region. The fact that they are the largest producers/processors of cocaine tends to exacerbate consumption because in both countries illicit drugs are easily available at low prices. Researchers have produced fairly systematic studies of consumption in both Colombia and Peru in the last eight years. Corresponding data for Brazil and Panama are less precise.

A. *Colombia*

The first serious epidemiological study of illicit drug use in Colombia appeared in 1987 (Torres and Murrelle, 1987). Unfortunately, the authors took a sample of 2,800 subjects in the four major cities (700 in each of the following: Bogotá, Medellín, Cali and Barranquilla) and applied their conclusions to the country in general, a methodologically unsound approach. Two years later a further study of Bogotá was carried out (Pérez Gómez, Correa and Salazar, 1991) with the objective of correcting some of the methodological errors in the previous study and of offering empirical support to a major primary prevention project. In 1992 and 1993, three new studies were undertaken: one analysed drug use in Bogotá and is referred to here as EPI-II (Pérez Gómez, Aja and Correa, 1993); the other two analysed data collected nationally (Rodríguez, Duque and Rodríguez, 1993; Ministerio de Salud, 1993). The last two studies are referred to as Santa Fe and Min. Salud respectively and, together with EPI-II they form the basis of Figure 1. The statistics include alcohol and tobacco, which for the purpose of this chapter will also be considered as drugs.

Figure 1:
Lifetime Prevalence of Drug Use in Colombia, 1993
(as percentage of adults)

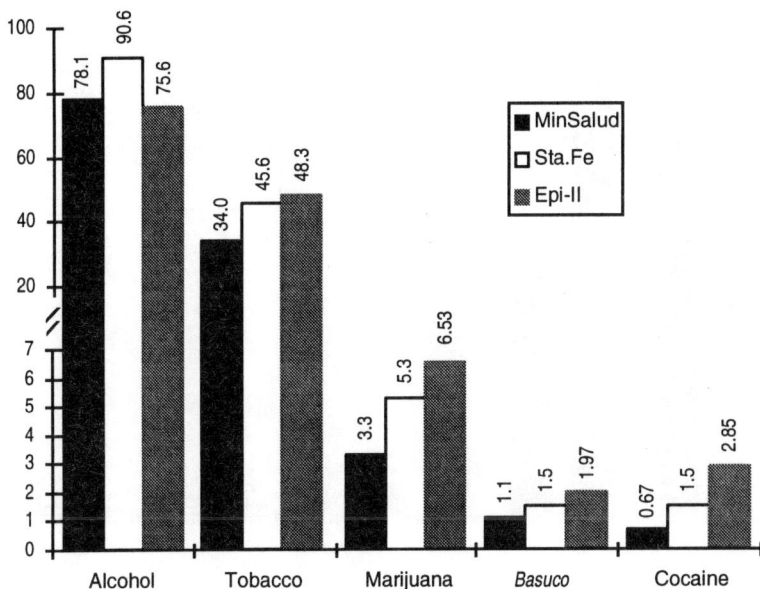

As was to be expected, alcohol is the most widely used drug in Colombia (see Figure 1); amongst the illegal substances, marijuana takes first place, followed by cocaine and cocaine base (*basuco*).[3] Some of the discrepancies in the data can be explained by the fact that EPI-II refers exclusively to Bogotá, where the concentration of drug users is probably greater than in the country as a whole. What is striking is that, in the case of all substances except alcohol, the Ministry of Health (Min. Salud) has less data than that available in the two other reports.

Each of the three surveys found the same tendencies when those surveyed were asked about their drug consumption habits in the previous year (see Figure 2), although there were substantial differences in the absolute numbers. Such differences can be more clearly observed in Tables 1 and 2, which are statistical projections of the percentages presented in Figures 1 and 2.

Figure 2:
Prevalence of Drug Use in Colombia, 1993 (Year Prior to Survey)

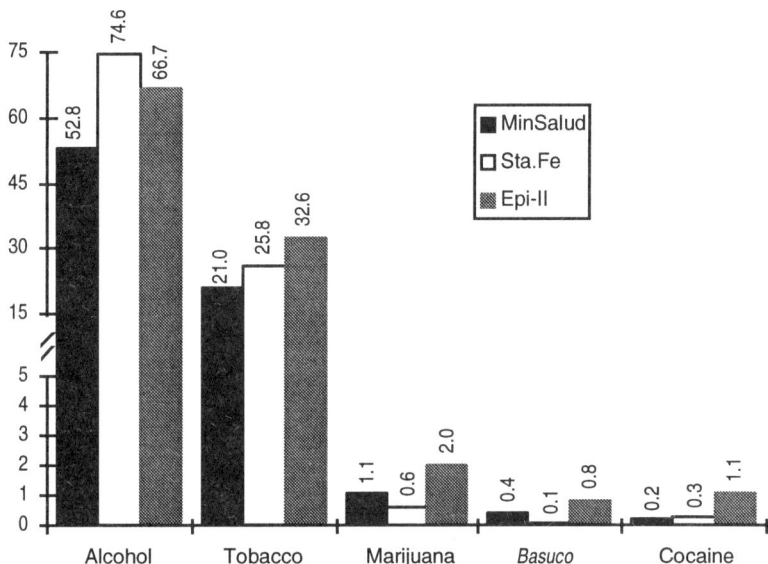

Table 1:
Estimated Number of Colombians Aged 12-45 Years Using Drugs at Some Point in Their Life: 1993

	Drug Users in Bogotá (Epi-II)	Drug Users, National (Santa Fe)	Drug Users, National (Min. Salud)
Alcohol	2,646,000	18,120,000	15,620,000
Tobacco	1,550,050	8,860,000	6,800,000
Marijuana	227,500	1,000,000	660,000
Basuco	70,000	300,000	220,000
Cocaine	101,500	300,000	134,000

*Sources:*Pérez Gómez, Correa and Aja (1993); Rodríguez, Duque and Rodríguez (1993); Ministerio de Salud (1993)

The data refer exclusively to members of the population between the ages of 12 and 45 years, taking 3.5 million as the minimum population in Bogotá of people of that age range, and 20 million for the country as a whole. Although Table 1 suggests much higher rates of drug use than Table 2, the lower figures are still surprisingly high in view of Colombia's reputation as a producer rather than consumer country.

Table 2:
Estimated Number of Colombians Aged 12-45 Years Using Drugs in Year Prior to Survey: 1993

	Drug Users in Bogotá (Epi-II)	Drug Users, National (Santa Fe)	Drug Users, National (Min. Salud)
Alcohol	2,331,000	14,920,000	10,560,000
Tobacco	1,141,000	5,160,000	4,200,000
Marijuana	70,000	120,000	220,000
Basuco	28,000	20,000[4]	80,000
Cocaine	38,500	60,000	40,000

The most reliable statistics are those for Bogotá, as reported in EPI-II. This survey was also very detailed, making it possible to develop a more precise picture of drug users. For that reason, the remaining figures for Colombia will be drawn from this survey.

It can be seen (see Figure 3) that, with the exception of tranquillisers, men use more pyschoactive substances, both legal and illegal, than women. Even where the differences pertaining to the use of alcohol are not apparently very great, analysis of the quantities ingested and frequency of ingestion reveals that in reality these differences are considerable. The ratio of men to women for the three main illegal drugs is : marijuana, 3:1; cocaine, 4:1; and *basuco*, 5:1.[4] In the case of inhalants, the ratio is 8:1.

A comparison between the different age groups (see Figure 4) shows that a virtually identical pattern emerges for the three main illegal substances: the number of users increases progressively with age up to the age group 25-34, but drops thereafter. This pattern of drug use appears similar to that found in a number of European countries (see Chapter 1).

Figure 3:
Prevalence of Periodic Drug Use in Bogotá, by Gender: 1993
(as percentage of adults)

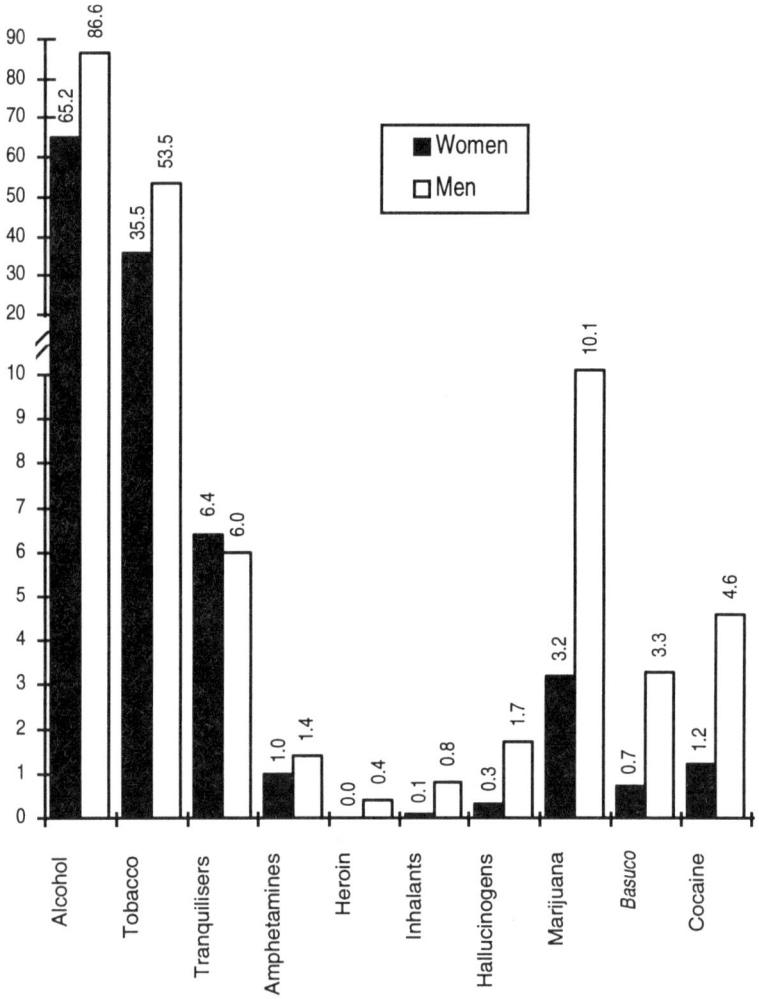

Source: Pérez Gómez, Aja and Correa (1993)

Figure 4:
Lifetime Prevalence of Drug Use in Bogotá, by Age: 1993
(as percentage of age cohort)

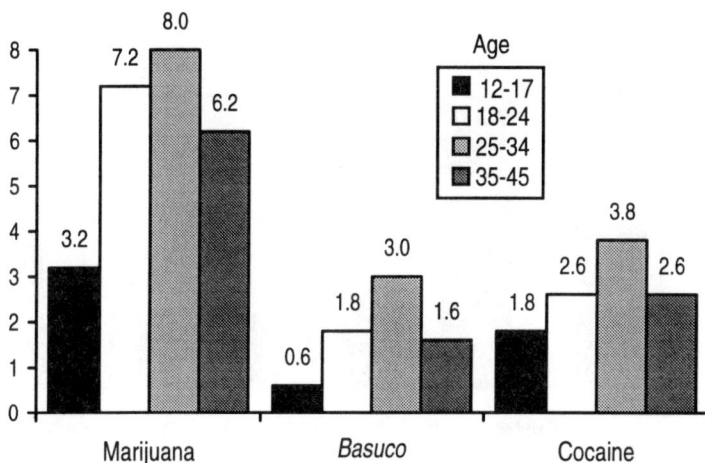

Source: Pérez Gómez, Aja and Correa (1993)

The EPI-II survey for Bogotá distinguishes between drug users not only by gender and age, but also by socio-economic status. The main findings are shown in Figure 5. The highest frequency of marijuana use occurs in the upper classes, while the use of *basuco* is associated with the lower rather than the middle classes. The use of cocaine is directly related to social class: the higher the socio-economic level, the greater the use of cocaine. In absolute terms, however, the situation is obviously completely different, since in Colombia the upper class is very small and the middle class not much larger.

These results show that Colombia has a significant illicit drug consumption problem; the situation is not so grave as in the USA (see Chapter 1), but it is indisputably a serious one. No country can afford to allow a substantial proportion of its active population to become addicted.[5] If Colombia was the only country in Latin America facing this problem, it might be different. As we shall now see, however, circumstances are not so different in Peru.

Figure 5:
Prevalence of Drug Use in Bogotá in Year Prior to Survey, by Socio-Economic Status: 1993 (as percentage of adults)

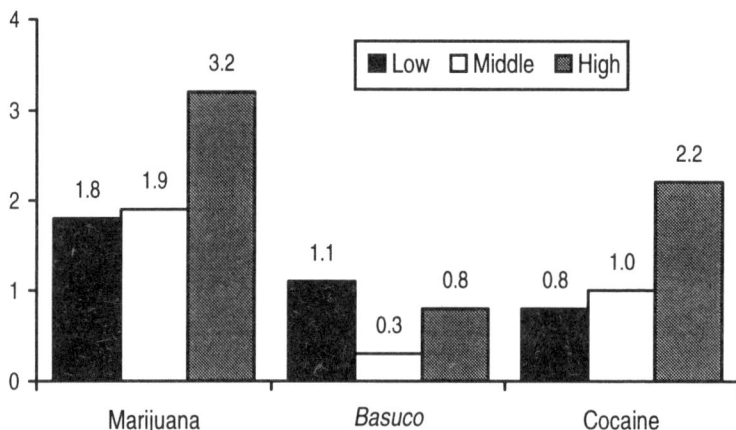

Source: Pérez Gómez, Aja and Correa (1993)

B. Peru

Peru, like Colombia is a major producer of drugs. The impact of drugs on Peruvian society has been the subject of a considerable amount of research. Until recently, however, Peru's role as a consumer of drugs was ignored. This has begun to change and now research has revealed the scale of the problem.

The main results for Peru are shown in Table 3. The estimates of drug consumption are very similar to Colombia, as can be seen by comparing Table 3 with Figure 1. The main difference is that the use of coca leaf (not included in the Colombian questionnaire) is of major importance in Peru, with nearly one-quarter of all adults estimated to be users in 1992.

It is difficult to explain the apparent fall in consumption in 1988 for all drugs (see Table 3), but it is likely that there was a problem in the sampling: the differences between the results of the 1986 surveys and those of 1992 are very slight, and there is no social or economic reason which could explain the drop and subsequent increase in consumption.[6]

Table 3:
Drug Consumption in Peru by Substance: 1986, 1988, 1992
(as percentage of adults)

Substance	1986 (%)	1988 (%)	1992 (%)
Alcohol	89.7	84.8	94.0
Tobacco	72.4	59.2	73.1
Marijuana	10.5	5.8	8.4
Basuco	4.7	3.3	4.4
Cocaine	3.3	1.5	2.7
Licit/Prescribed Drugs	28.7	24.5	25.1
Inhalants	4.0	2.3	3.3
Coca Leaf	18.2	14.0	22.7
Hallucinogens	2.4	1.2	2.5

Source: Fernando *et al* (1993)

El Salvador and Mexico

Research on drug consumption in these two countries is still quite limited, although *prima facie* evidence suggests that drug use is far from negligible. We will begin with El Salvador, where research was hampered in the 1980s by civil war.

The first significant attempt to complete a serious study in El Salvador (Castro Aguilar and Hernández, 1991), was at the beginning of the 1990s. This research can nevertheless be criticised on two grounds: first, more men than women were selected for the sample, making the *a priori* assumption that the former consume more; second, it is not known with any certainty whether the proportions of the sample, in terms of socio-economic levels, correspond to the general population.

Despite these shortcomings, the Salvadorean data (see Table 4) are quite surprising in view of the fact that the country is not a producer of drugs (unlike Colombia and Peru) and must therefore import narcotics from elsewhere.

Table 4 refers to the metropolitan area of San Salvador, capital of El Salvador, and reveals a high number of marijuana consumers. According to the authors, 80% of those who smoke do so at least once per week, 48.9% smoke daily and 63.3% smoke at least twice a week. Obviously, the number of consumers of cocaine and cocaine-derivates is lower than in the Andean countries, but in any event it is higher than might be expected.

Table 4:
Drug Consumption in San Salvador (El Salvador): 1991
(as percentage of adults)

Substance	Periodic prevalence	Habitual consumption
Alcohol	90.0	42.9
Tobacco	78.9	27.4
Marijuana	23.3	2.9
Cocaine	3.2	0.36
Tranquilisers	34.4	6.0
Stimulants	29.3	15.0

Source: Fundasalva (1991)

Figure 6:
Drug Consumption in Mexico, Periodic Use: 1992
(as percentage of adults)

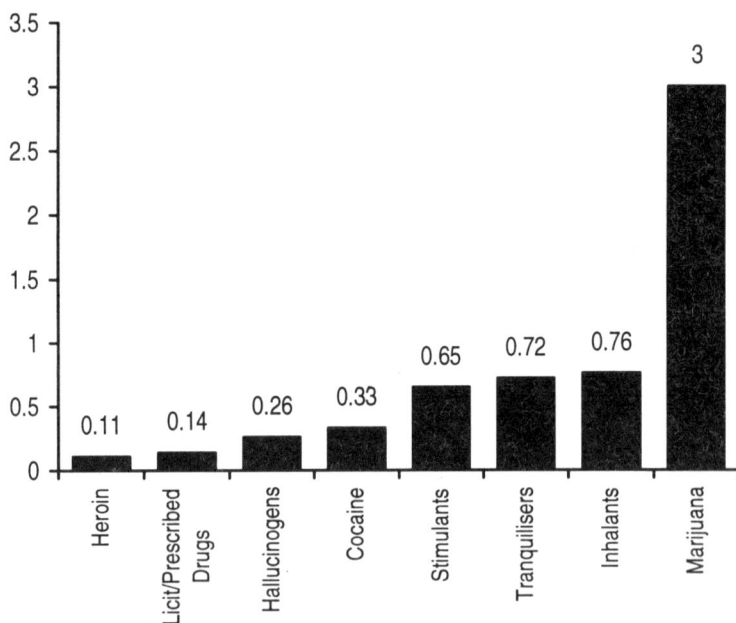

Source: Centros de Integración Juvenil (1992)

Mexico, unlike El Salvador, has for many years been heavily involved in the production and transshipment of drugs to the USA. It would seem natural, therefore, to expect high levels of consumption in comparison with other parts of Latin America. Yet some swings appear to show that there is really no consumption problem in Mexico, since fewer than 1% of inhabitants (see Figure 6) have used an illicit drug at any time, with the exception of marijuana, the use of which is estimated to reach three per cent.

However, more detailed analysis of particular regions indicates otherwise. For example, the results for Baja California, Southern Baja California, Sonora and Sinaloa, were as follows:

Table 5:
Drug Consumption in Baja California, Southern Baja California, Sonora and Sinaloa: 1992 (as percentage of adults)

Substance	At least once (%)	Previous year (%)	Previous month (%)
Marijuana	15.4	7.9	4
Cocaine	4.9	3.4	2.8
Inhalants	3.3	1.4	0.5

Source: Centros de Integración Juvenil (1992)

This regional survey shows that the lifetime prevalence of marijuana use is five times higher, and that of cocaine use 15 times higher, than in Mexico as a whole; indeed with reference to use during the previous month, the data indicate that consumption is proportionately greater in these regions of Mexico than in Peru or Colombia as a whole.

The data from the regional surveys present a very different picture to that provided by the national survey. If the national figures (see Figure 6) are almost certainly under-estimated, it is possible that the regional consumption pattern is biased upward by the focus on four states in close proximity to the USA. The truth is likely to be somewhere in between, leaving Mexico below the levels of drug consumption found in Colombia or Peru, but above those in the rest of Latin America.

The Southern Cone

There has been little research on drug use in the countries of the Southern Cone. Some data are available for Buenos Aires (the problem most frequently cited, apart from alcohol, is heroin) and Santiago (marijuana appears to be the most frequently used drug:), derived from Argentine and Chilean national health systems data. From these, it appears that illicit drug use remains at a very low level. Miguez, Pecci and Carrizosa (1992) carried out a study in Paraguay which produced similar findings.

Conclusions

The data discussed above show that most Latin American countries have a drug consumption problem, a condition that is often denied or ignored in international discussions. The debate presumes that only developed countries suffer the negative consequences of drug consumption. This chapter has shown that this assumption is false.

For those who wish to promote a greater emphasis in Latin America on law enforcement and control of trafficking to prevent illicit drugs reaching those developed countries, the Latin American consumption problem is largely irrelevant. At most, it can be presented as a minor incentive to governments to increase repression. For those who wish to encourage the view that drug use is the preserve of the affluent and 'decadent' cities of the North, evidence of similar patterns in the South is an inconvenient fact to be glossed over or ignored.

Latin Americans are consuming large quantities of both licit and illicit drugs and, although the problem is greater in some countries than in others, its current prevalence suggests that it will, in the future, probably become yet another obstacle to development in the region. However, notwithstanding the problem of illicit drug consumption, the data appear to demonstrate with a reasonable degree of certainty that alcohol abuse is the greatest problem, given the way in which alcohol is consumed in many South American countries.

The illegal drug consumption levels shown here are not equal to those of the USA (see Chapter 1). However, the Latin American drug consumption problem is greater than in many European countries: many Latin American drug users consume more cocaine and cocaine-derivatives, more inhalants and more hallucinogens (except LSD) than their European counterparts. Problems associated with some types of marijuana use are also manifested more frequently in Latin America than in Europe. In spite of this, when Latin American drug use is discussed, very few people listen with any interest.

The problem of drug consumption in Latin America must be urgently addressed by governments' social policies. Consider the following:

a. Drug use is undeniably related to an increase in social disintegration, violence and criminality. In contrast to what is stated in certain European countries – namely, that drugs are in themselves 'harmless', and that what leads to crime is the need to obtain them by whatever means available – there is more than sufficient evidence on the effects of certain substances on the body to show that they are inherently dangerous and threaten both physical and mental health.

b. The consumption of illicit drugs, particularly in accordance with complex patterns of use in Latin America such as the so-called 'ABC' syndrome (alcohol, *basuco*, cannabis), is associated with a number of problems relating to health, domestic instability and economic difficulties.

c. One must remember that Latin America is currently experiencing a big increase in AIDS, particularly in Mexico, Brazil, Colombia, in some Caribbean islands and countries of Central America. This situation is directly or indirectly related to the consumption of illicit drugs: the intravenous use of heroin is becoming more frequent, and, as elsewhere, the consumption of illicit drugs is closely related to heterosexual and homosexual prostitution, as well as unsafe sexual practices. It is worth recalling that in certain Asian countries with no prior tradition of intravenous heroin consumption – Thailand, Vietnam, Myanmar – and with a very low (virtually non-existent) incidence of HIV infection, a sudden change in habits related to heroin consumption unleashed one of the most serious AIDS epidemics in recent times, between 1991 and 1994.

d. The subject of alcohol should be tackled seriously and in depth. In many South American states, taxes on alcohol and tobacco serve to finance health and education projects; this may seem morally unjustifiable, but the same is true of a sizeable number of European countries. Inappropriate consumption of alcohol is associated with the same problems of health, domestic instability, violence and criminality as illegal substances. The legalised status of alcohol should, in principle, facilitate its social control, but this does not appear to be the case in the majority of countries worldwide.

Notes

*   Translated by Patricia Roberts.

1.   Some years ago, my conclusions about Latin American drug patterns were substantially different (Pérez Gómez and Escallón Emiliani, 1990). In Latin America, consumption and trade patterns change rapidly. Five years ago, Bolivia had a consumption problem similar to Colombia's – at least in La Paz, Cochabamba and Santa Cruz de la Sierra – whilst in Panama and Brazil the problem was only nascent. Now, consumption in Panama and Brazil appears to be almost on a par with Colombia and Peru, and in Bolivia consumption appears to have diminished. Within a few years, Colombia moved from being a country which processed basic cocaine paste to become the world's leading producer (Thoumi, 1991, p. 133). And it has become the second producer of heroin in Latin America, after Mexico.

2.   These factors have led some experts to conclude that:

a.   Different survey strategies are required, including in-depth investigations within small sectors of the community.

b.   Even where it is not scientifically acceptable, many experts consider that lifetime prevalence (those who admit to drug use at least once in their lives) reflects use during the previous year, and that the data on the 'previous year' would, in fact, represent current use. It is true to say that, if the survey data were taken as accurate, in many cases it would indicate that at the present time there is not a single consumer of psychoactive substances in certain countries or regions of South America. But it should be noted that 'current use' does not necessarily imply daily use (as tends to be the case with heroin): specifically, in the case of cocaine, we must remember that a particular pattern of consumption exists which is characterised by the use of massive quantities during a relatively short period – one or two days – followed by abstention which can last days or even weeks.

3.   Basic cocaine paste, or *basuco*, is a sub-product of the cocaine production process. A crude, smokable drug, it is most commonly a dried mixture made from coca leaves that have been treated with a solvent and sulphuric acid. Cigarettes containing *basuco* are known as *pitillos*.

4.   The Santa Fe story appears to have underestimated *basuco* consumption since it suggests that there are fewer users of cocaine base in the whole country than the EPI-II survey found in Bogotá alone.

The Santa Fe finding is further brought into question by provisional data provided by 52 treatment centres across the whole country which show that the number of persons soliciting therapeutic aid for drug problems in 1992 was approximately 20,000.

5. Since 1993, there has been evidence of increasing drug use among young adolescents aged 14-16 years, particularly among females. Changing patterns of drug use also include the increasing prevalence of some drugs not previously popular in Colombia. These include benzodiazepines, especially rohypnol, and some cases of heroin use. Clinical evidence has produced a small but not negligible number of heroin cases; as yet there has been no systematic study of these changes.

6. Roberto Lerner (the author of Chapter 5) has observed that the most recent study suffered from serious methodological deficiencies since conclusions had been drawn on the basis of an incomplete sample. Lerner accepted the conclusions on stable consumption in Lima, but disputed the findings that pointed to an increase in provincial consumption.

PART II

DRUGS IN LATIN AMERICA: THE PRODUCER COUNTRIES

CHAPTER 3

THE DRUG TRADE, POLITICS AND THE ECONOMY: THE COLOMBIAN EXPERIENCE*

Jorge Orlando Melo

For Colombians today, drugs are probably the phenomenon which has had the greatest impact on national life. In different ways and with varying degrees of accuracy, all kinds of effects are attributed to the drug trade. For some, one of the main causes of the upward trend of the economy over the last 20 years has been the resources generated by the drug trade. For others, the violence, which has affected the country to a degree unparalleled in any society not at war, is primarily attributable to the large groups of criminals created by the narcotics industry. The destruction of the judicial system, customary impunity for criminal offenders and growing corruption are usually attributed to the influence of the drug traffickers. Many believe that the money and resources have in their turn allowed drugs to influence popular culture, the management of the media, political campaigns and parties, and the distribution of power in general. It is not only foreign journalists or US government rhetoric that characterise Colombia as a 'narco-democracy'. Every day Colombians see on the news how Congress, mayors from remote regions, the judicial system or the bureaucracy are penetrated, influenced and directed by the 'narcos'.

As always happens in complex and dramatic situations, these characterisations hold much truth, but at the same time they are part of a rhetoric which has rarely had such force in other areas. The drug trade globally is a little understood but much denounced phenomenon in which immediate perceptions stubbornly resist contrary evidence. The interests of governments and the media favour sensationalist and extreme views which paradoxically fail to capture the real magnitude of the drug trade, and fail also to analyse the complex causal links and influences that affect it.

In this chapter I give a brief schematic presentation of the issues relating to the drug trade in Colombia in recent years, while not losing sight of the nuances of the problem. I will attempt to follow the development of this trade and its varied influences on Colombian life, taking as my central theme its impact on the politics and economics of the country.

The Transformation of Colombia

It is appropriate to mention, as a starting point, that Colombia is a society which has faced accelerated change in all aspects of its economic, social and political life. The drug trade has emerged in a country which has experienced a rapid change in economic structures, patterns of population distribution, urban structures, the form and function of the state, social and ethical values and customs and beliefs. These changes have been accompanied by very high levels of violence and disorder and by the development of all types of conflict, which periodically throw the country into situations from which there seems to be no way out. For Colombians there is nothing so familiar as the sensation that the nation is in permanent crisis, at the point of collapse or on the verge of chaos (Leal and Zamocs, 1990).

At the same time, there are reasons to believe that behind this apparent crisis there is a relatively solid and stable system, capable of adapting to the most varied situations, and one in which crisis, violence and agitation seem always to be accompanied by economic development, social change, and political progress. Intransigence and polarisation go hand in hand with dialogue and negotiation. Destroyed cities rise from their ashes: Medellín, following, the death of Pablo Escobar (leader of the Medellín cartel), has been transformed from a place where its inhabitants did not want to live – the most violent city in the world – to one whose image is of a paradise in the making. Those who one day seem to be irreconcilable enemies are willing to co-operate with one another. Liberals and Conservatives, after promoting confrontations which caused the deaths of between 100,000 and 150,000 people between 1947 and 1957, signed a pact to share public power for 16 years. Guerrilla groups, such as the M-19 (*Movimiento 19 de Abril*) or the EPL (*Ejército Popular de Liberación* – Popular Liberation Army), after fighting landowners and paramilitaries to the death, had no problem in making pacts not only with government agents, but also with the victims of their actions.

Furthermore, the existence of far-reaching processes of rapid change makes it difficult to determine the extent to which they have been brought about by drug trafficking, or whether drug trafficking accelerated and promoted them. When one analyses the changes in values and conduct which allowed the corruption of state institutions, how can one separate the influence of cultural changes such as the church's obvious loss of the capacity for social control, from the role of the efforts of the drug traffickers, backed up by immense sums of money, to subject the state to their control, or from the influence of the images of wealth and conspicuous consumption associated with the drug trade? How can levels of violence associated with drugs be evaluated in a society in which before the drug trade there was already vigorous guerrilla activity and in which, in many rural sectors, taking the law into one's own hands was a frequent occurrence, in which the police and army had developed methods of dealing with the enemy which were outside the legal norms, but in which drug trafficking, and its wider effects, would have been absent? Such judgements are not easy: there are serious arguments, backed by academic research, which maintain that the drug trade is the principal source of violence, while others claim that only 2-3% of homicides in Colombia are drug-related. Many of the previously mentioned factors can be seen both as elements that favoured the emergence of the drug trade and as outcomes of its existence. The weakening of religious values, secularisation, the desire for enrichment, the toleration of corruption, the use of violence and the absence of penal sanctions for crimes can all be seen this way.

Some of the processes of accelerated transformation which have occurred in Colombia since 1960 and which were already fully underway when the drug trade gradually emerged include:

1. A process of rapid urbanisation, which moved hundreds of thousands of peasants to the cities and placed them in a new cultural and social context. Within 40 years, Colombia changed from having a rural population of 70% to having one of 25% today. The population of Medellín increased twelvefold in 30 years.

2. A concomitant economic transformation, which diminished the importance of the agrarian sector, modernised the industrial sector and with great speed expanded the service sectors. This transformation was accompanied, especially in the last two decades, by rapid growth in the informal sectors of the economy.

3. A breakdown in the traditional forms of social control. Colombia was a society without extensive armed forces, in which traditional cultural and moral values, forms of authoritarian or societal sanctions, and religious conviction or oppression, maintained public morality. Even today, after 50 years of fighting the guerrillas, the Colombian army is not one of the largest in Latin America, and there are more than 120 urban centres which do not have even one policeman. The church's loss of power was rapidly expressed in its incapacity to impede the process of widespread acceptance of birth control mechanisms (Colombia moved from a birth rate of 4.4% in 1970 to one of 1.8% today), but also in the spread of illegal and 'immoral' behaviour by the majority of the population. Despite the fact that many of the country's philosophers and social analysts have called for the creation of a 'civil ethics' to replace the lost religious ethics, this has not taken

place.

4.   Social structures have changed rapidly and a new middle class has emerged, together with new political leaders, new business leaders, and new dominant economic sectors.   What remained of the traditional oligarchy has, in many cases, been supplanted by ascending groups from diverse backgrounds, although in some sectors of national life there remain some continuities identifiable as oligarchic.   The press and politics are both areas of public life that remain dominated by prominent 'traditional' families.   The sons of ex-presidents appear as candidates for the presidency or other political posts in disproportionate numbers; the same applies to the sons of senators and regional leaders.

5.   As I have shown, violence has always accompanied this process of change, although with varying degrees of intensity.   The violent upheavals of 1948-53 gave way to a period of declining violence and growing pacification.   Levels of violence reached their lowest point around 1965-70 when homicide figures were almost as low as those of the United States.   However, since then there has been a continuous increase in violence, which affects the whole climate of life in the country.   This rise may have somewhat preceded the drug trade, but the main phases of its growth, without doubt, coincided with the consolidation of the drug cartels.   Until 1976, the numbers of homicides increased slowly, and between 1976 and 1985 they gradually accelerated.   From 1985, a new wave of violence was unleashed, with a rapid growth which lasted until 1991/92, when a stabilisation or slight decline began.   But let us not forget the levels that had by then been reached: in 1994 there were some 26,000 violent deaths, excluding traffic accidents and the like, in Colombia; that is to say approximately 75 people per 100,000 of the population.   In cities like Medellín, 2.5 in every 1,000 inhabitants died that year, after three years of continuous reduction in the level of violence, which had reached rates of four in every 1,000 in 1991.

This violence is perpetrated by all sorts of agents: confrontation between the guerrillas, the private anti-guerrilla groups ('paramilitaries') and the state accounts for between 3,000 and 4,000 deaths annually;[1] urban violence of all types for some 15,000; and rural violence for another 4,000 or 5,000.   Of the violence that is not directly linked to confrontation with the guerrillas or to rural power conflicts, a small part is caused by confrontations between groups of drug traffickers, in the settling of old scores, etc.   The greater part is the result of the action of indeterminate criminal groups, homicides committed as a result of hold-ups and robberies, and minor fights and attacks concentrated in socially marginalised groups.   All these forms of violence are interlinked and difficult to separate.

Lastly, the country has had a complex and difficult constitutional evolution. Despite a long tradition of electoral democracy and high levels of civic participation in politics, the Colombian democracy was controlled by relatively small, close-knit groups until the middle of this century. When, in 1957, the only military regime of this century was overthrown, the social changes necessary for the functioning of a mass democracy coincided with the pressing need to find a *modus vivendi* between Liberals and Conservatives. What remained was a democratic system with significant limitations which lasted until 1974, and a political structure which did not adapt with sufficient speed to social change and its citizens' demands for participation. To a large extent, the conflicts of the last 30 years shifted towards extra-legal social confrontation – community protests, minor riots – while the political parties consolidated a power structure centred on relatively pliable clienteles. This prompted repeated accusations – imprecise but based on realities – that the political system was undemocratic and that power lay in the hands of a small dominant oligarchy. Although the usually respected legal and constitutional norms defined a representative and democratic system, the Colombians' propensity for resorting to violence was obstructing social and political action and inhibiting participation. Such ideas have also been the basis for the rhetoric with which the guerrillas to this day justify their armed action against the system, which has usually been accompanied by participation in elections by indirect representatives of the guerrilla groups themselves. It is significant that in the middle of the paroxysm of violence of 1989-91, there should have been an attempt to resolve this problem thoroughly *via* constitutional reform with a very participatory and decentralising orientation, intended to create extensive mechanisms for the defence of individual rights.

The Drug Trade: An Outline of its Evolution

Several stages can be identified in the history of the drug trade and its political context in Colombia.

A. The Marijuana Bonanza

Small-scale cultivation of marijuana began around 1960. It found an initial market in the USA, and by the end of the decade represented an important source of wealth and a marginal, but not negligible, source of foreign currency in an economy which had frequently been weakened by foreign exchange crises. Although laws prohibiting drug consumption existed, they were not regularly applied. Society noticed the 'entrepreneurs' of this initial boom, but tended not to condemn them. The men of Santa Marta or the Guajira on the Caribbean coast who enriched themselves through marijuana were seen largely as colourful characters, benefiting from Colombians' traditional affection for those who have managed to compete with the great traditional fortunes by unorthodox means. The trade generated violence, but initially it appeared only to affect members of the still small organisations that promoted it. The large-scale export of marijuana expanded until approximately 1981, and coincided in its last ten years with the first phase of the trade in cocaine.

B. The Emergence of the Cocaine Cartels

The experience of marijuana provided Colombians with some operational expertise, and a knowledge of the markets, contacts and routes which in 1973-75 were first applied to refining and exporting cocaine processed in Colombia. At this early stage, the dominant patterns of the commerce in cocaine were defined. The Colombians imported cocaine paste from Peru and Bolivia and the chemical elements for its processing from Europe and the USA (together with the arms for the control of the business). They refined it in laboratories which were initially located in city centres but which, by the end of decade, had been relocated to rural areas and sometimes the jungle. They then exported the cocaine to the USA, usually by air (smaller quantities flew with normal airline passengers, large shipments were sent by light planes which stopped off, if necessary, in the Caribbean or in Central America). Initially, a relatively high proportion of the Colombians' income must have been imported into Colombia, but soon this proportion decreased rapidly, and the majority of the money spent on cocaine in the USA remained there or was moved to the financial centres of Europe or the Caribbean.

The business rapidly appeared to acquire the structure of an oligopoly: a limited number of organisations (although never one single cartel, as the media image suggests) controlled access to the large distribution networks of the USA, giving them a position of pre-eminence in Colombia, but the import of cocaine paste and the processing were carried out by hundreds of small groups. The export was handled by the large groups which, nevertheless, constantly took organisations or individuals into partnership ('signed them up') on specific shipments – either their own or of other exporters who would then pay a share. The power of Pablo Escobar's cartel over other Medellín cartels seems to have had much to do with its ability to organise and enforce respect for the routes between Colombia and the USA. The capacity to have their decisions respected, of course, originated from the rapid formation of an armed organisation that applied the bullet to those who did not accept the export regulations. Competition and private initiative were acceptable, but only within the precise norms of operation and compliance. Armed violence also started to extend to those who stood in the way of the business: from 1974, the deaths of policemen and judges active in the fight against drugs became more frequent. However, the predominant mechanism for gaining state tolerance was essentially corruption, which enriched thousands of state officials and members of the security and justice services.

Between 1974 and 1978, the main groups of Colombian exporters were formed: in Medellín two or three large cartels; two major cartels were created in Cali, led by José Santacruz and the Rodríguez Orejuela brothers, together with a number of minor organisations; the groups from the north of Valle; Carlos Lehder's operation; the coastal groups and those from the Eastern Plains; Gonzalo Rodríguez Gacha's group in the central-east of Colombia; and the organisations in southern Colombia. Judging by their actions and their assertions, the administrations of Alfonso López Michelsen (1974-78) and Julio Cesar Turbay Ayala (1978-82) did not consider the drug trade a serious problem for Colombia. Although López Michelsen made several declarations about its dangers, in 1975 he opened up a conduit for the 'legal' laundering of dollars when, in a country characterised by strict foreign exchange controls, he made it possible to make anonymous withdrawals of dollars from the Banco de la República. The Turbay Ayala government, characterised by a great tolerance of corruption and political clientelism, seemed to view the internal role of the drug trade with indifference and even with sympathy. Probably because of the importance it assigned to maintaining close ties with the USA, the government did launch some military campaigns against marijuana. Although they were ultimately more efficient and damaging to the traffickers than had been expected, they were not followed up. The Turbay Ayala government also signed the 1989 extradition treaty with the USA, which opened the door to the extradition of Colombians and became the central source of conflict between the state and drug traffickers.

This period of growth in Colombian trafficking reached its first peak around 1982. At that point the drug traffickers managed a business which, according to more extensive estimates, allowed them to import foreign exchange ranging between $800 million and $2 billion, that is to say between 10% and 25% of the country's total exports (apart from the amount of capital accumulated abroad, which was obviously greater). A very concentrated income with an extremely large capacity for influencing daily economic life was made available, for a narrow sector of society.

Those involved were the great consumers with luxury houses, vehicles, security systems and arms imported from the USA. The country, despite some bizarre violent incidents, still seemed fascinated by the economic success, the conspicuously high levels of consumption and the generosity of the *narcos* who financed newspapers, donated dwellings and sports centres in poor areas, built safari parks in the countryside, paid high salaries and bought the loyalty and admiration of many people. In collaboration with the drug traffickers, many Colombians enriched themselves by working for them in sectors such as the construction of housing, the import of luxury consumer goods and the provision of entertainments and security. Extensive areas of rural property were sold to the drug traffickers, as were many of the houses which, in elegant neighbourhoods such as El Poblado in Medellín, had been symbols of the economic power of the great industrialists.

By the end of the 1970s, coca plantations were beginning to be set up in the Ariari area in the department of Meta. They were extended to several inconspicuous areas of settlement or to relatively remote centres of peasant communities, above all in the Eastern Plains and the regions of Caquetá and Putumayo. They never represented a large proportion of the supply of coca paste, but undoubtedly they served to regulate prices and supply, and created an additional social base for the drug traffickers. They also created the complex relationship with the guerrillas which I will describe below. They were constantly attacked by the government, which every year from the mid-1980s has attempted to eradicate the coca crops by aerial spraying of the weedkiller glyphosate. While some police officials announced great successes in the destruction of the crops, other reports showed that the total area planted continued to increase. By 1994, the National Directorate for Narcotics Control estimated that there were some 40,000 hectares of coca in the country, some 20,000 hectares of opium poppies – a crop that started to appear around 1989 – and some 8,000 hectares of marijuana. These estimates, like the majority of Colombian official reports, are usually incompatible with those that the same authorities have presented in previous years and contradict those of other state agencies.

C. Confrontation and War

The period 1980-84 saw the start of the confrontation between society and the state. The drug 'barons' consolidated their fortunes, acquired political power and were able to buy their own judicial impunity or obtain it by force. The governments of neither Turbay nor Belisario Betancur (1982-86) seem to have considered the rise of drug traffickers such as the Ochoas, Escobar, Lehder and Santacruz a serious danger. Indeed, several of these traffickers attempted to legitimise themselves or gain additional impunity by entering Congress. In the 1982 electoral campaign, the only consistent opposition to the 'barons' came from the Luis Carlos Galán camp in the Liberal party. In the case of Betancur, his nationalist perspectives and search for a policy more independent of the USA initially caused him to reject extradition on ideological grounds. As the issue had acquired considerable sensitivity within US politics, the refusal to enforce the mechanisms of the 1979 extradition treaty obliged him to intensify internal efforts of control. The seizure of the huge laboratory of Tranquilandia in March 1984 – at a time when the police and judicial anti-drugs campaign was led by Justice Minister, Rodrigo Lara Bonilla, a Galán supporter – was the incident that provoked the beginning of open war between the government and the traffickers. The following month the drug 'barons' assassinated Lara Bonilla. The Betancur government abruptly changed its policy and began extraditing Colombians to the USA. This raised the stakes for the cartel bosses. It also marked the start of a ritual which was to accompany the fight against the drug trade in moments of greatest confrontation: state retaliation as soon as there was an assassination of an important figure such as that of Lara Bonilla in 1984 or of Luis Carlos Galán in August 1989, centring on the arrest of thousands of suspects within a few hours, the confiscation of vehicles and aeroplanes, the occupation of properties and estates, many of which were returned to their owners – after they had been cleared by the courts – within a few months or years. These bursts of activity rapidly subsided to be replaced by periods of indifference and calm, in which the drug lords once again appeared in their roles as football promoters or conspicuous consumers, and in which state action concentrated on the search for laboratories and the seizure of shipments, or in which there was an altogether more pusillanimous response to crime.

The period of violence which began in the mid-1980s accelerated and rapidly increased until 1991 when the number of killings began to decline. These seven years could be called the 'extradition war'. Strong government action against the drug trade, by means of vigorous operations and the destruction of large laboratories, put pressure on the drug traffickers to which they responded with various acts of violence against public officials. And if, until 1984, the destruction of laboratories was the motive for retaliation by the *narcos*, from then on it was the threat or the reality of extradition that became the principal driving force in the traffickers' fight against the state. This conflict turned into an open war with an effort by the traffickers, led by Escobar and Rodríguez Gacha, to demonstrate that they could force the government to comply with their own rules by means of a campaign of widespread terrorism. The details of this bilateral escalation which took place between 1984 and 1990 are extremely complex. Suffice to say, between 1987 and 1990, during the government of Virgilio Barco (1986-90), the war was characterised, particularly after the assassination of Attorney General Carlos Mauró Hoyos in 1987, by the drug traffickers' resort to terrorism and, from August 1989, by a new wave of state activism which again included a large-scale campaign to confiscate traffickers' assets.[2]

The drug traffickers usually responded to the state's progressively more drastic measures with both terrorism and proposals for an accord,[3] using terrorism as a means of exerting pressure in negotiations. What the 12 leading drug traffickers who called themselves the 'extraditables' proposed – and many prominent Colombians such as ex-President Alfonso López Michelsen and Nobel Prize winner Gabriel García Márquez regarded it as a reasonable proposal – was in essence that the government would guarantee that they would not be extradited for trial in the USA, that their fortunes would be respected and that they would receive a total judicial amnesty. In exchange, they offered to retire from the business and even to exert pressure on the relatively independent groups (which represented and continue to represent a very high proportion of the Colombian drug business)[4] to scale down their commercial activity.

This period of confrontation ended in a kind of stalemate: it became clear that Escobar's group and those associated with him were not able to force the government to accept these terms of negotiation and that in the face of terrorism the state's response was not to negotiate but to take an increasingly hard-line approach. This is what happened in 1989 when the drug traffickers killed Liberal presidential candidate Luis Carlos Galán (and two other presidential candidates at the beginning of 1990),[5] blew up a civilian aircraft in mid-flight and destroyed, with dozens of fatalities, the offices of the Departamento Administrativo de la Seguridad (DAS). It was obvious that unless the 'barons' felt they could negotiate complete guarantees of impunity, no agreement would be possible. For its part, the government could never, on legal, political or ethical grounds, justify negotiating with those who were bombing the civilian population and assassinating its officials. Meanwhile, the state's own actions in confronting the drug trade were, despite repeated partial government victories, largely ineffective. The trade continued and the terrorists remained at large. The only notable success was the death of Gonzalo Rodríguez Gacha, 'the Mexican', at the end of 1989. Public opinion, tired of the violence, increasingly lost sympathy for the previously popular drug 'barons', but attributed a good part of the responsibility for the violence to the government for not granting the traffickers' sought-after concessions. Alternatively, the violence of the war ruled out a solution which had always had considerable support in Colombia: to maintain that drugs were above all a problem of the consuming countries, generated by demand, and that the drug 'war' should therefore be fought in the schools, hospitals, prisons and rehabilitation centres of developed countries and not those countries that produced drugs.[6] Barco's government, by insisting on a total war against drug trafficking in 1989, opened up an irreparable rift between the traffickers and principal sectors of Colombian society and for many years made the sort of concessions demanded by the traffickers unthinkable. It created divisions within the army and the police, by reducing the previously widespread tolerance towards those on the payroll of the cartel bosses, especially those in Medellín. And with the extraditions, the massive confiscations of assets, the detention of thousands of people (although this was never systematic or judicially sound), the government put the drug traffickers on the defensive and thus brought them to the realisation that it would be convenient for them to reach an agreement with the state, albeit an agreement in which they would themselves have to make some significant concessions. Lastly, the Barco government, in launching this radical confrontation, drew in the design of its policies a clear conceptual distinction between 'narco-terrorism' and 'narco-trafficking' (see Introduction to this volume). Although this distinction was not applied with any rational coherence, it did allow for the coexistence of a total (according to public opinion quite legitimate) crackdown on drug-related terrorism, and more flexible policies in relation to the drug trade itself.

D. Towards a Truce

The next stage in drug control involved attempts to secure the voluntary surrender of traffickers to the Colombian judicial system. It has to be remembered that, until 1990, various efforts to bring traffickers to justice had proved totally futile. When it had been possible to bring any of them to trial, one after the other had been acquitted by corrupt or intimidated judges, or by judges devoted to judicial formalities that worked in the traffickers' favour. On the few occasions that some determined judges attempted to imprison Escobar or other traffickers, they and their families were assassinated and new trials were ineffectual. For this reason, extradition became the most effective internal mechanism of serious confrontation with the traffickers. But it was precisely the significance of the fear of extradition that raised the value of a compromise agreement with the government. When, in September 1990, President César Gaviria announced a series of legal reforms guaranteeing those drug traffickers who surrendered and confessed to their crimes immunity from extradition and reduced sentencing, the traffickers, although they were looking to pressurise the government into further extending the concessions, accepted the terms. To spend a few years in prison with the guarantee of immunity from extradition was reasonable.

For the government, it represented an undoubted success, to the extent that its concessions, rather than seeming to weaken the judicial institutions and moral and ethical principles, actually acknowledged the validity of the justice system and its rulings. And, at the same time, the arrangement provided a political victory that created the basis for the extraordinary popularity which President Gaviria enjoyed throughout most of his mandate. Colombians felt that the epoch of terrorism and outright confrontation had definitively ended. Finally, and as an important part of its strategy, with the main drug bosses in prison, the government counted on gaining time to consolidate its administrative mechanisms for eradicating the drug trade (by, for example, improving and reforming the police force). Above all, it attempted to change the fundamental structure of the judicial system in the hope that it would begin to function efficiently, would prevent the rise of a new generation of traffickers protected by the same impunity as their predecessors, and would re-establish a certain judicial legitimacy.

The application of this policy was not easy, nor was it always coherent. After some initial successes and the surrender of the leading members of the Ochoa family, Escobar preferred to wait until the 1991 Constituent Assembly had definitively ruled against the extradition of Colombians before he handed himself in. He was not convinced that a simple agreement with a judge would preclude the possibility that in some arbitrary trial other authorities would hand him over to the USA. Escobar's procrastination seriously weakened the government politically and morally. It began to seem as if the state wanted Escobar's surrender and possible extradition because it had been intimidated by the abduction of important national figures, including the sister-in-law of the assassinated presidential candidate Luis Carlos Galán, the son of the owner of *El Tiempo* and the well-known journalist Francisco Santos, as well as the blackmailing and bribing of members of the Constituent Assembly.

Subsequently it became evident that, although well conceived, the policy's secondary operational stages were carried out with remarkable negligence and irresponsibility. This incompetence resulted in catastrophe in June 1992, when Escobar, who had spent a year in prison, escaped in an operation which left many of the state institutions looking ridiculous and put into question the president's control over the surrender policy and his seriousness about countering the drug problem. During the following two years, the state concentrated on recapturing Escobar, using all possible military measures, but leaving the way open for the other traffickers to surrender to the authorities of their own volition, on certain modified conditions. The intensity of the hunt for Escobar and the flexibility of the negotiation mechanisms induced several traffickers, including some of those who had fled with Escobar, to give themselves up, thereby breathing new life into the negotiation mechanism. However, that mechanism never totally recovered from the image promoted by Escobar's luxurious lifestyle in prison and the impression that the terms of surrender had been proposed by the *narcos* for their own benefit.

After Escobar's death in December 1993, the government sought to defend its credibility by reinforcing its pursuit of the so-called Cali cartel, after years of relative indifference. This pursuit frequently seems to be on the verge of bringing about numerous surrenders – some traffickers did indeed surrender – but it is evident that the government considered the concessions which Prosecutor-General Gustavo de Greiff was offering the traffickers to be legally and politically unacceptable. The government's qualms were, of course, also heavily influenced by the need to maintain credibility with the USA. The government ultimately found itself in confrontation with the Prosecutor-General and not achieving results in this area of its anti-drugs policy.[7] The policy of surrender offered extremely lenient sentences to some traffickers. Consequently, it appeared that government action was dictated by their demands. What was needed was an improvement in the institutions in charge of the internal anti-drug campaign. Many efforts were made and institutional changes adopted by the police and army, but the results were limited. Although coca seizures increased between 1991 and 1993, a fact well-received by the US administration, the major drug 'barons' were not apprehended. Worse still, improvements in the justice system and penal sanctions against the accused remained far below the government's expectations, and of course below those of the USA.

A somewhat unforeseen development of the crisis which faced the country as a result of the intensification of the terrorist conflict, was the attempt radically to confront the problem of the democratic limitations of the political system. Ever since the Barco government was first besieged by the drug trade and the guerrillas, alternative notions emphasising the need for a strengthening of the state accompanied the emergence of proposals to take a great leap forward: to take measures to re-legitimise the state, to re-establish the broken ties between the citizens and the public sector and to open channels for the broad participation of all social groups.

Thus, between 1988 and 1991, Colombia was balanced on a knife edge. At the same time as policies of a repressive nature were adopted, which advanced the possibility of military or police management of the terrorist conflict, the Barco and Gaviria governments promoted the redrafting of the constitution. The new 1991 Constitution included reform of the judicial system, the recognition of the rights of Colombia's different ethnic and national groups, the institutionalisation of mechanisms for the protection of individual rights, all of which have made a surprisingly substantial impact, such as the resort to 'protected trials', or a system of constitutional revision of the law which has led to a libertarian interpretation of individual rights. The Constitution, which professed to be a kind of peace treaty between all Colombians, also banned extradition. Thus, the traffickers' ultimate demand was met: the only judicial sanction from which they had anything to fear was removed from the legal order. And the state thereby lost one of its most effective negotiating tools, and relied more than ever on the efficiency of its own law enforcement institutions to pressurise the drug traffickers.

E. The Undermined Beginnings of the Samper Government
President Ernesto Samper (1994-) had made a name for himself between 1976-77 and 1981 when, as director of the National Association of Financial Institutions, he called for the legalisation of marijuana with the declared objective of removing the incentives that maintained trafficking. Thus it was ironic that, on assuming the presidency of Colombia in 1994 and having repudiated his earlier declarations on legalisation, he should have begun his term in the middle of such a succession of vacillations *vis-à-vis* public opinion and the USA with regard to the drug problem. Before even taking office, he was accused of having received a substantial contribution to his election campaign from the Cali cartel. This led to strong US pressure on the new president, which eventually resulted in the removal of the chief of police and other gestures, giving the impression of a complete subordination of the Colombian anti-drugs policy to US objectives. The USA, taking advantage of the change of government, wanted to obtain the greatest possible collaboration from the new Colombian administration, obliging it to demonstrate convincingly its innocence of any ties with the drug traffickers.[8]

     Samper's government was not able to do this. Shortly after the new government took office in 1994, Samper's Conservative election rival Andrés Pastrana produced tape recordings – the *narcocassettes* – which allegedly proved contacts between the Cali cartel and those who had run the President's election campaign. A Congressional investigation into whether the President had known about the contributions concluded in December 1995 that he had no case to answer. In January 1996, former Defence Minister Fernando Botero was arrested and claimed that Samper had been aware of the funding, but a second protracted enquiry by the House of Representatives' Committee of Accusations which lasted throughout the first half of 1996 produced the same conclusions as the first. The integrity of the Samper administration had, however, been irredeemably tainted[9] and not only within Colombia. US-Colombian relations reached their nadir in March 1996 when President Clinton 'decertified' Colombia.[10] It had become obvious that the USA was opposed to Samper himself. US officials even tried to draw a distinction between Samper's government and other Colombian institutions, saying that decertification was applied to the former for its lack of support to the latter (Joyce, 1996). Samper's room for manoeuvre was severely constrained; he was obliged to take a hard line on drug control where otherwise he might have sought alternative solutions. Consequently, by the standards the USA used to judge effective drug control, Colombia's record under Samper was rather good. In 1996 there were more arrests, drug seizures and crop eradication by force than ever before, none of which appeared to placate Washington. Any debate with the international community about new approaches to drug control would have to be set aside at least until Samper was succeeded by a new president. The option of autonomy for Colombia in the formulation of its own drug policies was, for the time being, foreclosed.

Attempts at Judicial Reform
An essential part of President Barco's effort in his war against the *narcos* was to establish judicial mechanisms to indict and sentence them. Consequently, his government repeatedly resorted to declarations of a state of emergency, which modified penal categories, in particular that of terrorism; increased penalties; created new offences; and above all radically changed penal procedures to speed up the process of prosecution. Furthermore, Barco tried to modify the general system of justice by creating an Office of the Prosecutor-General of the Nation, which would collate evidence and indict traffickers and terrorists. Generally these reforms failed, partly because implementation was largely improvised as a reaction to various crises, and partly because, with a Congress he could not rely on, the President consistently resorted to state-of-siege regulations to implement the reforms, creating great instability within the system. Reforms that required constitutional change failed because they were linked to the movement to put an end to extradition which had the support of important members within Congress. However, the measures that were adopted

gradually generated a coherent programme that was shaping a clear judicial policy on the drugs trade.

Based on this, the Gaviria government, with the same objective of reforming and strengthening the justice system, issued a series of decrees that consolidated a special jurisdiction for the crimes of terrorism and the most serious crimes of drug trafficking. This, modelled on Italian counter-terrorism methods, was presided over by anonymous judges. The Gaviria administration also managed to persuade the Constituent Assembly to create the Prosecutor-General's Office, which would transform the judicial system from an accusatory to an inquisitorial system, and in the performance of which the government placed all its hopes. Finally, there was a progression from merely rhetorical to financial support of the justice system. Resources practically doubled, likewise the salaries of its officials, during the four years of the government's mandate.

Nonetheless, few advances were made. The government, which relied on the results of its reforms and the swift progress of the justice system, as part of its aim of reforming the political system to make it less authoritarian, promoted a series of restrictions limiting the possibility of modifying judicial legislation by emergency decrees. This deprived the government of essential tools, the need for which remained apparent in view of the persistence of judicial shortcomings. When, for example, the Prosecutor-General's Office was unable to conclude within the legal terms any of its investigations into the drug trafficking and related crimes of some 1,000 suspects under arrest, the government twice extended the terms of the procedural code by decreeing a state of emergency, until the Constitutional Court, probably with good reason, declared that it no longer had the constitutional power to do so. In 1994, three years after these cases were handed over to the judicial system, almost none had been fully prepared and the accused remained under arrest, but their release was imminent because of the expiration of the time limit. Almost symptomatic of this failure was the fact that the preliminary investigation of Escobar on giving himself up in July 1991 for illegal possession of weapons, based on his confession and the handing over of the actual weapons, had not been concluded by the time of his death in December 1993. Not even for this crime, where reliable evidence was available, was Escobar taken to trial.

The weakness of the justice system continues to be one of the main factors preventing Colombia from pursuing an autonomous anti-drugs policy. This has created conflicts between US and Colombian judicial and diplomatic authorities. Efforts to share evidence in crimes have been unsuccessful, despite occasional declarations of good intent. It was this weakness that made extradition so important to the Barco government and which made extradition the only credible threat for traffickers arrested in 1990 and 1991. Because of this weakness, Gaviria had to propose voluntary surrender under preferential terms: if there were no judges who would convict traffickers against their will, at least in this way they would allow themselves to be convicted in exchange for being exempted from trial in the USA. Today, when extradition is not possible, the Colombian drug traffickers again enjoy impunity for almost any crime.

It is important to remember that the inadequacy of the legal system owes much to the direct and indirect effects of the drug trade. Intimidation, bribery, assaults and violence laid siege to the legal system from 1975 onwards. At the same time, the exponential growth of crime (caused in good part by the emergence of armed gangs on the payroll of the traffickers, the more widespread carrying of arms and a general increase in individual criminality for which indirect causes can be found in the boom of the drug trade), generated levels of congestion in the courts and additional work loads which, given the traditional formalist nature of the Colombian system, became impossible to deal with, and which have generally meant that, since no single trial can be delayed, all trials were delayed. At present, after many reforms and other efforts, and increases in spending, probably not even 2% of the homicides committed in the country are brought to trial. Of course the cycle of mutual reinforcement is inescapable and, faced with the inefficiency of the legal system, the cost of committing a crime – to the criminal – in terms of the calculated risk of punishment, has become close to zero. The economic incentive to commit a crime is very high.

One of the least satisfactory aspects of investigation and detection concerns the tracing of property and financial operations of the drug traffickers. Although the creation of a special unit for financial investigation within the DAS, which functioned as the anti-drug trade intelligence headquarters, has been proposed at least since 1987, hardly any steps have been taken in this direction. When, from the end of 1990 onwards, Escobar, the Ochoas and another 15-20 immensely wealthy traffickers gave themselves up, not only did the DAS have practically no evidence to indict them, despite having investigated them for years, but it was for the most part also unaware of the details of their fortunes and how they ran their businesses.

Guerrilla Involvement in the Drug Trade

The expansion of coca plantations in rural areas produced an ambiguous relationship between the traffickers and the guerrillas. Given the right climatic conditions, the areas most suitable for cultivation were those which were previously deserted but which attracted large numbers of displaced, colonising peasants, and where the state had little presence and capacity for control. Such areas tended, for the same reasons, to be under guerrilla influence or control. The high incomes coca generated proved extremely attractive for peasants in areas that did not have the roads and communications to make the commercial cultivation of other products viable. The guerrillas did not openly confront the peasants, but tried to regulate the process by limiting the number of coca plantations and forcing them to continue growing alternative food crops. But they also decided to take advantage of the drug production business: a fixed rate, usually estimated at 10%, was imposed on coca leaf or paste transactions in exchange for protection of the crop.

In this way, the guerrillas and traffickers formed a pragmatic alliance, although their politics were very different. They were united against state control and for their mutual economic and military benefit. The guerrillas received resources and access to contacts who provided them with arms, while the drug trade gained a means of protecting crops. Occasional disputes over specific issues sometimes created tension: the guerrillas tended to insist on maintaining a basic level of prices for the peasants, even at times when market prices fell; the drug traffickers were not prepared to pay fixed rates in areas they could guard themselves, such as airports and laboratories (although sometimes they agreed to contract guerrilla groups). There was also friction between particular guerrilla groups and individual drug traffickers; the guerrillas and the traffickers were not homogeneous groups.

In addition to the operational disputes, there were underlying political differences. The entrepreneurial traffickers in their rural strongholds tended to have right-wing and authoritarian tendencies. They sought and, in many parts, enjoyed the enthusiastic backing of local army units when they were prepared to confront certain guerrilla activities. They were also reconstructing a sizeable network of rural properties which, in practice, constituted a profound agrarian counter-reform. Essentially, traffickers and guerrillas represented contradictory political projects, each requiring relatively comprehensive control of their geographical areas of influence. Reconciling these conflicting aspirations was difficult. At the beginning of the 1980s, the appearance of networks of anti-guerrilla defence organisations, financed in good part by the *narcos* and viewed approvingly and supported by the army, was evidence of the conflicts between these two groups in areas like Magdalena Medio (1982-85). However, from 1986 the leading drug 'baron' of the central eastern part of the country, Rodríguez Gacha, under whose direction cooperative activities between the guerrillas and the traffickers were carried out, fell out with the guerrillas. The critical moment came in 1987 with the assassination of the presidential candidate supported by the guerrillas in the 1986 elections, the Communist Party militant Jaime Pardo Leal, after disputes over alleged guerrilla actions against the drug traffickers, which had included military attacks, kidnappings and appropriations of the same assets they were supposed to have been protecting. From then on, political groups connected to the guerrillas, especially the *Unión Patriótica* movement, were the victims of an intensive campaign of extermination which was largely coordinated and promoted by the drug traffickers, but always counted on the more-or-less secret support of members of the state security bodies, in particular the army.

The complexity of the relationship between traffickers and guerrillas was as complicated as those between the traffickers and public officials, members of the army and the police. These relations also included occasional tactical agreements in spite of fundamental opposition. The official rhetoric, boosted by Washington, created an image of a united *narcoguerrilla* front, suggesting that the objectives of both groups, and even their operations, had been unified. The term was first applied in March 1984, when the cocaine-processing laboratories of Tranquilandia were discovered and found to be guarded by guerrillas. It was applied again in 1985 during negotiations with the FARC (*Fuerzas Armadas Revolucionarias de Colombia*), which critics tried to sabotage by characterising the group as common criminals. They tried to demonstrate that the guerrillas were involved in the management of laboratories and that consequently they had ceased to be mere vigilantes and were interested in taking direct control of the business. The term was again used in 1993 and 1994, when the government came to the conclusion that the FARC's income from coca could reach US $20-30 million annually. A new wave of accusations emerged when the plane of former Defence Minister Fernando Botero, accompanied by the US ambassador, was attacked from a laboratory site, in which 10 tons of coca were found, allegedly guarded by the FARC. The evidence, as always, was tenuous and was handled according to standard police practice: relatively imprecise 'leaks' which the newspapers exaggerated for a few days.

There is no doubt that the FARC benefits from the levies on cultivation and from other occasional coca operations. It is possible, although significant conclusive proof is again lacking, that, given the FARC's financial decentralisation, some of its fronts do have laboratories. No one has really described how the guerrillas enter into the drug business or what they actually do. This makes it difficult to believe, without further proof, that the guerrillas have managed to penetrate the cocaine marketing networks overseas, which is where the greatest profits are made. In any case, the extortion of drug traffickers is just one source of guerrilla financing. They also collect levies from cattle ranchers, banana and African palm producers, and oil and gold exploration companies, among others. The importance of all this is that, if public opinion can be persuaded that the guerrillas are coca producers, the room for manoeuvre of the Colombian government, which for the last ten years has negotiated with them to secure a peace agreement on the basis that their crimes are political, is much reduced and it is possible for opponents of the negotiations to summon up the spectre of violence and US opposition, or for Washington to encourage active covert opposition.

The Political Impact of the Drugs Trade

In the 1980s, the level of violence in Colombia increased rapidly. Obviously this trend was only partly due to the drug trade, but there is little doubt that the wave of violence between 1985 and 1991 was to a large extent generated by trafficking. The drug traffickers, with their extensive rural power base in areas adjoining those of guerrilla influence, were an essential part of the paramilitary operations that dramatically raised the number of homicides and forced disappearances from 1985 onwards. By consolidating permanently armed groups, following the example of the emerald traffickers, they created private armies, most but not all of which were rural. In Medellín in the mid-1980s Pablo Escobar managed to mobilise armed gangs which numbered at least 1,500 people when the city's police force was only 2,500 strong. The spread of methods such as the use of motor cycles, the arming of all kinds of gangs with automatic weapons and machine guns, the use of adolescents to carry out crimes, and the promotion of young criminals into gangs ready to carry out contract killings, were all a direct and immediate effect of the drug trade in several cities, but above all in Medellín. The violence can be seen as partly the result of common criminality and partly political; those involved seek to influence or change the way the state functions. The assassination of political candidates and judges, and the efforts to destroy groups with suspected ties to the guerrillas are some of the political actions in which the traffickers play an essential role. At the same time, the illegal but frequent ties between traffickers and middle- and in some cases high-ranking members of the military and police hierarchy have had much to do with the human rights crisis in Colombia and with the public forces' loss of credibility.

Although the Colombian justice system had already displayed symptoms of crisis and inefficiency in the 1950s and 1960s, when it proved relatively incapable of confronting the legal challenges related to political violence and the guerrillas, this became more patently obvious with the increase in drug-related crimes. The traditional system – appropriate for a society of small towns where everybody knew each other and where there was a low crime rate – did not adapt easily to the new challenges. It was a judicial system primarily based on oral testimony, with very formal procedures and, theoretically, with a high level of protection of the procedural rights of the accused, who was aware of all the evidence and witnesses at every stage of the investigation. Organised crime, determined to intimidate and buy off witnesses and judges and capable of doing so, was by definition almost immune to such a legal system.[11] The absence of any tradition or experience of investigation and detection – crimes were solved on the basis of confessions and testimonial evidence, and contradictory evidence was practically inadmissible or there was uncertainty about how to assess it – guaranteed the police's ineffectiveness in solving crimes committed with the deliberate intention of concealment.[12]

Corruption existed before the rise of the drug trade but, without doubt, the high levels of corruption in recent years can be explained fundamentally as a consequence of the opportunities created by drugs. The payment of bribes to look the other way, the infiltration of the intelligence services, and links in the fight against the guerrillas and their allies were all aspects of a process which converted an important sector of the police and army into an ally of the drug traffickers, while other sectors within these institutions firmly opposed them. The difficulties of this situation – the internal distrust; the conflicts between *esprit de corps* and the need for integrity; between the concern for maintaining unity and the risk of infiltration – are obvious but their precise nature can scarcely be imagined. The police, because of this greater involvement in drug control operations, were more subject to temptation and frequently succumbed to it; the army tried to maintain a relative distance. As early as 1979, several senior army officials insisted on distancing the army from the fight against the drug trade to avoid the risks of corruption which would affect their ability to fight the guerrillas. However, this was impossible: the army participated in almost all of the major anti-drugs operations and, in each case, there emerged the obvious symptoms of corruption. The army and police, facing discredit because of this, responded with what could be called a metaphysical distinction between the institution and its members. Never mind the fact that the police is the Colombian institution with the highest proportion of criminals amongst its ranks, or that when gangs of delinquents or kidnappers are discovered there is all too often evidence of police complicity in their activities. The same disingenuous litany is always repeated: the institution itself is excellent, its success rate outstanding, its activity worthy of the citizens' appreciation; it is only its members who sin, commit crimes or are inefficient. While the police or the army as institutions are above all suspicion, their members – how could one expect anything else? – share the weaknesses of their fellow Colombians.

The drug trade produced a profound crisis of state legitimacy. Its influence intensified already declining respect for legal norms and the gradual disappearance of a sense of obligation to comply with the law. The increase in corruption, the crisis in the judicial system and the growing resort to private, often violent, solutions to conflicts were other consequences.

At the national level, open attempts at influence were aborted and opposed by the nation's leaders. However, it is clear that the traffickers possess the ability to influence large sectors of Congress and municipal and local authorities. It is 'influence' rather than full control and merits a more detailed description. Influence on electoral campaigns is exerted in various ways. Many traffickers became important *de facto* authorities in regional politics. Their property, wealth and operations have influenced thousands of people, and their resources help finance electoral campaigns. Thus, a substantial number of local politicians became a kind of political clientele of the traffickers. In areas like Cali, the most important cartel figures distanced themselves from direct political activity but, from the late 1970s, they maintained close links with a wide and diverse group of high-ranking political agents of both parties, although with greater influence over the Liberal Party than the Conservatives.

In areas like the Atlantic coast and the new national territories, where such a powerful network of protection did not exist, the combination of activities was closer, and it was not strange to discover politicians dedicated to drug-related activities, while others simply received a 'slap on the back' from the traffickers. In 1981 and 1982 in the city of Medellín and the department of Quindío, Pablo Escobar and Carlos Lehder attempted to participate directly in politics. Escobar sought to represent Liberalism and initially even tried, unsuccessfully, to be admitted into Galán's movement, which resolutely opposed the drug trade. He did, however, briefly serve as an 'alternative' member of Congress. Lehder rapidly moved towards the formation, without much possibility of attracting anything but a small following, of his own political movement, based on a confused blend of populist and authoritarian ideas. Both traffickers seem to have been partly motivated to seek direct political participation by the possibility of immunity afforded by congressional status, but their calculations about their political prospects were inaccurate. Although the regional political leaders were not opposed to accepting the traffickers' money and even to maintaining amicable and cooperative relations with them, they preferred not to have the uncomfortable daily presence of known and very powerful traffickers in Congress, and looked upon these efforts with apprehension rather than sympathy. Escobar's summons to court forced the House of Representatives to revoke his immunity, at a time when anti-drugs pressure had increased, thereby ending his political career and signalling the beginning of his life as a fugitive.

The Economic Impact of the Drugs Trade

It is beyond the scope of this chapter to analyse in detail the economic magnitude of the drug trade and its impact on the national economy. Several studies have addressed this subject, and although there are extensive divergences in the estimates of different authors, in general the image that emerges from studies is one of a trade of much lesser magnitude than media reportage and politicians' statements suggest. Evidently at certain times when there is a lack of foreign exchange, the earnings from narcotics can help maintain favourable conditions for foreign trade, import of consumer goods, debt management, etc. Equally, the demand for certain products – luxury housing, entertainment, expensive vehicles – generates economic dynamism and employment. But for an economy like Colombia's, which has been struggling for several years to prevent an *increase* in its reserves, these flows are expendable or replaceable with others. And the distortion which drugs have introduced into the economy should be taken into account as costs: military and judicial costs and other state spending on drug control, distortions in the range of public investment, and the impact of corruption on the efficacy of the state, are all difficult to estimate but nevertheless real costs.

Between 1978-82, the first drugs boom coincided with an industrial crisis: the application of resources from drugs, above all to the import of contraband goods, aggravated this situation. Nowadays, the impact of high levels of contraband, still one of the favourite ways of converting dollars into pesos, seems less important. The impact of drugs on the Colombian economy seems secondary and expendable: in economic terms it can sometimes be positive and at other times negative.[13]

Various estimates have been made of the size of Colombian drug exports. Considerable divergences can be explained by the methodology and by what Colombian earnings are considered to be. Although the media and the police often define the value of drug seizures, for example, in terms of their street value in the areas of consumption, it is essential to differentiate between the price put on the crop in the country of production, a price which represents the direct earnings of the Colombian drug traffickers, the price of the crop paid by distributors (part of the difference between these two prices corresponds to the earnings of the Colombian 'entrepreneurs') and the final price paid by the consumer, of which the part that corresponds to the Colombian exporters is but a small proportion. Also it is essential to emphasise that the Colombian traffickers' national earnings are not the same as the global Colombian foreign exchange earnings, insofar as an important part of those earnings remain in the USA, or other countries suitable for investing money of illegal origin or which offer relatively discreet banking facilities: for example, Panama, some Caribbean islands, Switzerland.

1.   The total earnings of the Colombian traffickers for 1981-88 have been calculated as $14 billion (Gómez, 1990). This in essence represents the value of drug exports upon arrival in US ports, and ignores the role the Colombians might play in wholesale and retail distribution in the USA. The starting point for Gómez's calculations was production of cocaine base, the volumes imported into Colombia and processed there, eventual exports to the USA and prices given by the DEA.

2.   Earnings totalling $18 billion have been calculated for the five year period 1988-92 (Kalmanovitz, 1994). These calculations represent net earnings, because the author has made a deduction of 30% on the values exported abroad.   This figure, substantially higher than that of other analysts, supposes that cocaine exports to Europe represent almost 70% of those to the USA, which is debatable.   This author was attempting to demonstrate that this figure is credible from the point of view of national economic aggregates, implying net earnings of $3-4 billion annually, close to 10% of GDP and 70% of Colombia's legal imports.   For this reason he argues for the existence of high levels of contraband entering Colombia (through illegal imports and under-invoicing). Additionally, these resources would have financed capital flight: they are converted into assets in dollars abroad, in the hands of the traffickers themselves or those who have sold their property to the traffickers.[14]

The traffickers bring only a portion of their incomes into Colombia (Thoumi, 1992, pp. 60-1). In principle, they only need to convert (and in some way launder in Colombia) dollars into national currency for some of their activities.   There is no sense in accumulating dollars in Colombia (especially if the devaluation rates of the peso to the dollar are, as in the 1990s, consistently lower than internal inflation) except as an emergency measure. Given the size of the Colombian economy, the efforts to convert large quantities of dollars into pesos generated from 1975 onwards an unofficial or parallel dollar exchange rate which was almost always lower than the official rate; it raised the internal price of the goods most desired by the traffickers, such as real estate. It should not be forgotten that the dollar purchaser must spend the dollars abroad: by simply converting them into assets abroad (the capital which theoretically arrives does not in reality come in, and therefore enters the accounts as capital 'flight'), by using them to bring in illegally imported goods, or by using them to travel. Those, according to Kalmanovitz, are the main uses of foreign currency from the drug trade (Kalmanovitz, 1994, p. 35).

Activities which require payment in dollars include the following:

1. The local costs of drug trafficking. Payment for the raw materials are usually made in Peru and Bolivia, although Colombia itself is now an important source of coca leaf; in Europe for the precursor chemicals, and in several countries for many of the costs of security services and matériel, such as weapons, communications equipment, etc., which are obtained illegally. Local costs include the wages of Colombian growers, the costs of refining and transport, payment for security equipment, vehicles and planes when they are legally imported and acquired on the local market, and the illegal payment of public officials. In Kalmanovitz's calculations the total costs are equivalent to 30% of gross earnings.

2. The conspicuous consumption of the traffickers and their associates, which includes luxury housing, vehicles, consumer goods and high expenditure on recreation, as well as the expenses motivated by generosity, philanthropy or the desire to gain the personal or political support and friendship of others: a typical example of this was the investment in housing for low-income sectors by Pablo Escobar in Medellín.

3. Investment in other activities, including rural property, urban real estate, and innumerable and uninvestigated commercial and industrial economic activities: processed food firms, transport companies, and a variety of retail stores.[15] There appears to be a consensus that in general investment was kept outside the large financial and industrial groups, with some exceptions at the beginning of the 1980s.

This situation generates a system of balance between assets held abroad and inside Colombia, in which the major part of is probably abroad. When the financial conditions of the country make the repatriation of assets attractive, or when political or law enforcement conditions put capital held in Europe or the USA at risk, the flows to Colombia accelerate, and *vice versa*. In a rough approximation, the traffickers' expenditure supplements the internal economy to the extent that it finances the import of extra goods and services (including debt repayment of legitimate debtors, export of profits, capital flight, etc.) and increases internal demand for goods and services. Some assets imported into the country leave again, as happens when those who sell real estate, sometimes under pressure because of internal insecurity, complete the cycle by investing the earnings obtained outside Colombia, often moving abroad themselves.

Estimates of resources which did enter the country fluctuate between an average of $800 million and $2,500 million per annum over the past ten years, excluding the foreign currency which served to realise the flight of capital. This represents between 2% and 8% of GDP. Based on these figures, trafficking is not a decisive element of Colombia's economic activity, but neither is it negligible. In macro-economic terms it undoubtedly contributed to the fact that a country traditionally affected by exchange crises caused by an insufficient supply of foreign currency, should have become a nation with large reserves and a surplus of dollars. Within the Latin American context, the relative abundance of dollars in Colombia helped the country finance part of its obligations without resorting excessively to international credit. The reasonable equilibrium of the economy during the 1980s and the modest impact of the foreign debt crisis which affected Latin America without doubt owed something to these phenomena.

The economic effects of the drug trade also contributed to the stabilisation of macroeconomic policies, despite the difficulties provoked by inflationary pressures caused by the massive influx of foreign currency. However, we must not forget that at the same time as the coca boom (1974 to the present) there was a gradual reorientation of the economy. From being a country whose economic policy was centred on the protection of national industry, by means of a very complex system of tax and administrative controls, Colombia moved to almost total economic liberalisation very much in line with global changes. The first attempts at liberalisation (1975, 1978-82) ran into grave difficulties and provoked serious industrial crises: the boom in imports affected national producers, insufficiently prepared for competition, while the real prices of imported goods fell rapidly, boosted by tendencies to revalue the peso. On these occasions, drug earnings could be considered negative for the overall economy, because for the most part they stimulated demand for imported goods which competed with high-cost domestic industrial production. Moreover, they reorientated demand towards goods such as luxury housing and rural property, initially for unproductive use, while other claimants of these goods (popular sectors without housing, rural producers) saw prices rise to unattainable levels.

In recent years, when Colombia was able to adopt a policy of external liberalisation without excessive trauma, it is more difficult to judge negatively the macroeconomic impact of the drug trade. The policy of reducing import prices in order to force local industry to become more efficient was in fact reinforced by the drug trade. In the same way, many of the risks of liberalisation were reduced by the abundance of foreign exchange generated by the drug trade. Drugs continued to finance the expansion of imported consumer goods and even led to the return of very large volumes of capital between 1990-93, when there was a combination of high internal interest rates, a revaluation of the peso and a positive reading by the traffickers of President Gaviria's policy of submission to justice.

If one wants to analyse more closely the differences between various sectors of the economy, it has to be acknowledged that certain producers of finished industrial goods, who would have encountered difficulties in adapting to liberalisation, saw their situation aggravated by the easy terms for financing contraband which has characterised the Colombian economy. Because of this, they had to make a greater effort to modernise and increase competitiveness. More than a few small- and medium-sized industries have disappeared in the process.

From another point of view, it has been calculated that some 45,000 people in Colombia depend directly on the cultivation of drugs and some 20,000 on their processing. Taking into consideration top level personnel – lawyers, financiers, accountants – it has been calculated that direct employment generated by the drugs business reaches 70,000 people, who represent less than 0.5% of national employment, but who account for 6%-7% of income (Kalmanovitz, 1994).

The economic costs generated by drug trafficking must also be considered as consequences of the drug trade. If, in the early years (1970-85), the direct expenditure of the Colombian state on the suppression of the drug trade was not very high, gradual recognition of the threat trafficking posed brought about an increase. The army and police force grew rapidly, above all in the last few years, and central government spending on these institutions rose from 1.7% of GDP in the 1970s to nearly 3% in 1994. There has been an equally significant change in judicial expenditure, particularly since 1991, with the creation of the Prosecutor-General's Office and the efforts to expand and increase the security of the prison system. Other costs derived from higher levels of crime and violence in the country have to do with the number of lives lost each year. Approximately one in every seven deaths in Colombia is caused by violence, and this phenomenon affects, above all, young people at the beginning of their productive life. In the opinion of hospital administrators, the costs of attending to the victims of violence have converted the majority of urban hospitals into 'war hospitals', greatly expanding the work of accident and emergency units. Insurance against robbery and terrorism become part of the normal accounting on the part of citizens and businesses. Wealthy individuals – and at times even ordinary members of the population – resort to private protection and spend, in addition to what the state already spends, immense amounts on personal security, bodyguards and security guards. Although there are no calculations of their economic importance, industries that provide private security services (legal and illegal), armour-plating of vehicles, the manufacture of security grating and alarms, etc., have acquired central importance in Colombian life. In a less direct way the impact of the drug trade can be observed in the economic costs for the education system (affected by changing values but also by the arming of pupils in poor neighbourhoods) and the general inefficiency of the judicial system, as discussed earlier.

Conclusions

One of the most peculiar effects of the war against drugs is found in social communications. As much for the US government as for the Colombian government what matters is not so much what is done as what the people see or believe is done. Actions are not taken to achieve results, since the only result, or at least the one of most interest, is to persuade public opinion that the problem is being taken seriously. Therefore, the mid-term opinion polls which are necessary to evaluate the results of policy are not of interest. If a policy does not work, it is not a serious problem: it has already served its purpose of demonstrating the political intention of the state, particularly prior to elections. Perhaps it is even more convenient that it should not have had any results, since it allows for the promise of something more novel than the continuation of a policy which produces necessarily modest results.

This interest in the impact of public opinion generates greatly distorted forms of discussion and debate about the subject. The debate which took place in the Colombian media, or the statements by political leaders, including those of the President, about a May 1994 Constitutional Court ruling which decriminalised the private consumption of drugs, was an exercise in distortion. Few read the ruling, almost everyone refuted things that it did not say, and it was portrayed as a proposal for the liberal use of drugs to promote an emotionally-charged plebiscite in favour of the penalisation of individual consumption. In this case few of the politicians promoting the debate were concerned that drug consumption should be penalised. The concern above all was to send a signal to the USA (probably over-estimating its effect, since that government is not particularly worried about consumption in Colombia) at a time when the efficacy of the Colombian anti-drugs effort and the independence of the Colombian state from the traffickers was in question. From this point of view, one of the effects of drugs on Colombian society recently has been to make public debates concerning anything related to the traffickers more emotional and less analytical. In the debates about how the drug trade affects economic life, the accumulation of fortunes, the financing of political parties, and daily street violence, the drugs element frequently becomes pre-eminent and displaces the really important issues.

Emotional and distorted debates have, with some exceptions, masked the absence of far-reaching strategies to confront, or even to acknowledge, the problems generated by the drug trade. Put simply, no government has had a serious strategy with regard to the economic impact and the penetration of national economic activity by assets from the drug trade, a subject which has always been treated with relative indifference and superficiality. The new capitalists were acquiring immense rural properties, purchasing retail chains, providing the country with luxury vehicles and supplying the contraband markets where all middle- and upper-class Colombians obtained their electro-domestic appliances. In addition to the constitutional difficulties of establishing a basis for a system of controlling these resources and their possible expropriation, there were also the vested interests of the majority of regional politicians, who depended for their survival on contributions from the owners of the new capital. Various governments preferred to avoid combining the fight against the drug traffickers' main criminal activity with any attempt to control moneys obtained from the drug business. For this reason rather than proposals for expropriation or punitive taxation mechanisms, the new capitalists could take advantage of measures which, although they were not necessarily intended to benefit them, did so in an obvious way: the elimination of inheritance tax and the frequent tax amnesties.[16] The debate about the alliance of the drug trade with the army in confronting the guerrillas was always associated with the subversive intentions of those who raised it, and it only caused concern to those state institutions dedicated to the promotion of respect for human rights.

Neither has a coherent or comprehensive strategy for confronting the penetration of political life by the drug trade been sought. The debates about the state financing of political parties have carefully avoided this problem and the present norms can indirectly reward the beneficiaries of previous illegal donations, since these norms are based on reimbursement according to results. Even the norms regarding campaign expenditure curiously continue to depend on the good will of the parties themselves: while they are required to keep detailed accounts of their income and expenditure, donors are not asked to include their contributions in their accounting and tax documents.

Only in two areas has there been a serious and at times costly effort by national governments. The first, obviously, is the fight against violence generated by the drug trade. In this sphere, after years of indifference, the administration of Belisario Betancur (1982-86) started to act from 1984 onwards, but even then in a reactive and unmethodical fashion. The government of Virgilio Barco (1986-90) for the first time defined a comprehensive policy on this point, directed at destroying the cartels through the capture and extradition of their bosses. The Barco government also defined several conceptual elements that helped to shape a policy which, although seemingly very different, was in essence very close to that of César Gaviria (1990-94). It openly distinguished between the urgent necessity of standing up to narco-terrorism and real scepticism about the fight against the narcotics trade itself.

With regard to the latter, the main concern of the Colombian government is international policy. In effect, the general perception in the country is that the problem of local drug consumption is not very serious. With regard to the problem of drug exports, although there is a great diversity of positions, the most common opinion tends to point out that it is a problem which fundamentally affects the countries of consumption, and that it affects Colombia only to the extent that it produces secondary effects. For the Barco government, the most serious effect was probably the impact on the effective functioning of democracy, the risk that it would generate such levels of corruption, violence and disorder that it could endanger the constitutional order. For the Gaviria government, the central problem was violence. In all of these cases, the logical conclusion is that Colombia's real responsibility is not to control drugs but, rather, their damaging effects on the country. Drug control is primarily the responsibility of the countries of consumption or of the international community as a whole. It should be, as Barco and Gaviria insisted, a collective and cooperative multinational effort.

In addition to national considerations, the efficacy of Colombia's individual struggle against the drug trade has to be taken into account. In general, even those Colombians who consider that Colombia, as a responsible member of the international community, should make an effort to control the trade regard with considerable scepticism the results that a national effort could produce. It is easy to argue that the destruction of crops, laboratories and airports and the persecution of the cartels can produce results in the short term, but as long as demand is maintained, that which has been destroyed or seized will be replaced in Colombia or, if local anti-drugs measures are very effective, in other countries.[17] This argument easily leads to the conclusion that the costs assumed by Colombia in the struggle against drugs could be disproportionate to the results achieved. Among Colombian analysts, there is frequently a sense that the efforts at crop substitution or crackdowns on the drug cartels are relatively inefficient, and that above all they represent operations which have to be conducted because it is necessary to demonstrate to the USA that efforts are being made.[18] Furthermore, it seems strange to Colombians that there should be such an emphatic attempt at attacking the supply of drugs from Colombia, when the supply on US streets is not suppressed very vigorously, since from an economic point of view the priorities should be reversed.[19]

Notes

*   Translated by Pam Decho.

1.   The number of deaths from this cause may well have risen in 1996 following the major guerrilla offensive in the middle of the year.

2.   For a more detailed account of the way in which the confrontation between the traffickers and the state was conducted in those years, see Melo and Bermúdez (1994). There is an immense body of literature on drugs in Colombia; some general introductory surveys of the subject include: Arrieta et al (1990), Bagley and Tokatlián (1990), and Vargas (1994).

3.   The first proposals for negotiation came from the traffickers Escobar and Lehder in 1983 in a meeting with Attorney General Carlos Jiménez Gómez and talks began in 1984.

4.   The usual figure that Cali controls 80% of Colombian cocaine trafficking is little more than Drug Enforcement Administration (DEA) rhetoric.

5.   The circumstances surrounding the assassinations of the two left-wing presidential candidates Carlos Pizarro, a former M-19 guerrilla, and Bernardo Jaramillo of the left-wing coalition Unión Patriótica remain

murky. Escobar was blamed for the killings but protested his innocence more loudly than usual (Strong, 1995, p. 236). The possibility cannot be ruled out that the murders were planned by the secret services opposed to government policies, or that they were carried out by groups linked to both the secret services and the paramilitary anti-guerrilla organisation run by the drug traffickers.

6. Most Colombians concur with this prescription but, not being able to influence US demand for drugs, can do little about it. Rather, they have to consider the impact that the growth of the drug trade has on all aspects of their national life; on its institutions, its social structures and values and on the levels of violence. Without a serious anti-drugs campaign in Colombia, the traffickers would eventually have subjected the country completely to their control.

7. De Greiff himself was a controversial figure throughout his period as Prosecutor-General (*Fiscal General*), variously hailed as the man who had delivered Colombia from narco-terrorism, and condemned for suspected links with the Cali cartel. For details of those allegations, see Strong (1995). By the beginning of 1994, the Colombian government was in conflict with de Greiff over the implementation of the surrender policy while at the same time trying to defend him in Washington where he was the object of deep suspicion. The US Department of Justice was particularly reluctant to cooperate with him. This period – notwithstanding the popularity in Washington of de Greiff's successor, Alfonso Valdivieso – marked the start of a serious deterioration in US-Colombian relations.

8. Although the US government firmly supported the election of Gaviria as Secretary-General of the Organisation of American States (OAS), this did not completely erase the memory of the relatively low-key disagreement over the surrender policy for drug traffickers. The conflict between the Colombian government and Prosecutor-General de Greiff over his leniency in negotiations with the Cali cartel was probably decisive in Washington's agreement to support Gaviria in the OAS.

9. It was not only the credibility of the president that was damaged. More than 100 politicians, including three government ministers and other senior figures, were implicated. The campaigns of both Samper and his rival Pastrana were investigated by the Consejo Nacional Electoral (CNE) in 1996 on the grounds that both the Liberal and Conservative parties had far exceeded the legal limit of 4 billion pesos in their campaign spending.

10. Colombia was decertified for failing to cooperate adequately with the

USA on drug control. The compulsory consequences of such a measure are the suppression of 50% of bilateral aid, with the exception of some humanitarian and drug-related aid; a negative US vote for loan concessions in six international financial bodies, including the Inter-American Development Bank and the World Bank; and denial of access to Export-Import Bank credits for US exporters selling to Colombia. Most US aid to Colombia is related to drug control and would be unaffected by the sanctions. The effect of the negative vote in financial bodies will be limited, partly because the US vote is not decisive in all of them and partly because Colombia is not heavily dependent on their credits.

11. It is worth noting that, despite serious functional limitations, the other judicial sectors (civil, labour, family) work in a reasonably acceptable way. However, considering the relative inefficiency of the judicial and administrative systems in protecting the rights of the individual, the impact of new forms of 'exceptional justice' such as the *juicios de tutela* or 'protected trials' created by the 1991 Constitution, has been surprising. *Juicios de tutela* are a form of legal appeal which allows any citizen who believes that his/her fundamental constitutional rights are threatened by actions or omissions on part of the state to file a claim with *any* judicial authority and seek immediate redress (rather than going through normal legal procedure).

12. Still today, despite almost a decade of international advice on setting up systems and laboratories for the collection and scientific analysis of evidence, and the development of systems of investigation, those responsible for crimes are practically never identified unless they are apprehended in the act of committing the crime or there is reliable testimonial evidence. Of the on-average 25,000 homicides each year, suspects are not named in more than 2% of cases, and these are mostly people who have committed the crime without premeditation, or members of state institutions who have killed someone in operations of dubious legality.

13. This is far from what the DEA seems to believe. In one of its recent studies it claims that if Colombia continues to undermine legal exports and to allow illegal ones to increase 'it could be the first country to be economically dependent on the narcotics industry'.

14. The existence of these resources diminishes the pressure on foreign currency from legal origins, but we must not forget that a good part of the 'capital flight' was caused by conditions of personal insecurity created by the drug trade itself (Kalmanovitz, 1994).

15. Alejandro Reyes has carried out a detailed study of the acquisition of

real estate by the traffickers (Reyes, 1992). In this case, apart from the purely economic impact, it is essential to take into account the political and economic implications of the process. The drug traffickers support paramilitary activities, are key figures in local politics and a source of finance for legal state activities (a frequent form was to donate petrol for military vehicles).

16. The most important tax amnesty was approved in 1983. It had been proposed in 1982 initially with the support of Justice Minister Bernardo Gaitán Mahecha and National Association of Industrialists (ANDI) President Fabio Echeverri Correa. On that occasion it was clear that the amnesty was declared specifically to legalise moneys from the drug trade.

17. A corollary of this argument is the frequent complaint in Colombia about the weakness of US efforts to reduce domestic demand.

18. The case of the Samper government has proved unexpectedly dramatic and almost tragi-comic. Given Washington's growing lack of confidence in the Colombian government, there was a perceived obligation to demonstrate results which, compared with previous governments, were noteworthy: while Barco had no more to show than the death of Rodríguez Gacha, and Gaviria only just achieved the surrender or capture of the Medellín cartel bosses, Samper in less than a year managed to imprison the leading drug 'barons' of the Cali cartel and has substantially increased the volumes of drugs seized and crops destroyed. However, the greater his results, the less convinced about the seriousness of his efforts the USA appears to be.

19. Whereas an attack on supplies in Colombia should produce an increase in the price of drugs and create an incentive for trafficking, suppression on the streets of the USA should have the effect of intimidating consumers, thereby reducing final demand.

CHAPTER 4

THE ECONOMIC AND POLITICAL IMPACT OF THE DRUG TRADE AND DRUG CONTROL POLICIES IN BOLIVIA*

Andy Atkins

No country in South America is more dependent on the drug trade than Bolivia, but not because Bolivia is teeming with 'narco-terrorists' in league with a criminally-inclined population. Bolivia displays a number of characteristics which distinguish it from other countries in the region, and which have encouraged its participation in the drug trade while determining the effect that the trade has had on Bolivia itself. At the same time, Bolivia has been the focus of intensive international efforts to control the cocaine trade and these efforts have significant consequences of their own.

More academic attention has been given to the impact of the drug trade on the economy and politics of Bolivia than to its consequences in any other Latin American country. The first half of this chapter reviews the principal ways in which illicit drug production and trafficking affects Bolivia's economy, political system and society. By contrast, little academic attention has been devoted to the political and economic consequences of measures to *control* the drug trade. Yet these consequences are far-reaching and potentially damaging to Bolivia. Thus, the second half of the chapter will assess the political and economic effects on Bolivia of current drug control policies.

First, however, let me remind readers of some salient socio-economic features of Bolivia. While they may appear rather random at this stage, their significance to a discussion of the drug trade will emerge as the reader progresses.

Bolivia is the poorest country in South America, in terms of *per capita* income and a range of social indicators such as infant mortality.[1] Compared with Colombia and Peru, the other two major Andean countries involved in drug production, Bolivia's population is the smallest at 7.7 million and the most rural, with 45% of the population residing in the countryside. Bolivia also has the least diversified economy of the three Andean countries, with agriculture accounting for 44% of employment and manufacturing only 10%; other employment is concentrated in the commercial and service sectors

(Economist Intelligence Unit, 1994, p. 12). Bolivia experienced a profound economic recession in the 1980s, with Gross Domestic Product (GDP) contracting every year between 1980 and 1987, in part because of the collapse in prices for its chief exports, tin and natural gas. In 1985 inflation reached 11,850%, one of the highest rates ever recorded in the world.

The government subsequently undertook an extremely stringent economic stabilisation and structural adjustment programme, which, although it stabilised the economy, initially exacerbated the economic recession and social deprivation. Yet, compared with Colombia and Peru, Bolivia has been by far the most peaceful of the three countries in the last ten years: guerrilla movements have been small and very short-lived; neither criminal nor political violence nor human rights abuses have reached anything like the chronic proportions they have attained in Colombia and Peru. Finally, Bolivia is the Latin American country with the strongest cultural attachment to the coca leaf. Coca has been cultivated for at least 1,500 years and used for a variety of traditional purposes but, most notably, for the practice of chewing or *acullico* (Carter and Mamani, 1986). Coca may be grown legally in parts of the country to supply the traditional market and legal coca accounted for about 6.5% of agricultural production in 1992 (Economist Intelligence Unit, 1994, p. 13).

The Economic and Political Impact of the Drug Trade

Perhaps the most visible and obvious impact of the coca-cocaine trade on Bolivia was the rapid expansion of illegal coca cultivation during the 1980s. This took place mostly in the tropical zones of Cochabamba department, in an area known as the Chapare, far from the principal area of legal coca cultivation for the domestic market, in the zone of Los Yungas in the department of La Paz. Calculations of the rate of increase in coca cultivation can differ markedly, but show the same trends. According to Bolivian government estimates, cultivation expanded from approximately 22,788 hectares in 1980 to 60,956 hectares by 1989.[2] The US State Department, on the other hand, estimates the increase to have been from 35,000 hectares in 1980 to 55,400 hectares in 1989 (US Dept. of State, 1994, p. 94). What is clear is that the expansion of cultivation in the 1980s, particularly in the Chapare, was dramatic.

The fundamental reason for the boom was the high price of coca relative to other agricultural products. This was due in part to the increase in demand for coca to supply the US 'cocaine boom', and a series of factors which depressed the prices of other crops. Rising unemployment in Bolivia's formal economy provided a ready-made supply of labour. Calculations of how much could be earned from coca in the 1980s vary, but a number of studies from the early to mid-1980s suggest a minimum annual return of $5,000 per hectare. Depending on the study and the year it was undertaken, coca appears to have been anything from four to nineteen times more profitable than the next most profitable crop in the Chapare.[3] Although this did not make coca cultivators rich, it reduced their degree of misery compared with relatives in the highlands.

The coca boom sharply accelerated the colonisation of the lowland jungle Chapare, attracting tens of thousands of migrants from arid *altiplano* or high plains departments, and the high valleys of Cochabamba. Between 1967 and 1981, the Chapare's population increased from 24,000 to 84,000. By 1987, however, just six years later, it exceeded 200,000 – eight times the population of two decades earlier (Painter, 1994, p. 4). Thus the Chapare became, and remains, the hub of coca production for the cocaine trade in Bolivia – and the primary focus in Bolivia of internationally-supported drug control efforts. Coca became, and remains, the motor of the Chapare's economy. According to a 1992 survey, 95% of farmers in the Chapare cultivate at least some coca (Office of National Drug Control Policy, 1993, p. 20). Nevertheless, few peasants grow only coca and it is rarely grown on more than a quarter of a peasant's cultivated land. Coca tends to provide a comparatively reliable and regular source of cash which subsidises the production of less profitable food crops. And although, by 1994, the profitability of coca had fallen to between $2,800-$3,840 per hectare, UN sources suggest it still provided four times the income of bananas or pineapples[4] – two crops which have been seen, by some at least, as potential substitutes for coca.

The drug trade has boosted Bolivia's national income significantly over the last 15 years. This income derives from Bolivia's role as the world's second producer of coca after Peru,[5] and its growing importance in recent years as a producer of fully-processed cocaine. Estimates of the financial value of the coca-cocaine trade to Bolivia vary greatly, given that they depend on numerous other variables, including judgements about how much of the final value of coca and cocaine is retained by Bolivia and how much accrues to producers and traffickers in other countries. Former Bolivian Government Minister Samuel Doria Medina stated that the coca-cocaine trade was worth $1.5 billion to Bolivia in 1987, of which $600 million (40%) remained in the country (George, 1992, p. 42). A more conservative estimate found that the coca-cocaine trade was worth around $800 million to Bolivia in 1988, of which a minimum of $500 million (roughly 62%) remained in the country (Campodónico, 1989, p. 234). Even this minimum would have equalled the value of Bolivia's legal exports in that year.

There is broad agreement among researchers that the coca-cocaine trade made its greatest relative financial contribution to the Bolivian economy around 1987 and 1988, at a time of poor performance in Bolivia's legal economy and just before the price of coca fell sharply in 1989. Since then the value of the coca-cocaine trade has fallen, although it should be noted that its absolute value has declined less steeply than its 'relative value', as a proportion of legal exports and GDP. Discrepancies between studies underline the difficulty of calculating the exact value of the cocaine trade and make comparisons of one year with another somewhat hazardous, but they suggest a clear trend. USAID, for example, estimated that illegal coca-cocaine exports were still worth $732 million to Bolivia in 1992, but this represented a much-reduced 37% of the value of legal exports (Economist Intelligence Unit, 1994, p. 29). Government sources claimed the coca-cocaine trade was worth $600 million to Bolivia in 1994, although this by now represented only 8.5% of GDP.[6]

The declining value of the coca-cocaine trade since the late 1980s has been a function both of a fall in the price of coca and growth in Bolivia's legal economy. The average annual price for coca fell from $1.6 per kilo in 1986 to $1.2 per kilo in 1989, then slumped to $0.46 per kilo in 1990. Although it subsequently rose again to reach an annual average of about $1.00 in 1993-1994,[7] this is still less than the pre-slump price of five years earlier. Between 1989 and 1994, on the other hand, the Bolivian economy grew at an average rate of more than 3.5% per year and legal exports have increased, from $608 million in 1992 to $1,181.2 million in 1995.

Despite decreasing coca prices from the late 1980s to 1991, the fall in the absolute value of the coca-cocaine economy has been relatively slow. This is due firstly to the fact that an increasing proportion of Bolivia's coca is being processed into cocaine within the country, offsetting the income loss from lower prices. Secondly, since the price slump of 1989-90, coca prices have risen again, from a low of $0.46 per kilo in 1990 to around $1 in 1993-94. Of the total value of coca-cocaine production, all studies agree that only the smallest fraction falls to coca growers. A study by Frank, for example, suggests that in 1990 the coca farmers between them earned only 7% of the total value of coca-cocaine falling to Bolivia and somewhere between 0.65% and 2.15% of the final street value of cocaine manufactured from their coca (Frank, 1992, p. 40). It is worth stressing that this amount is shared between them.

Nevertheless, the coca-cocaine trade is still very significant for the Bolivian economy, particularly for specific regions. Despite economic growth, Bolivia remains desperately poor. Between 1985 and 1993, according to the government, the terms of trade for Bolivia's major exports worsened by

60%. The gap between Bolivia's exports and imports continued to fluctuate between $500 and $600 million in 1992-94. Moreover, despite wiping out its debt service arrears, Bolivia's total foreign debt still remains high for such a small country, and the debt service ratio (expressed as a percentage of exports) remains above 20%.

Against this economic background, the slowly dwindling income Bolivia earns from the coca-cocaine trade remains of greater relative significance to her economy than the much larger illicit incomes earned by Colombia and Peru. And coca remains as important as it ever was to the Chapare region where, despite the fall in prices since the mid-1980s, it is still by far the most profitable and reliable crop. Moreover, much enterprise in and around Cochabamba, the regional capital and Bolivia's third city, remains reliant on the income from the coca-cocaine trade.

Another obvious economic effect of the cocaine trade, also with important political implications, has been to provide employment. The amount of agricultural employment generated by the cocaine trade is closely linked, of course, to the area under coca cultivation. At the peak of coca cultivation, in 1988-89, conservative estimates suggest there were at least 60,000 rural families or 300,000 people directly dependent on coca cultivation in the Chapare. In the same year the Bolivian government estimated that a total of 0.5 million people, or between 25% and 33% of Bolivia's economically active population was employed in some part of the coca-cocaine economy (George, 1992, p. 41). Other studies suggest this figure was exaggerated. A survey of all research, using a selection of the more serious investigations, gives a range between 120,000 and 243,000 people employed in some aspect of the coca-cocaine trade for the two year period 1989-90 (Painter, 1994, p. 40). This produces a median average of 181,500 or about 10.1% of the economically active population. But even this lower figure is significant. Even if 'only' one in ten of Bolivia's workforce was directly involved in the coca-cocaine chain, the number whose livelihoods indirectly depended on it, through the multiplier effect stimulating service industries, construction etc., would obviously have been much higher.

The current level of employment provided by the coca-cocaine trade is difficult to calculate. In contrast to the situation in Peru and Colombia, the area under coca in Bolivia has been reduced in recent years. According to Bolivian government estimates, by the end of 1994 there were less than 37,000 hectares of 'excess' coca (that is coca not reserved for legal, traditional use), due to government eradication efforts. This represents a net reduction of approximately one third in five years.[8] This has undoubtedly led to a significant drop in agricultural employment in the Chapare.

As important as the monetary value of the coca-cocaine trade to Bolivia has been the complex role it has played in the real economy. Although the coca-cocaine trade has provided less income for Bolivia than for Peru or Colombia, it has played a more critical role in the economy precisely because Bolivia is the poorest and least diversified economy of the region, dependent for its legal income on the export of a small range of primary commodities and inflows of cheap credit and foreign aid. From the early 1980s, as Bolivia's legal economy nose-dived, the coca-cocaine economy acted as a parachute, sustaining tens of thousands of people who were ejected from the formal and informal economy elsewhere. First, from the early 1980s, persistent drought and increasing land shortage in the populous highlands created a pressure to migrate to the lowlands in search of new land and a higher income from coca. Then, in the mid-1980s, the economy contracted further with the introduction of a tough economic stabilisation and adjustment programme, known as the New Economic Plan (NEP) and a crash in the price of Bolivia's two main exports, tin and natural gas. In 1985 alone, some 60,000 public sector workers, including 17,000 tin miners, were made redundant. For many, joining displaced highland peasants in the Chapare to cultivate coca was the most logical survival option.

Many analysts believe that Bolivia's cocaine income made a second critical contribution by providing revenue with which to finance the external debt and imports. The Paz Estenssoro government (1985-89) passed measures allowing the Central Bank to buy dollars at the free-market rate. It also relaxed the rules governing the repatriation of dollars and the identification of origin of deposits made at private banks. While such changes may have been orthodox instruments to control the money supply and encourage foreign investment, they allowed the government to 'soak up' cocaine dollars through the banking system. Thus, Bolivia's cocaine income probably oiled the implementation of the NEP. Indeed, many observers believe that the lack of serious social unrest in Bolivia in the 1980s, despite an almost apocalyptic recession in the legal economy, was partly thanks to the ability of the coca-cocaine trade to provide replacement employment and badly-needed foreign exchange.

The economic consequences of the drug trade were not all positive for Bolivia. The injection of cocaine dollars into the economy is thought by many economists to have caused an over-valuation of the boliviano (national currency) which undermined the competitiveness of Bolivia's legal exports, a phenomenon known as 'Dutch Disease', apparent also in the Colombian economy in the 1980s. The over-valued boliviano encouraged imports, as did the common practice of laundering drug money by the importing and reselling of foreign consumer products. As a result, many Bolivian industries struggled to compete even in the domestic market.

It is customary in some circles to claim that the presence of an illegal industry such as the drug trade dissuades potential investors in legal enterprise. It is possible that the drug trade has dissuaded domestic investment in the zones most affected by the coca-cocaine trade, such as the Chapare. But it is debatable whether it has frightened away significant foreign investment at a national level. From the mid- to late 1980s, when the cocaine trade was making its most significant contribution to the Bolivian economy, the formal economy was experiencing a profound recession. Under such circumstances, added to Bolivia's historical poverty, geographical isolation and poor transport and communications infrastructure, there was little foreign interest in investing in Bolivia in the first place.

With the economic gains to be made from Bolivia's involvement in the drug trade, it is inevitable that the coca-cocaine complex should influence the country's politics. It has done so in numerous ways, some obvious, some more subtle. The most obvious effect of the drug trade has been to encourage corruption. This has infected almost every sphere of the state, from the executive, legislature and judiciary, through law enforcement bodies to state-owned companies. The most notorious case is that of General Luis García Meza who seized power in June 1980 in what has become known as the 'cocaine coup'. During the year he was in power, he and his Minister of the Interior, Colonel Luis Arce Gómez (widely dubbed the 'Minister for Cocaine') used the apparatus of the state to set up a cocaine production and export network. García Meza was tried *in absentia* for corruption and human rights abuse. In December 1994, after much legal wrangling, he was finally extradited from Brazil to commence a life sentence in Bolivia for conspiracy to murder and corruption.[9]

Since the García Meza regime, there have been a succession of corruption scandals involving individuals in high office. In 1993, for example, charges of drug-linked corruption were made against the President of the Supreme Court and another Supreme Court judge. They were subsequently impeached and dismissed in 1994. Another scandal with serious political implications was the so-called *narco-vínculos* or 'drug-ties' case. This emerged in early 1994, when an investigation by the Fuerzas Especiales en la Lucha Contra Narcotráfico (FELCN) led to accusations that politicians close to former President Jaime Paz Zamora, and possibly Paz Zamora himself, had accepted bribes from convicted drug trafficker Isaac 'Oso' Chavirría to finance the 1989 presidential campaign. Enigmatically, Paz Zamora initially admitted that he may have made mistakes but denied committing any crime. Then, in May 1994, he announced his retirement from politics. In December 1994, following its own investigation into the matter, Congress determined that several politicians, including Paz Zamora and two siblings, should be charged with drug offences under Law 1008. Then, in January 1995, Paz Zamora, declaring his innocence, presented himself to the Palace of Justice and announced his return to politics. The case rumbles on. While such high profile cases make the international headlines, corruption at lower levels is rampant. There are, for example, widespread accusations of corruption within the drug-control forces themselves. This concerns not only the bribery of officials to 'turn a blind eye' to illegal activities, or to alert traffickers to impending operations against them. There are cases of military or police officials themselves trafficking drugs. In January 1995, for example, drug-control police detained a Bolivian navy captain transporting 480 kilos of cocaine in military vehicles between La Paz and Oruro. Evidence exists of widespread misappropriation of goods confiscated from traffickers. In June 1994, a Bolivian government report announced the disappearance of millions of dollars seized from the drug trade, owing, according to the report 'to negligent action by members of FELCN, certain citizens nominated by the Prosecutor's Office (*Fiscalía*) as custodians of the goods, and certain ex-subprefects'.

It is often assumed that such corruption breeds political instability and the García Meza coup is presented as the example *par excellence*. Yet the 'cocaine coup' was probably exceptional. In a country notorious for the frequency of its military coups, the armed forces have rarely needed the incentive of immense illegal enrichment to induce them to rebel; political ideology and inter-institutional feuds have always been sufficient. Neither were these elements absent from the 'cocaine coup'. Most significantly, however, since the fall of García Meza, Bolivia has enjoyed 15 years of elected civilian government. And during this same period the influence of the cocaine trade in the Bolivian economy reached its peak.

A brief review of Bolivian politics over the last decade suggests that the most obvious instability has arisen not from the drug-linked corruption itself but from the political repercussions following revelations of such corruption in high places. Such incidents tend to provoke bitter clashes, accusations and counter-accusations in Congress. The political parties most associated with the accused person attempt to rally to his defence or to limit the damage, while that party's political opponents attempt to take advantage of their discomfort. Such battles have caused serious rifts between different political parties complicating and impeding normal legislative business, as the acrimony surrounding the accusations of *narco-vínculos* against Paz Zamora and several of his colleagues showed. In mid-1994, when the congressional commission set up to investigate the charges failed to meet successive deadlines to deliver its verdict, exasperated members issued independent reports and charged that a cover-up was being attempted. According to

Bolivian press reports, strongly denied by the new Movimiento Nacional Revolucionario (MNR) government, the MNR was offering to ensure that charges against Paz Zamora were dropped in exchange for another favour.[10] The favour was that the former President's party support the impeachment of the two supreme court judges and desist from its own investigations into an earlier unresolved scandal. This was the notorious 'Huanchaca Case', which the MNR was widely suspected of covering up.

Whatever the truth of these particular press reports, it was hard to avoid the conclusion that the congressional commission was more of a political battle field than an impartial investigation. The drug trade has no doubt increased the rewards of corruption for those so placed to extort or attract bribes, but the temptation to make drugs a scape-goat for all corruption in Bolivia needs to be kept in check. As any who have lived or travelled in Bolivia can testify, petty corruption is an everyday affair. This is nothing new in impoverished countries with weak democratic traditions. It existed in Bolivia long before the cocaine trade and is likely to outlive it, if these conditions persist.

The Economic and Political Impact of Drug Control Measures

Clearly the illegal drug trade has had major economic and political consequences for Bolivia. But Bolivia has long been a focus for international drug control efforts which have their own consequences, intended or otherwise. I suggest, therefore, that in the interests of obtaining a more complete picture of the wider impact of the drug trade, the impact of drug-control measures merits much closer scrutiny.

In the case of Bolivia, successful coca eradication has diminished the importance of the cocaine trade as a provider of employment and income. Views on the degree of the income loss diverge wildly. In 1991, Minister for Social Defence, Gonzalo Torrico, stated that eradicating Bolivia's 50,000 hectares of coca would reduce Bolivian GDP by $4 billion, cut foreign exchange earnings by $200 million a year and cause the loss of 175,000 jobs.[11] Different estimates suggest that between 1989 and 1991 alone, between 10,000 and 22,000 families left the Chapare, as a result of the drastic fall in the price of coca and the eradication of some 8,000 hectares of the crop in 1990.[12] Eradication slowed thereafter, at least until mid-1994, while coca prices have risen. This combination could be expected to slow the migratory outflow.

Between 1987 and 1990, new planting of coca probably exceeded that eradicated each year. Subsequently, however, the balance has tipped in favour of eradication, to bring about a net reduction of at least 20,000 hectares between 1987 and the end of 1994. This would suggest a reduction in direct employment in coca cultivation of at least 20,000 families and many thousands more involved in the subsequent stages of coca paste and cocaine production.

While Bolivia has lost income because of its declining share of the coca-cocaine trade, it has nevertheless gained some compensation. From the late 1980s, the Bolivian government, along with other Andean governments, appealed to the international community to help them reduce drug production. They appealed, in particular, for aid and trade concessions. Their hope was to boost their legal economies generally and, in particular, to fund 'alternative development' programmes in zones of drug production. To some extent, their demands were met.

Any form of economic assistance that can diminish a country's reliance on illegal drug production can reasonably be classified as 'alternative development' aid. Consequently, it is difficult to disaggregate drug control assistance from other types of aid. The United States has changed its account-headings three times in the last six years, making year by year comparisons difficult. The European Union (EU) clearly regards general development aid as making a contribution, albeit indirect, to overcoming the drug trade by targeting the poverty that encourages people to engage in drug-related activities. By invoking the need to substitute the drug economy, Bolivia has almost certainly been able to attract more aid. Politically, this ability to attract high levels of drug-related aid has been a double-edged sword, although it has had some economic benefits.

Bolivia attracts more bilateral aid from the United States, the EU and the EU member states than any other country in the Andean region. Much of this aid has been explicitly or implicitly linked to the drug control effort. US drug-related aid soared in 1989 when President Bush launched his Andean Initiative. This promised $2.2 billion in economic and security aid to the Andean countries over the five years, 1990-94. Of this total, $830 million was originally allocated to Bolivia, much more than that proposed for either Peru or Colombia. Owing to budget changes and delays in disbursement, the amount actually delivered has almost certainly been less. But the figures demonstrate that Bolivia remains the main Andean beneficiary of US drug control and general development aid: for the last three fiscal years (1993-95), Bolivia has been allocated a total of $238 million in aid, compared with $142.7 million for Colombia, and $117.5 million to Peru.[13] For the 1995 fiscal year, the Clinton administration asked Congress to set aside a total of $134.1 million in aid for Bolivia (second only to Peru for which $150.5 million was requested). But of this, $68 million was tied to drug control measures, more than that so designated for either Peru or Colombia (Office of National Drug Control Policy, 1994, p. 134).

No doubt the balance of payments relief that the United States offers Bolivia is welcome. One presumes it has allowed the Bolivian government to make savings or divert public expenditure to other social priorities. However, only a small proportion has been spent on direct attempts to replace the coca-cocaine economy, for example, through alternative development programmes in the Chapare. From 1992-94, the US aid package included an allocation of between $50 million and $100 million per year in balance of payments support. But aid allocated for development projects on the ground was a mere $20-$24 million per year.[14] Moreover, the Bolivians have complained that, although the United States, has been quick to disburse security aid, it has been very slow to disburse balance of payments and development aid. The presence of the drug trade has enabled Bolivia to attract more aid, but much of this assistance, particularly from the United States, has been security aid. And while the economic aid has been useful, it has made little difference to the average coca farmer who still lacks attractive alternatives to coca. Of the 24,000 hectares of coca eradicated as part of so-called alternative development programmes between 1987 and 1994, only 6,513 hectares, or one in four hectares, were substituted by other crops, according to Bolivian government sources.[15]

Although Bolivia has received some benefits from aid, it is less certain that it has benefited from trade preferences. In 1990, the European Community (EC) granted Bolivia, together with Colombia, Peru and Ecuador, special trade preferences under the EC's Generalised System of Preferences (GSP) as part of its economic support for drug control in Latin America. This allowed for the reduction or removal of tariffs on a range of manufactured and agricultural goods for a period of 4 years (January 1991 - December 1994). Preferences were renewed in 1995, for one year only on agricultural products and three years on manufactured goods.

Yet, while these may assist Bolivia in the future, the evidence suggests that by comparison with the other Andean countries, Bolivia has benefited least from the trade preferences so far.[16] The bulk of Bolivian exports to the EC (or European Union – EU – as it is now called) are traditional exports of primary agricultural or mineral products. These already entered the EU with a zero or very low tariff. The lowering of tariffs on manufactured and non-traditional exports, therefore, offered little to Bolivia in the short term. Neither has Bolivia been able to diversify its economy rapidly to take advantage of the improved opportunities for non-traditional products.

Bolivia has been hamstrung in its efforts to diversify by lack of investment, poor transport and communications infrastructure, as well as by its land-locked position. Thus, the country most in need of export incentives as a way of substituting its illegal economy for legal enterprise, has been the least able to benefit from the EU's trade arrangements.

It is in the political sphere that international drug control efforts have had their greatest impact on Bolivia. Most studies have concentrated on assessing the effectiveness of drug control policies, but heated debates over this issue have distracted attention from the less obvious political side-effects of these policies.

An issue of increasing concern to jurists and human rights specialists is the serious erosion of civil rights and due process occasioned by efforts to defeat the drug trade. An important strand of international efforts to reduce drug production in developing countries has been to promote the strengthening of local anti-drug legislation and more effective law enforcement. It is entirely appropriate that this should be attempted, not just in the hope of reducing drug supply but also to eliminate the noxious effects of drug-related corruption and violence on democracy and the rule of law. But in Bolivia at least, while the strengthening of law enforcement has led to the capture of some major traffickers, it has also had some perverse consequences largely for the poorer sectors of the population. The drug trade carries on relatively undiminished, but legislation introduced to reduce it has instead restricted civil rights and encouraged human rights violations.

The prime example of this is the *Ley del Régimen de la Coca y Sustancias Controladas* (Law of Coca and Controlled Substances Regime), or Law 1008 of 1988. This is extremely crude, defining certain 'crimes' imprecisely, and at worst explicitly criminalising a range of activities which would not be considered misdemeanours elsewhere. Moreover, it has dangerously reduced both the evidence required to sentence the accused and the rights of the accused to a defence. Someone found innocent of a charge under Law 1008 in one court cannot expect to be released until both the Appeals Court and subsequently the Supreme Court have also come to the same verdict. This process is supposed to take no more than 95 days but, in practice, usually takes much longer and in some cases has taken in excess of two years (Pettersson and Mackay, 1993). In any country, such clumsy laws should be of concern to democrats. In countries like Bolivia, with a history of political intolerance and social polarisation until as recently as the early 1980s, such 'catch all' legislation is particularly dangerous and open to abuse.

Already the law has led to a dangerous and inhumane overcrowding of jails. In 1994, 52% of detainees in Cochabamba's San Sebastián men's prison, and 61% of detainees in the women's prison were charged under Law 1008.[17] According to a 1994 report by the *Pastoral Social* of the Catholic Church in Bolivia, 65% of prisoners charged under Ley 1008 were held on remand (in 'preventive detention') and had not been tried.[18]

Not only is the legislation clumsy, it is also being enforced by police and military forces notorious for their corruption and disregard for due process. Drug control legislation has endowed these historically undemocratic forces with even more control over civic life while providing no safeguards against the abuse of that power. Well-substantiated allegations of serious human rights abuse, including arbitrary detention, theft, torture, rape and murder, are made with increasing frequency against UMOPAR, the para-military rural drug control police. On 18 August 1994, an unarmed coca farmer was beaten and summarily executed by UMOPAR troops who initially claimed that the deceased was a dangerous trafficker killed in an armed confrontation. This lawlessness of the law-enforcers should be of concern not only to human rights specialists. As its effect is to alienate the local population and generate the public opposition to the police, it can only impede future efforts to combat drug trafficking.

The drug trade has undoubtedly increased the power of the undemocratic in Bolivia but, perversely, the drug control effort has done the same. US attempts, under the Bush administration, to involve Bolivia's armed forces in the 'war on drugs' presented the Bolivian army with a new pretext for involvement in matters of civilian government and law enforcement. This threatened to reverse years of delicate work by elected civilian governments to bring the army firmly under civilian democratic control and to accustom them to a role of external defence rather than internal social control.

The Bush administration pressured the Bolivian government into signing a bilateral drug control treaty in 1989, whose top secret Annex III apparently provides for US troops to train Bolivian troops for counter-narcotics activities. The Bolivian army carried out just one fruitless drug control operation in 1991. Subsequently, the Bush administration's hopes of involving the Bolivian army in serious drug control foundered in the face of determined Bolivian government and public opposition to a 'militarisation' of the 'war on drugs'. The Clinton administration has continued to take a hard line on foreign drug control and has pressed for renewed Bolivian military involvement, under its declared aim of shifting US interdiction efforts away from US borders (a strategy which it acknowledges has failed) to the 'source countries'. In mid-1994 and early 1995, Bolivian troops took part in drug control operations in the Chapare.

A consequence of intense international attention to the drug trade has been what one could might call the 'narcoticisation' of Bolivia's external relations. In effect, the drug issue affects all others in Bolivia's foreign relations. While this has enabled Bolivia to appeal successfully for foreign aid, it also has negative consequences. Above all, the linking of such a sensitive issue to other matters introduces an extra element of instability into Bolivia's foreign relations and severely restricts the Bolivian government's freedom of manoeuvre in domestic and foreign politics. This makes the task of government ever more difficult. A practical example of this, and one that causes profound resentment in Bolivia, is the way US balance of payments assistance is conditioned on Bolivia's 'drug control performance' and, in particular, to Bolivia attaining annual eradication targets of between 5,000 and 8,000 hectares of coca. Another is the way that the US administration annually certifies countries as cooperating with US drug-control efforts. Under the terms of the 1988 Omnibus Law on Drug Abuse, if a country is 'decertified' the Executive must instruct its representatives on the international financial institutions to vote against loans to that country.

Bolivia remains critically dependent on foreign assistance. Thus, the Bolivian government is under intense pressure to accede to US wishes in matters of drug policy for fear of jeopardising economic assistance not only from the United States but from equally important multilateral sources. This frequently presents the Bolivian government with a dilemma: La Paz must choose between following its preferred course of action and taking a course necessary to placate Washington. Successive Bolivian governments have found themselves trapped between the peasant federations, with which there is a long-standing agreement that coca should be eradicated voluntarily in parallel with alternative development programmes, and the United States, pressing for eradication by any means necessary on pain of a withdrawal of aid. In April 1994, President Sánchez de Lozada was led to complain publicly that 'the dependence of the nation is terrible'.

This 'narcoticisation' of external relations causes domestic social instability. In June 1994, it was announced that Bolivia would lose $20 million in US aid if it did not eradicate a further 3,400 hectares of coca by 30 September.[19] On 13 July, the government launched Operation New Dawn, involving 700 FELCN troops, 240 police and US Drug Enforcement Administration (DEA) advisers. The purpose was to establish sufficient control over the Chapare to enable forcible coca eradication, and to break up trafficking networks. The effective 'militarisation' of the Chapare, coupled with attempts to eradicate coca in apparent contravention of the accord between the government and peasant federations, provoked strong protests by the peasants. The government attempted to suppress these. Reports of widespread human rights abuses by UMOPAR forces increased public criticism of the operation. This was exacerbated when the government arrested elected peasant leaders. On 29 August, the clash between the government and peasant federations intensified, when some 5,000 coca farmers set off on a 600 kilometre march from the Chapare to La Paz. Under the banner of 'For life, coca and sovereignty', the peasants arrived in La Paz 22 days later. By this time, the coca growers had won overwhelming public support, including that of leading politicians, intellectuals and the Archbishop of La Paz. The intensity of public opinion and the determination of the marchers forced the government to return to the negotiating table, in order to preserve national stability and its own authority. Forcible eradication in the Chapare ceased (temporarily at least) and, on 22 September, the government signed a 54-point accord with Bolivia's trade union federation, the *Central Obrera Boliviana* (COB), to which the Chapare peasant federations belong. This agreed, among other things, on the need to reformulate Law 1008 and to end the linking of sustainable development assistance to the prior eradication of coca. In the course of events, public trust in the government had been severely eroded, complicating its efforts to reach a national consensus on the issue of eradication, sustainable development and alternative uses of coca.

Any hope of swiftly rebuilding consensus was shattered in early 1995 when President Sánchez de Lozada declared a temporary State of Siege. Ostensibly the justification was to allow the government to break a prolonged strike by the country's teachers who were opposing a reform of the education system. But it was no coincidence that the government was simultaneously facing a real threat of 'decertification' by the United States over drug policy. On 18 April 1995, the Bolivian authorities arrested Evo Morales, elected leader of the Chapare peasant unions, along with other Bolivian, Colombian and Peruvian delegates who had gathered for the annual assembly of the Andean Council of Coca Growers. Although they were actually detained several hours before the State of Siege was declared, the Bolivian peasant leaders were held under State of Siege provisions and informed they would be charged under Law 1008. After two weeks in detention and considerable international protest, Morales and his colleagues were released without charge. While he was held, however, effectively as a hostage to dissuade resistance by the peasant federations, the government sent the army into the Chapare to register coca cultivation in preparation for eradication.

There is a widespread perception in Bolivia that the USA is not only infringing Bolivia's sovereignty in pursuit of its drug control objectives, but that it is manipulating the drug issue in pursuit of other objectives. There was particular controversy surrounding President Paz Zamora's decision in 1990, apparently under US pressure, to authorise the entry of US troops for drug control purposes, without first seeking the required congressional approval. Another incident which did not escape public notice was that, when the State Department named Bolivia in March 1993 as one of the less cooperative countries on the drug issue, the White House proceeded to 'certify' Bolivia because of other, unnamed 'vital interests'. The US decision may well have been determined by the judgment that 'decertification' would provoke a strongly nationalist response from many sections of Bolivian society which would further complicate drug control cooperation, and possibly destabilise the democractic government and harm its programme of economic liberalisation and privatisation.   Nevertheless, in Bolivia, the phrase confirmed belief in other more recondite explanations.   Typical was the conviction that the USA, seeking to dominate the bio-technology industry of the future, was determined to ensure its control of the Amazon basin's unique biological resources and regarded Bolivia as a vital strategic base from which to do so.

Suspicions of US intentions have been fuelled considerably under the Clinton administration by the notable frequency with which high-level US visitors have arrived in Bolivia, among whom have been successive commanders and senior officers of the US military's Southern Command, and Vice-President Al Gore.   Whatever the truth of these suspicions, they reinforce public concern about the side-effects of drug control policy generally, to increase public rejection of the current drug control strategy. This has now generated a social and political backlash against the Bolivian government.

One manifestation of this backlash is the increasingly widespread and vociferous support for the proposal that coca should be removed from Schedule I of the UN's 1961 *Single Convention on Narcotic Drugs.*   This would allow the export of a variety of coca products, such as *mate de coca* or coca tea, which are already marketed commercially within Bolivia and Peru. Of course, behind the re-emergence of this idea over the last few years is a popular reaction against the way in which the international community has misunderstood what is, to many millions of Andean citizens, a sacred plant, stigmatising its traditional users.   In addition, however, for many Bolivians the campaign to depenalise coca also provides a symbolic banner with which to express their much broader concerns about the so-called 'war on drugs' to which they feel subjected.   Bolivian peasant federations may have been distrustful of President Sánchez, but they would find some agreement with him on the issue of depenalising coca.   When in Washington in March 1994, he declared 'The coca leaf, when it is not processed, is like coffee or tea without any narcotic effect' and he complained that 'the United States needs more imagination and openness if we are to find viable solutions [to the drug problem]'.[20]   In May 1994, Law 23780 was passed, regulating the industrialisation and commercialisation of coca products within Bolivia, although it explicitly excludes the use of coca from the Chapare for this purpose.   Another manifestation of this backlash has been the movement to revise Law 1008.   In October 1994, a congressional commission was set up to make proposals for the reformulation of this law.

The US embassy in La Paz represents this backlash as inspired by drug traffickers and opposition politicians. It would be surprising if some politicians did not use the drug issue as political ammunition. But serious concerns about drug control policy are expressed by a broad range of totally independent sectors, including leading establishment figures. To dismiss them all as politically motivated or under the influence of drug traffickers is unrealistic. It is also dangerous because it risks further polarising an increasingly charged situation by criminalising democratically expressed dissent.

The extent of this dissent is revealed by a public opinion survey, carried out in La Paz and the adjoining city of El Alto, in August 1994. According to the survey:

- 63% of those questioned were against the forced eradication of coca;
- 72.6% were in favour of the depenalisation of coca;
- 75.1% were against the participation of the United States in the 'war on drugs' in Bolivia; and
- 93.7% thought Law 1008 should be reformulated or abandoned.[21]

Conclusions

The economic impact of the drug trade on Bolivia has been immense. Although Bolivia's income from the drug trade has diminished slowly in recent years, and the legal economy has grown, illicit production and trafficking nevertheless remain important to this, the weakest of Andean economies. It is particularly important in zones such as the Chapare and the region around Cochabamba. The political impact of the drug trade has been much more negative, but has never produced the kind of violence that it has in neighbouring countries.

Bolivia has certainly had more success than either Peru or Colombia in reducing coca cultivation. In terms of the area under cultivation, it has now almost certainly fallen into third place behind Colombia. It has also had some success in capturing key traffickers (although others have replaced them). Despite its relative success, Bolivia remains under unparalleled pressure within the region to intensify drug law enforcement against rich traffickers and impoverished coca-growers alike. At the same time, international willingness to fund alternative development programmes, designed to provide peasants with viable livelihoods other than coca, is waning. Both the US Congress and the European Parliament, for example, are increasingly sceptical about the value of such programmes (European Parliament, 1995).

Thus, an avenue which could allow more peasants to make a peaceful and dignified exit from the drug economy is in danger of being closed off. This is likely only to increase the combativeness of the coca-farmers as well as their support among large sectors of the population, among which they have attained almost folk-hero status. Add to this clumsy Bolivian laws, heavy-handed law enforcers and the sensibilities of most Bolivians concerning US interference in their country, and the situation becomes volatile.

There is now, in this author's view, a serious risk that further crude US pressure on Bolivia to play to its drug control game plan 'or else', may seriously harm Bolivia. In no way should this be taken as a defence of the drug trade. But it should raise questions about the appropriateness of some of the tools used to grapple with it, and the manner in which those tools are applied. In the long run Bolivia would be better off without the drug trade. But it has survived the last decade with it, strengthening its democracy, stability and peace despite a legacy of military rule and excruciating poverty. It would be a tragic irony indeed if the fight against the drug trade now eroded these precious achievements.

Notes

*   The author would like to thank James Painter, to whose book *Bolivia and Coca: A Study in Dependency* (1994) this chapter owes a great debt.
1.   Indicators are from the United Nations Human Development Index (cited in Economist Intelligence Unit, 1994, p. 8).
2.   The figures are from the Ministerio de Asuntos Campesinos y Agropecuarios (Quiroga, 1990, p. 81).
3.   Author's extrapolations from Painter (1994, p. 10).
4.   Sandro Calvani, director of the United Nations International Drug Control Programme (UNDCP) in Bolivia, cited in CEDIB, *Coca y Lucha Contra las Drogas*, Vol. 4, No. 8 (Cochabamba, Sept. 1994), p. 4.
5.   Reliable statistics are hard to come by, but Bolivia may have been pushed into third place by the recent growth of coca production in Colombia.
6.   Author's interview with Bolivian foreign ministry officials, February 1994.
7.   *Coca y Lucha Contra las Drogas*, Vol. 4, No. 8, p. 4.
8.   *Ibid.*, p. 4 gives a figure of 37,000 hectares and there has been further eradication since then.

9. Arce Gómez was sentenced by a US court to 30 years imprisonment for cocaine trafficking.
10. CEDIB, *Coca, drogas, narcotráfico y desarrollo*, No. 1 (Cochabamba, 15 June 1994), p. 2.
11. Quoted in *Hoy*, La Paz, 5 September 1991.
12. 1991 estimates by Government Minister Samuel Doria Medina (10,000) and USAID (22,000) (Painter, 1994, p. 42).
13. This includes aid disbursed (1993), aid approved (1994) and aid requested by the President, awaiting approval by Congress (1995) (US Dept. of State, 1994, p. 60).
14. Author's calculations from data in Washington Office on Latin America, *Andean Initiative Legislative Update* (Washington, July 1992 and August 1993).
15. DIRECO and IBTA, cited in *Coca y Lucha Contra las Drogas*, Vol. 4, No. 8, p. 1.
16. According to the Institute for European-Latin American Relations (IRELA), between 1990 and 1993 the number of Colombian export products covered by the GSP quadrupled. Bolivia's product coverage during the same period increased from four to seven. Less than 5% of Bolivia's total exports benefit from the GSP (for Colombia, the figure is 51%).
17. Andean Commission of Jurists, *Drug Trafficking Update* No. 51 (Lima, July 1994), p. 3.
18. *Coca y Lucha Contra las Drogas*, Vol. 4, No. 10 (October 1994), p. 1.
19. *Coca, Drogas, Narcotráfico y Desarrollo*, No. 1 (15 June 1994), p. 2.
20. *Coca y Lucha Contra las Drogas*, Vol. 4, No. 4 (April 1994), pp. 1-2.
21. *Coca y Lucha Contra las Drogas*, Vol. 4, No. 8 (August 1994), p. 2.

CHAPTER 5

THE DRUG TRADE IN PERU*

Roberto Lerner

After decades of frustration, Peru in 1990 appeared to be on the verge of dissolution; the prospect of territorial disintegration was by no means inconceivable. Institutions were failing to discharge their official roles, the state was in danger of being overthrown by forces which found no formal means of political expression (Matos, 1988) and which discharged their resentment by creating alternative channels (De Soto, 1987), the ruling class lacked long-term objectives, political subversion was growing rapidly, and vast areas of national territory were being converted into coca plantations.

In 1990, Ricardo Belmont, a man with no party affiliations who spoke in simple, rudimentary language, was elected mayor of Lima. Later that year, Peru's internationally-renowned novelist Mario Vargas Llosa was defeated in the presidential elections by an unknown citizen, Alberto Fujimori. During the next two years, an economic stabilisation and adjustment programme supported by international financial organisations, combined with the increasingly brutal onslaughts of subversion and a political imbroglio that showed no prospects of a solution, pushed Peru further towards crisis.

It is not easy to establish unequivocally to what extent the crisis was 'allowed to come to a head' by the new Fujimori government, which desperately needed the support of the army for a President who had no firm political base and few allies within civil society. An additional cause for concern was that the army already had *de facto* control over vast areas of Peru as a result of its counter-insurgency campaign.

However, largely as a result of international pressure, democracy prevailed and a process of institutional strengthening began. A Constituent Assembly was formed, and municipal elections and a constitutional referendum took place. The Constitution was amended to allow for the possible re-election of the president, a prospect which seemed to consolidate the people's rejection of the traditional political class, and President Fujimori duly won an overwhelming victory on 9 April 1995.

It is important to acknowledge that since 1992 remarkable changes have taken place in Peru. After the capture of *Sendero Luminoso* leader Abimael Guzmán – thanks to the daring and intelligence of National Police special agents led by General Ketin Vidal – counter-subversion policies began to produce results and the security situation improved significantly. Special tribunals, faceless judges, the *Arrepentimiento* (Law of Atonement) and rural patrols undoubtedly led to the strategic defeat of *Sendero Luminoso* and the *Movimiento Revolucionario Tupac Amaru* (MRTA).[1] The reduction in inflation, a more or less consistent privatisation programme, and the inflow of foreign capital – largely speculative but beginning to stimulate productive investment – opened up prospects of economic improvement amidst severe unemployment and acute poverty for a significant section of Peruvian society.

Peru, an extraordinarily heterogeneous and complex country of 23 million inhabitants, has over recent decades experienced profound changes in its demographic, social, economic and political circumstances. In many ways, it has become a modern state. As in other Latin American countries, the process of modernisation has manifested itself in various ways. In 1940, the population of Peru was predominantly rural – 65% of inhabitants lived outside urban centres, and around 61% lived in the Andes. Today, 70% of people live in cities, with an over-concentration of inhabitants in the capital, Lima.

In spite of the enormous problems which Peru faces, it enjoys relatively low rates of illiteracy, which dropped from 60% in the 1940s to a current rate of 11.2%. Similarly, it has witnessed a certain slowing down in demographic growth rates, with a marked trend towards smaller families, and an increase in the life expectancy of all inhabitants. All people, and especially the young, see education to be the best means of progress, and many seek to complete their education in universities – currently, about 500,000 people are studying in institutions of higher education – and have sought, at least over recent years, to qualify for technical or middle management careers. However, many university graduates are unemployed or underemployed despite the rapid growth in the economy between 1991 and 1995.

Migration from country to town and from the mountain ranges to the coast has generated a trend towards cultural miscegenation in Lima, where 39% of the population of Peru is concentrated, while the distinctly centralist nature of its society has become more marked. Lima contains people of many different races and origins, who maintain their cultural distinctiveness while giving rise to new linguistic forms. At the same time, modernity has arrived rapidly, through the considerable influence of the media, telecommunications and technology, and of other formerly unknown services.   During the 1960s, colonisation occurred at the rim of the rainforest (*selva*) and within it, but successive economic crises and the absence of agroindustrial development converted the new centres into magnets for migrants which resulted in the formation, at a later stage, of peasant communities dedicated to the cultivation of coca.

Peru has been characterised by a pendular movement in the management of the economy and also in politics, swinging between economic populism and orthodoxy, and political authoritarianism and democratic practices. From 1911 onwards, an oligarchy which was the legacy of the colonial period and which was allied to the army predominated. Between 1930 and 1963, there was a succession of military and civilian governments.   Towards the end of that epoch, a young architect, Fernando Belaúnde, came to power heralding a renovation programme which quickly sank in the mire of peasant revolt and scandals of every kind. In 1968, a period of redistributive populism was initiated in the wake of a reformist military movement which aspired to redefine power relationships in the country and also to avoid the political explosion of social forces identified with the left. After six years, there was a return to economic orthodoxy. At the same time, the army returned to their barracks, surrendering political power to an elected non-military regime led by Fernando Belaúnde, the same President they had deposed twelve years earlier.

During the second presidential mandate of Belaúnde (1980-85), the economy was managed using a combination of limited liberalism and controlled populism, which failed in the midst of natural catastrophes and a guerrilla uprising with Maoist tendencies and overtones of the messianic movement of the Andes (Gorriti, 1990). The return to populist heterodoxy and the use of anti-imperialist rhetoric raised great hopes as a result of the eloquence of a charismatic leader – Alan García – who had risen through the ranks of APRA (*Alianza Popular Revolucionaria Americana*), a social democratic party which had been in opposition, whenever it was not banned, for 60 years. After two years of growth based on the redistribution of income, low prices for public services, differential rates for the dollar, the partial suspension of international debt repayments and a protectionist policy, the model began to collapse. President García opted to nationalise the banking system, a measure rejected by the population amidst growing disorder, corruption, and an intensification of *Sendero* subversion.

At that moment, novelist Mario Vargas Llosa offered to modernise and 'clean up' Peru's national institutions. For a time, this political outsider was a breath of fresh air. Vargas Llosa's mistake was to allow himself to be surrounded by elderly conservative politicians, the traditional political élite that had lost influence, while the social democrats and the left were ranged against him. The image of Vargas Llosa gradually became associated with figures perceived as *passé*, with the possibility of a government deaf to the demands and difficulties of the most needy classes. His campaign was thwarted by the advance of a hitherto unknown candidate, another political outsider who, unlike Vargas Llosa, remained untainted by associations with the social elite. Alberto Fujimori, son of Japanese immigrants, a man of few words, surrounded by simple people, swept to victory in the second round of presidential elections in 1990 in the face of the impotence of many of the supposedly powerful institutions of Peru, amongst them the Catholic Church.

The new President continued, tentatively, to assemble his team and his programme, making and breaking alliances as he went. He managed to implement one of the most severe economic adjustment programmes ever – petrol went up 36 times in a single day – with the assistance of sectors of the right and left of centre. Those who helped him to defeat Vargas Llosa, the legal left and APRA, were left by the wayside. Since that time a section of the armed forces and very small groups of relatives and advisers have held the reins of power.

The Effects of Drug Trafficking in Peru

The Economy

Peru is the world's primary producer of coca leaf. According to some estimates, Peru produces around 60% of all coca destined for conversion to cocaine, despite evidence of increased cultivation in Colombia. Bolivia and Peru each produce 500-700 tonnes of coca paste every year. In Peru, much of the coca is grown in the remote Upper Huallaga Valley. Although there are indications of greater Peruvian participation in the export and distribution of cocaine, it is still modest in comparison to Colombia.[2]

The estimate made for 1992 by Cuanto S.A. (1994), a respected private consultancy firm, was that 257,000 hectares were planted with coca. Of these, around 18,000 were legal and registered with the National Coca Company for traditional uses such as for the production of coca tea, an entirely legal and popular beverage in both Peru and Bolivia. The growth rate of coca crops between 1980 and 1992 was calculated around 6.4% annually, with a constant increase in productivity per hectare, which has now stabilised at 1.8 metric tonnes. The method employed for the above estimate was based on the economically-active rural population available in the coca areas, minus the number of workers necessary for legal cultivation.

Although Peru has traditionally produced coca, farmers have increasingly become involved in processing the leaf to produce cocaine. It is calculated that the annual increase since 1980 in the production of unrefined and refined basic cocaine paste is 9% and in fully processed cocaine hydrochloride, 15%. The biggest increases in refining were between 1987 and 1988, and between 1989 and 1990. These were both periods of acute crisis, which probably consolidated the full involvement of Peru in processing and exportation, activities in which it had played a relatively modest role during the first ten years of the cocaine boom.

With regard to the distribution of areas dedicated to cultivation, those which satisfy traditional demand under the law are situated in Cusco. The districts (departments) with the greatest proportion of coca plantation destined for illegal production are San Martín and Huanaco which together account for 57% of cultivated land.[3]

Prices for cocaine derivatives have fluctuated considerably in accordance with supply and demand. A peak was reached in 1989, when unrefined basic paste reached a value of 1,500 dollars per kilo and refined paste 2,000 dollars. Prices were significantly lower between 1991 and 1994. In the last quarter of 1994 prices rallied, but still only reached $100 for unrefined, and $500 for refined paste. The amount of revenue Peru gains from its participation in the cocaine industry has also been the subject of much debate and the figures vary between 2% and 11% of GDP; between 3% and 18% of the foreign debt; and between 14% and 80% of legal exports (Gonzales, 1994).

The economic effect of the production and processing of coca leaf and its derivatives is two-fold. First, it creates micro-economies in the producing regions, thereby ensuring financial security (but not necessarily high incomes) and steady employment, which the farming of licit crops cannot offer. The landless day labourer earns $200-300 per month; if he has some land, he will earn $400-550; and if he processes cocaine paste, he could earn $800-1,200. It is income above the national average and certainly above the average for the agricultural sector. Second, the main effect of the flow of foreign currency into the national economy is to keep down the parity of the dollar; although this has helped to reduce the rate of inflation, it has weakened the international competitiveness of the export sector.

Ecology

Drug-trafficking in Peru damages the environment. Indiscriminate tree-felling is carried out to increase the areas dedicated to the cultivation of coca leaf. According to some experts, around 10% of the deforestation witnessed in the Amazon regions is due to cocaine-related activity. Moreover, many farmers use cultivation methods that are harmful to the environment. They burn large areas of land and use huge quantities of herbicides and pesticides. The intervention of farmers causes significant environmental damage, while the processing of paste and cocaine hydrochloride has a damaging effect on the ecological balance of a region characterised by considerable biodiversity. It is estimated that in 1992 around 23 million litres of kerosene, 4.4 million litres of sulphuric acid, 1.1 million litres of ammonia, 1.7 million litres of herbicide, and 728 million kilograms of potassium permanganate were pumped into the water supply of Peru's coca-producing regions.

Politics
The political effects of Peru's involvement in the drug trade can be seen on two levels. First, many Peruvians depend directly or indirectly on the cultivation, processing and export of the coca leaf and its derivatives. A country with a high degree of unemployment and underemployment, Peru has seen over the last 20 years a considerable tendency towards migration from rural to urban centres, particularly Lima. But the regions on the rim of the rainforest and within it have also attracted immigrants from the *sierra*, or those who had previously attempted and failed to migrate to the capital. The coca plantation zones have experienced significant immigration and a demographic explosion which has caused many of their problems to increase. In certain areas, such as Tingo María and Tocache, the majority of inhabitants were born elsewhere. These are relatively rootless populations with non-existent social structures, a factor which makes them more conflictive. Around 160,000 families depend upon their participation in the cocaine industry, that is to say, between 800,000 and one million people, a very substantial percentage of the economically-active population in general and the agricultural population in particular. This large population inhabits areas where, in addition to drug trafficking, subversive movements and the armed forces have been very active, in conditions where the institutions of civil society have practically no validity.
    Second, some key players in the Peruvian drug trade wield considerable political influence. Most criminal organisations have not yet accumulated sufficient wealth to exercise political power directly. Peru is extremely centralised and the coca plantation zones are usually too distant from the capital. Nevertheless, certain figures managed, from the end of the 1970s, to set up influential networks with money from drug trafficking and the position which they occupied as intermediaries for the Mexican and

Colombian organisations. The political parties, who at that time were returning to the political arena as the military went back to its barracks, were their preferred targets. Carlos Lamberg, for example, had connections with important APRA leaders, and contributed generously to the party during the presidential campaign in 1980. Reynaldo Rodríguez López, known as the Godfather, approached prominent leaders of *Acción Popular* during the government of Fernando Belaúnde (1980-85). Both men were exposed by the press and brought to justice, and served sentences in prison.

Cocaine-related activity acquired a decisive political importance from 1980 onwards as civil institutions progressively lost authority – in effect surrendered it – across vast areas of national territory. The state of emergency declared in various regions, which placed large areas under the control of military units, was a decisive element in this process. This transformation was completed when the subversive organisations decided to follow the cocaine 'route'. The military, insurgents, the drug barons, their employees and the coca growers established from 1987 a system of shifting alliances, alternately attacking and protecting each other according to prevailing circumstances, while a weak and undermined civil society took refuge in the cities. In this way, the coca industry and its main players came to be key political actors. This became more pronounced from 1990 onwards, when the armed forces openly assumed the power which they had been wielding in practice ever since they had been given responsibility for counter-subversion.

The Legal System

Peruvian laws related to the production, traffic and consumption of drugs have tended to follow the lead set by international legislation (Rubio, 1994). Until the first half of the present century, the use and traffic of opium, heroin and morphine were criminal offences. Coca leaf was not considered a drug, although its production was taxed. Then, from 1949 until the middle of 1978, the consumption of coca leaves was prohibited in non-traditional areas, and its cultivation was controlled. The country committed itself to the elimination of consumption and cultivation within a period of 25 years.

The legal framework which applies in Peru with regard to psychoactive substances is Decree Law 22095, promulgated in 1978 by the military government under the presidency of Francisco Morales Bermúdez. Legal responsibility to regulate all actions regarding psychoactive substances is assigned to the Ministry of the Interior, whose representative presides over the Executive Office for the Control of Drugs that includes delegates from other departments.

The most recent legislation is related to money laundering, the social problem generated by the number of farmers involved in the illegal cultivation of coca, and the control of its processing. Although, strictly speaking, drug consumption is not illegal, and those found with less than five grams of a psychoactive substance can claim that it is for personal use, the number of prisoners committed for drug-related crimes – most of whom have not been sentenced – is considerable. In effect, the Peruvian legal system lacks coherence or authority on drug control.

International Relations
One of the most serious consequences of drug trafficking for Peru is the way in which it defines the country's international relations. The USA has made drug control an important element of its foreign policy since the end of the last century (Musto, 1973). Originally concerned with opium and its derivatives, US foreign drug control strategies gradually came to include marijuana and cocaine. The Andean countries and Mexico have suffered more than most the effects of the USA's abiding determination to stem the supply of illicit drugs from other countries.[4]   The division between those countries classed as producer nations and the USA becomes ever more apparent even as operational cooperation intensifies. The Andean countries feel that they are obliged to postpone other crucial policy objectives in the name of a struggle in which they have to carry too much responsibility for an evil they did not create. Meanwhile, the USA feels cheated by corrupt societies dominated by underground forces, with which they are forced to co-exist.

Successive Peruvian governments have used the issue of drug trafficking to modulate their relations with the USA, whilst at the same time pursuing their own objectives. The law that still governs all anti-drug activities in Peru was passed in 1978. At that time, intensive anti-drug operations were being carried out by the military working with the police in coca plantation zones.   However, both the legislation and the law enforcement operations had much more to do with the need of a government in retreat to secure the economic and political support of the Carter administration (1976-80) than with a genuine interest in drug control.

The supposedly anti-US government of Alan García (1985-90) accepted a good deal of the most repressive US strategies as a means of continuing anti-imperialist rhetoric in other areas. Finally, when Alberto Fujimori came to power in 1990, despite his need for US support, he relied heavily on Hernando de Soto, who was promoting a decriminalisation policy for coca-producers, alternative development strategies and an independent official body on drug-related questions.

Policy on illicit drugs is often the 'joker' in international relations, its value and function in relations between countries sometimes having little directly to do with the production, sale and consumption of the drugs themselves. The distortion and tension this creates often damage countries like Peru, whilst reinforcing double standards and stimulating institutional corruption.

Public Opinion

Drug trafficking in Peru generally takes place in the most isolated areas at the rim of the rainforest. The principal players are the coca-growing *campesinos*, the processors of cocaine paste, the guerrillas and members of the military. These activities are carried out far from the main centres of population and do not impinge directly on most people. However, anti-drug policies require the support of public opinion. From the mid-1980s, the government began to publicise the dangers that drug production posed for public health and Peruvians took notice. The addict became a concrete and threatening reality and is potentially more effective in winning public suppport for anti-drug policies in the area of production than an abstract reality which was remote from the majority of people.

It is appropriate to point out that a semantic confusion exists in relation to the drugs question. This is a phenomenon which is not exclusive to Peru, but which has acquired more pronounced characteristics there, bearing in mind the country's involvement in drug production and trafficking (Lerner, 1991). The general public in Peru, including its most qualified exponents (its leaders), identify the term 'drugs' with illegal drugs, particularly basic cocaine paste. In a free association test on the word 'drug', it was discovered that the most cited substance was basic cocaine paste, which is closer in composition to coca than to cocaine (Lerner, 1987). There appears to be a kind of semantic knot which ties coca to cocaine and cocaine paste.[5] The *cocainización* of the collective Peruvian mentality (Lerner, 1991) might have some bearing on the over-concentration of anti-drug operations on the cultivation of the coca leaf and in the production of its derivatives. Although the institutions which impart preventative education mention other psychoactive substances, coca or cocaine are the specific focus of most demand reduction campaigns. The importance and weight lent, above all, to basic cocaine paste in news on drugs in the mass media is enormous (Ferrando, 1989). This phenomenon has still not been studied in depth, but it is relevant to the design of preventative education campaigns which will be meaningful for a specific population, or in the assessment of on-going prevention projects (Ferrando, 1989b; Ferrando and Lerner, 1991; Lerner,

1989).

Various surveys of public opinion on drugs (Ferrando, 1988; 1989b; 1991; 1992; 1993; CEDRO, 1993) show similar results:

1.   Although Peruvians certainly attribute importance to the production, trafficking and consumption of psychoactive substances, we can say, without fear of contradiction, that they consider them to be third-order problems of less importance than economic matters or political violence.   In the most recent surveys carried out by market research companies, attention focuses on unemployment, since even political subversion and inflation now appear to be secondary considerations. Drugs do not figure as the primary problem.   With regard to the different aspects of the drug problem, Peruvians lend greater importance to consumption, that is to say, to the public health aspect, since it is their perception that the country is threatened by a drug abuse crisis.   The drugs considered to have the most dangerous impact are the illegal ones and particularly those derived from coca; those considered to be the least dangerous are the medical and so-called social drugs, with a significant number of citations for coca leaf.   It is clear that there is no support for the legalisation of illegal drugs, and that the degree of permissiveness with regard to the different substances – at least that which is open and explicit – is quite low.

2.   Peruvians perceive the drug problem, in its different aspects, to be increasing, and although they accept that the government is carrying out some kind of attempt to combat the phenomenon, very few appear to perceive results actually being achieved, and there is a significant 25% who believe that the government has achieved no tangible success.

3.   Public opinion believes that Peru is the greatest coca leaf producer in the world (this is the case) and that it is followed by Colombia (which was not the case until recently); a majority assert that the area under coca cultivation is constantly growing. Peruvians are more or less equally divided when it comes to an evaluation of whether the cultivation of coca brings benefits for Peru, and those who think it does affirm that it brings in foreign currency and has medicinal uses.   With regard to what should be done about the growers, the majority of those surveyed are of the opinion that they should be assisted, guided and provided with opportunities to substitute their crops.   The majority attitude is much more punitive and repressive towards producers of coca-derived drugs, and even more radical when it comes to drug traffickers. Peruvians are very clear about the fact that Peru is a producer country, and that the USA is a consumer country. Similarly, the perception is that drug trafficking has increased during recent years, although Peruvians see virtually no benefit in this activity which, furthermore, they link to subversion.

Thus, Peruvians have a complex perception of drug-related problems. This is connected to the kind of focus taken by the media, together with the strategies used by rehabilitation and prevention organisations (Lerner, 1992). The most dangerous aspect of public opinion is, as has been stated, that it has become 'cocainised' in accordance with the agendas of the consumer countries.

Public Health

The first drug-related epidemiological study, in a representative sample of the population of Lima and Callao between the ages of 12 and 45, was carried out in 1979 (Lerner and Ferrando, 1987). Seven years later, in 1986, research appeared that was based on a sample of persons between the ages of 12 and 45 who were habitually resident in homes in cities containing over 25,000 inhabitants (Jukowitz et al, 1987). Although in this case there were also methodological limitations (Lerner and Ferrando, 1987), the survey has the merit of being a landmark in the study of drug consumption patterns in Peru. In 1988, the second study of this kind took place (Ferrando, 1990), and it was the first in a series carried out by the Centre for Information and Education in the Prevention of Drug Abuse (CEDRO), on a sample constituted by a population aged between 12 and 50, and residents in private homes in cities of more than 25,000 inhabitants, and finally, in 1992, on a national sample of households (CEDRO, 1993). Research was also carried out on a young sector of the population, aged between 15 and 25 (Ferrando, 1992) while surveys were made in colleges (Ferrando, 1993).

The 1992 CEDRO study suffers from major limitations with regard to the nature of the sample upon which it was based, and it is difficult to take the findings seriously. However, the patterns in the use of psychoactive substances in Peru are probably quite stable, and resemble those which are prevalent in other Latin American countries.

It is possible to establish a classification of the different drugs in the following groups:

a) Those which are socially and legally accepted. These are the most frequently consumed substances which do the greatest damage to public health, although they have been dismissed in many of the prevention programmes designed to decrease the consumption of psychoactive substances.

b) Substances which fall, like coca leaf and hallucinogens, into the category of traditional use in certain regions. The consumption of the former is an ancient custom in Andean culture and the latter are quite well established within the framework of traditional medicine in the Amazon region and the northern coast of the country.

c) Medicaments the use of which is accepted in the practice of orthodox medicine, and certain industrial substances – largely solvents and glues – generally commercialised for purposes which have little to do with psychoactive substances. In the case of medicines, there are abuses which are not widely publicised, but which undoubtedly cause addictions. In Peru, this conforms to a lax prescription policy and the absence of control over dispensaries, which means it has become one of the countries in which self-prescription is possible with virtually any substance, including amphetamines and powerful analgesics. Inhalants are the drugs favoured by minors in very deprived circumstances (Lerner and Ferrando, 1994), and the use of them appears to have increased considerably.

d) Illegal drugs: marijuana, basic cocaine paste and cocaine hydrochloride. The use of the first of these appears to demonstrate a certain trend towards a decrease in drug use in the general population, although it continues to be the illegal drug which has been consumed by the greatest number of Peruvians on at least one occasion. The second, basic cocaine paste (*basuco*), is a highly-addictive substance, which has a very bad press (Ferrando, 1989), and the consumption of which, although still at a low level, has increased, especially amongst young people. The use of cocaine is stable and chiefly restricted to sections of the upper classes.

The consumption of drugs in Peru should not be underestimated (see Chapter 2, Table 3). It generates problems of a very real nature and has probably increased over the last two or three years, although there are no studies in existence which can prove this. The availability of drugs in general, and those derived from coca in particular, has been a decisive factor in this increase. Nevertheless, consumption patterns are still far removed from consumption rates.

The most problematic drugs in the USA are those which are legal, as in the rest of the world. In spite of this, and as a consequence of the role played by Peru in the global drug trade, a considerable number of prevention campaigns, especially those carried out during the 1980s, were concentrated on coca derivatives (Lerner, 1992). This fact, which is part of the phenomenon of the 'cocainisation' of public opinion, constitutes a serious distortion and can produce damaging effects. Prevention policies, promoted in many cases by non-governmental organisations, in terms of a subjective epidemiology and the need to convince public opinion that an epidemic was imminent, in order to secure support and specific measures in the field of production, have not sufficiently taken into account the realities of drug addiction in Peru.

This chapter has attempted to analyse, in brief, some of the main repercussions of drug trafficking in Peru over the last two decades. These are varied, and on occasion have unexpected consequences. The role which Peru plays in the global drug trade causes obvious distortions in every aspect of life, and not exclusively in those places where production and traffic are manifest, or in those environments which are traditionally related to the illegal trade in psychoactive substances. We must now pause to reflect upon the situation resulting from the new political, economic and security scenarios which have prevailed in Peru during the last few years.

After the Drug War

As noted at the beginning of this study, in certain senses there has been a unique change in circumstances in Peru. The neoliberal economic stabilisation programme is producing results and inflation has been brought under control. The chief political actors are relative newcomers; there are more independent figures – the three most popular candidates for the presidency in 1995 had no party affiliations – and the concept of presidential re-election is a feature of the Constitution which has been made law, by a narrow margin, by means of a referendum. At the same time, the armed forces have assumed crucial decision-making powers and a decisive role in maintaining political order in civilian life. Finally, subversion appears to have been strategically overcome and has ceased to be a perceived and actual threat to the state. Within this new context, what is currently occurring and what is likely to occur in the field of the production and trafficking of coca derivatives?

As always, when the war is over, there remain those whose chief *raison d'être* is to carry on waging it. In the coca plantation zones, members of the armed forces, guerrillas and communities involved in production and commercialisation remain in contact and foster each other. The fact that the majority of the emergency zones under political and military control are coca production zones is a crucial one, as is the fact that over the last two years the armed forces have had *carte blanche* in those regions – owing to the need for counter-subversion operations and their new political role. The military defeat of the guerrillas may simply indicate a greater involvement by all the protagonists in the processes linked to production and trafficking.

The economic situation will probably continue to be characterised for a considerable time by an improvement in the macroeconomic indicators, which will not be felt in all sectors and areas of the country. Those areas which are related to drug production and trafficking are amongst them. The coca plantation zones have been increasing considerably, and have reached into previously untouched areas.   On the other hand, the only crop substitution which appears to have functioned successfully is that based on the opium poppy. Journalists' accounts and those of certain researchers maintain that production of the poppy and its derivatives has become important in Peru. An estimated 14,000 hectares is under poppy cultivation. The *cuajada*, a subproduct of the poppy in the processing of opium, has been sold at $10,000 per kilo, while a kilo of refined basic cocaine paste only reaches $500 per kilo in certain areas of the rainforest. Opium poppy production, therefore, is likely to develop on a very significant scale. Repressive actions and a very harsh legal framework have been adopted in the face of this phenomenon. Those who dedicate themselves to the cultivation of poppy plantations and other related activities will be sentenced to prison terms varying between eight and fifteen years, and they will be denied any right to parole or pardon. Finally, poppy crops will be destroyed by any possible method, provided that it does not upset the ecological equilibrium.

At a global level, the sources of drug production and drug trafficking routes are changing. In Latin America, Brazil and Venezuela will probably become increasingly important to the global drug trade. Peru will respond to these changes. Its function as a cocaine exporter may expand, and its independence from Mexican and Colombian organisations, which have always been of central importance, may grow. In fact, an ever greater quantity of cocaine is refined within Peru and there are signs that more of the drug organisations will export it. These organisations may also begin to exert a greater influence on civil society and political institutions. This influence will be facilitated by changes in the economy which, as it becomes more liberal, deregulated, privatised and internationalised, will allow large quantities of 'hot' money to flow in, the provenance of which is difficult to corroborate and control. Profits resulting from illegal drug trafficking can be reinvested in a growing market to become a springboard for the infiltration of institutions.

The drug issue will continue to be the 'joker' in relations between the USA and Peru. After a period of tense relations caused by President Fujimori's *autogolpe*, during which US aid was frozen and the free flow of intelligence regarding surveillance of shipping and radar was interrupted, relations between the two countries returned to normal. The Peruvian government will continue to yield to some of the pressures, in order to demonstrate its political will to combat drug trafficking, but without becoming deeply embroiled in the matter. The armed forces will continue to be protagonists in the coca plantation zones, and will carry out operations of a more or less spectacular nature, such as the destruction of laboratories and clandestine landing strips, and ultimately the eradication of coca plantations, in which varying quantities of drugs are actually confiscated.

However, it is unlikely that an effective alliance will be forged between the government, civil society and aid agencies – whether multilateral, international or national – except in the case of limited projects, whether at the level of alternative development, or in the strengthening of institutions, such as the judiciary, or in the financing NGOS. Whether an autonomous authority will be set up which can centralise anti-drug operations – prevention, law enforcement and treatment – and if so, what the extent of its operating capacity would be, remain open questions. A two-fold movement could develop in the USA which would complicate matters: on the one hand, a greater social tolerance of drugs, and on the other, a falling away of interest in global schemes for boosting economies in favour of solutions based on forcible, and, as some suggest, even unilateral eradication.

Peru has changed rapidly in recent years. The dangers should not be underestimated. Values have changed as a result of years of insurgency and counter-insurgency – many Peruvians lived in a *de facto* state of war – and this will have its impact on attitudes to drugs.

The route to material success in the shortest possible time encourages economic activities at the outer limits of legality that attract people who would normally reject openly criminal activities. In addition, the frustration of expectations, the understandable desire to make up for lost time and the fear of returning to previously insecure conditions, as well as the virtually limitless availability of drugs, creates opportunities for considerable drug abuse. It is possible – although there is no firm evidence beyond hospital emergency statistics and the consistently biased assessments of health professionals – that the consumption of drugs is generally increasing. Certainly, the expansion of private rehabilitation and therapeutic enterprises in recent years has been striking. There is, however, no evidence to show that the prevention programmes of previous years, which were focused, as we have observed, on geopolitical questions and concerns over public opinion, rather than on epidemiological realities, have been of any particular value.

Notes

*   Translated by Patricia Roberts.

1. The MRTA, however, was able to capture international attention in December 1996 with the seizure of the Japanese Embassy in Lima.
2. The government claims that coca cultivation has fallen in recent years. In mid-1993, the Interior Ministry claimed that 19,000 hectares had been eradicated, approximately 8.6% of the total. In September 1994, the Foreign Affairs Ministry said 15% had been eradicated while, on the same day, the Justice Ministry put the figure at 8%.
3. Nevertheless, over the last five years, the coca crops have been greatly extended, and include new areas in the departments of the Amazon, Ucayali, Junin, Ayacucho and Puno. There are areas where growth has been explosive: the valley of the River Apurimac, the Pichis Palcazu and the tributaries of the Central Ucayali. But, in addition, further coca plantations are being opened up: Jaén-San Ignacio-Bagua, the high river basin of the Marañón and Madre de Dios.
4. Since 1988, they and other countries that Washington has classified as drug-producing nations have been evaluated by the USA for their drug control efforts in order to qualify for US aid. Those whose drug control performance is deemed unsatisfactory are 'decertified'. Peru, Colombia and Bolivia all narrowly escaped 'decertification' in 1995: the administration gave them conditional approval only on the grounds of US national security interests. In 1996, Colombia was fully decertified. See Chapter 3 for Colombia, Chapter 4 for Bolivia and Chapter 9 for a more detailed discussion of the US certification process.
5. Basic cocaine paste, or *basuco*, is a low-quality, low-cost coca paste that has not completed the refining process that would transform it into cocaine hydrochloride. Unlike cocaine, it can be smoked.

CHAPTER 6

THE POLITICAL REPERCUSSIONS OF
DRUG TRAFFICKING IN MEXICO*

María Celia Toro

The most widespread explanations given for the unprecedented rise in marijuana, heroin and cocaine trafficking in the Western Hemisphere during the last decade are that it is the inevitable result of a rise in the number of US drug users, and Latin American governments incapacity or lack of interest in putting an end to their production and export. This line of argument – as prevalent in academic literature as it is in political discourse – in which the existence and dimensions of drug trafficking ultimately depend on the decision of an individual, generally North American or European, to use drugs, and on the unwillingness and lack of resources of numerous Latin American governments effectively to enforce the prohibition of the narcotics market, has led to mistakes in national and international policies to combat drug addiction and trafficking.

The costly and unsuccessful programmes to destroy coca, marijuana and opium poppy plantations have demonstrated in Latin America, after fifteen years, that what happens in the fields has little to do with the behaviour of users. Although the consumption of marijuana, heroin and cocaine in the USA increased towards the end of the 1970s and began to diminish from 1985 onwards (see Chapter 1), no proven link has been made between variations in the number of consumers and the eradication of crops in Latin America. What remains beyond doubt is that the more fields are destroyed, the more are planted; and the cost of eradication programmes increases at an exponential rate.

Also without foundation and the cause of profound repercussions for Latin America was the US belief, translated into policy, that it was possible to ameliorate the public health problem which drug addiction represents by preventing drugs from penetrating US territory and by breaking drug dealing chains. Paradoxically, this approach can actually strengthen the position of the more powerful traffickers by pushing the smaller, weaker traffickers out of business. Those willing and capable of resisting increased enforcement can rely on their ability to buy protection or escalate violence.

The argument that more stringent prohibitions on the production, distribution and sale of narcotics are a significant influence on user behaviour cannot be sustained. There is no consensus on the precise relationship between penalisation policies and the number of drug consumers.[1] It appears that the effects of these policies on consumption have, in the majority of cases, been insubstantial. However, drug control over several decades has had notable repercussions on the quantity of drugs produced and, more importantly, on the ways in which both production and trafficking are organised.

This chapter aims to analyse the causes of the Mexican boom in drug trafficking in the 1980s and the national and international political consequences of the expansion of this unique business. The first part will analyse how prohibition policies that seek to reduce drug availability and effect a rise in retail prices have increased trafficking in Mexico, by making the drug trade a more lucrative and potentially attractive business. The second part will address the two most serious political problems that drug trafficking and drug control policies have generated, namely the weakening of the Mexican criminal justice system and of the Mexican state's capacity to preserve its monopoly over the administration of justice, in particular in relation to the USA.

The Increase in Drug Trafficking in Mexico

Although it is impossible to estimate with complete accuracy the size of an illegal market, assessments of the Mexican drug problem tend to indicate that the production and export of narcotics increased after 1984-5 (National Narcotics Intelligence Consumers Committee, annual; US Dept. of State, 1994; Ruiz Cabañas, 1989; Ruiz Cabañas, 1989a; Ruiz Cabañas, 1989b). The US government estimated that by the end of the decade Mexico was the principal supplier of marijuana, heroin and cocaine to the North American market, an estimate that the Mexican government never contested.

The list of reasons most often put forward to explain this change in the magnitude of drug trafficking in Mexico is extensive: negligence on the part of the Mexican authorities, widespread corruption, the adaptability of drug traffickers and, of course, the rise in US drug consumption. The negligence hypothesis is not supported by government spending on drug control: from the latter half of the 1980s, the Mexican government has spent around 60% of the budget of the Procuraduría General de la República (PGR – Attorney General's Office) on drug control. In 1983, President Miguel de la Madrid (1982-88) decided to increase further army participation in the campaigns to destroy marijuana and opium crops, since then extended over most of Mexico's states. In 1987, President de la Madrid, and some years later President Salinas de Gortari (1988-94), labelled drug trafficking a 'national security problem', thus justifying the need to combat it with greater resolution and with unsparing resources.

In absolute terms, the number of marijuana, heroin and cocaine users in the USA did not rise significantly during the 1980s, and US consumption began to decrease from 1985.[2] The concern that inspired the famous 'war against drugs' of Presidents Reagan and Bush stemmed rather from an increase for the first time in the number of deaths caused by overdose among the middle class. Institutional corruption, like the ability of drug traffickers to adapt to and evade various forms of control, has been a constant, rather than a variable, in Mexico and elsewhere, and should be seen as an inevitable and increasingly costly effect of penalisation policies or, in the case of bribery and official complicity, as a regrettable consequence of these policies, and not as a cause of their failure or as some strange 'knock-on' effect.

None of these factors had consequences as serious as those of the change in drug import prices in the USA, which are the prices that have the greatest influence on the calculations of Latin American drug traffickers (Toro, 1992). The big business in trafficking in Latin America is drug smuggling, not production. Although production is highly profitable, its profits are negligible compared to those made by exporting drugs.[3] The price that importers in the USA were prepared to pay during the 1980s for foreign marijuana, heroin and cocaine had a decisive influence on the quantity of drugs that were clandestinely transported from Mexico to the US market.

Prices are, of course, a function of demand. However, in the case of an illegal industry like drug trafficking, a drug trafficker's costs – which include the risks associated with illegally cultivating, transporting and, above all, exporting drugs – constitute the most important determinant with regard to prices. These risks, or costs, increased at the beginning of the 1980s as a result of the ambitious interdiction campaigns that the US government maintained throughout the decade and which raised the prices in the main US ports of entry (Reuter, Crawford and Cave, 1988; Kleiman, 1989).

From at least 1981 onwards, the USA spent a huge amount of federal resources on programmes that aimed to stop drugs entering its territory. Towards the end of the decade, the US government was spending around $10 billion on this activity which, while it did not stop the illegal import of drugs, certainly made smuggling more difficult and significantly increased the costs of its organisation. US sources report that the seizure of cocaine rose from only two tons in 1981 to 27 tons in 1986, and to 100 tons in 1989 (Bagley, 1992, p. 2). The clear rise in the risks of transporting drugs to the US market (also evident in the number of aircraft seized and drug traffickers detained) was reflected in a drastic price increase. In 1987, for example, the coca leaves required to produce a kilo of cocaine cost $500-700. After processing the leaves into cocaine, the price increased (in Colombia) to $3,000 – 6,000 a kilo. In the USA, the price per kilo of cocaine in bulk varied between $14,000 and $21,000 (Smith, 1992, p. 10). The price of heroin was, and continues to be, much higher, although the quantity demanded is lower. Clearly, the cost of drug control was absorbed by the traffickers through prices.

Increasingly, high quantities of drugs were therefore transported to the US market to compensate for possible losses in transit and in the hope (or the certainty) of being able to avoid surveillance and recover considerable sums of money. There were no governments capable of countering this market logic, which was the direct result of a prohibition policy that was in no way able to reduce the availability of drugs in the US market or to increase prices to the end consumer. The price of raw material – that of the plants used to produce the final product bought by users – has never amounted to more than 10% of the retail price, that is to say, of the price paid by consumers in the USA. Consequently, eradication programmes never have much influence on the price of marijuana, heroin or cocaine in US streets, schools and parks.[4]

As well as explaining the astronomical rise in Latin American exports, the intensification of US anti-drug campaigns also changed the routes and *modus operandi* of drug traffickers in the USA, Mexico and other countries of production. Drug traffickers changed their trafficking routes in the 1980s to confront the new risks of loss of goods, vehicles, arms (and, of course, their lives) or to reduce the possibility of arrest. US surveillance of the main drug import sites in Florida forced drug smugglers, particularly cocaine traffickers, the majority of whom are Colombian, to look for new channels into US territory. Mexico, therefore, became a useful place of transit for cocaine from 1983-4. The technical difficulties of preventing a huge influx of traffickers with increasingly large shipments of cocaine into national territory were similar in all the countries involved. Cocaine seizures in Mexico rose from virtually nothing in 1981 to more than 49 tons in 1990, which testifies as much to the magnitude of the resources spent by the Mexican government as to the uncontainable rise in trafficking caused by US drug control policies. By 1990, marijuana and cocaine trafficking in the Caribbean, ostensibly from Colombia, had been largely redirected towards the Mexican-US border, where from 1989 the operation to stop smuggling in this border zone has been centred.

The cultivation of marijuana and opium poppies in Mexico was also reorganised in the 1980s, only a few years after the Mexican government launched what was seen at the time, from 1976 to 1979, as one of the most ambitious crop eradication campaigns in history. The number of hectares of marijuana that were sprayed with herbicides in 1975 is similar to that of 1990, the difference being that, while the number of plantations targeted in 1975, for example, did not exceed 22,000, more than 100,000 were destroyed in 1990. Something similar occurred in the opium poppy fields. Cultivation was carried out on smaller and smaller plots of land, partly in response to aerial spraying campaigns which were to prove so successful in the 1970s and so costly ten years later.

The growth of drug trafficking in Latin America has caught the attention of a number of analysts who have hastened to interpret expansion in this business as one more economic boom, typical of a developing country. They have even calculated the economic consequences, which they imagine to be devastating, of a drastic decrease in the revenue derived from cultivating and smuggling drugs.

In Mexico, however, drug trafficking money does not, at present, seem to have a major influence on the national economy. There are no comprehensive studies of the effects of this illegal market on the Mexican economy, but the few estimates that have been made do not indicate that we are confronting a 'narcoticised' economy like that of Bolivia or a number of Caribbean countries (Maingot, 1988). In Bolivia, for example, the stability of the exchange rate depends to a large extent on foreign currency revenues from drug trafficking. In both Bolivia and Colombia, the central banks have at various times opened their doors to 'narcodollars' (the famous *ventanillas siniestras*). In Colombia, inflows of drug money are estimated to reach between 2% and 8% of GDP (see Chapter 3). The amount of money involved in drug trafficking in Mexico, which of course is considerable, is not as important. The Mexican economy is far larger than the economy of Bolivia or even Colombia. Moreover, the really big profits in cocaine smuggling were made in the 1980s when the business was largely in the hands of Colombians and North Americans; Mexican traffickers have only recently penetrated the market. The majority of drug trafficking revenue in Mexico, at least until 1989, came from the cultivation and export of marijuana and opiates.[5]

Although estimates of the size of this illegal industry in Mexico tend to be over-simplified, even arbitrary, they can provide an initial overview. According to Nadelmann, marijuana and cocaine exports generated around two billion dollars in foreign exchange for Latin America in 1987

(Nadelmann, 1988, p. 86). Around one third of this revenue, approximately $700 million, stays in Mexico and, given that the production and export of heroin generated at least $750 million,[6] the production and smuggling of these three drugs generated, at the most conservative estimate, around $1,450 million dollars in foreign currency for Mexico. However, according to the more detailed calculations of Peter Reuter and David Ronfeldt, Mexican revenues from drug trafficking in 1988 amounted to at least $2.1 billion, the equivalent of 1.25% of GDP and close to 5% of Mexican exports for that year. More than a third of this total would have come from marijuana export. Even if we accept that today this figure may be around $5 billion, as some civil servants privately believe, these estimates are nothing like the astronomic sums frequently referred to in the press.

In terms of the economic impact of marijuana and opium poppy cultivation, it is possible that up to 50,000 families depend on drug trafficking and that their annual earnings from the cultivation of these crops is around $12,500.[7] Moreover, there does not seem to be a clear crop displacement in areas of intense production. Sinaloa, for example, is both the richest agricultural state in the country and one of the most important centres of drug production. It is known that drug trafficking money has been invested in a variety of businesses, especially in cattle, root crops, stock exchanges, tourist and commercial centres; but it is also thought that a significant amount is deposited or invested abroad.[8] Be that as it may, there is no evidence at the present time that drug traffickers completely dominate any industrial or commercial centre, let alone the national economy. However, whatever their usefulness might be, these statistics do not reflect the ground that drug traffickers have gained on governments over the same period of time, in other words, the political repercussions. In the last analysis, the money generated by drug trafficking is important because it gives drug traffickers the means to subvert the legal order.

Domestic and International Political Repercussions

The profits offered by drug trafficking today are the result of increasingly tenacious prohibition, especially in the USA. The solution of the countries most affected by the expansion of this market has invariably been the same: to increase the resources available to combat it. No other crime has been so insistently persecuted in the last decade in Mexico. No other law in the country has been modified as much as the one that penalises the activities related to drug trafficking.

Faced with increasingly strong attacks from the state, drug traffickers have responded by creating their own security forces, bribing the authorities and, when it is deemed necessary, killing those who pursue them. Drug traffickers did not just reorganise in the 1980s by looking for new systems of production and organisation that would allow them to survive in the same clandestine world as before. Such a strategy became more and more difficult to sustain, not only because the government tried every means available to stop it, but also because competition between traffickers intensified. Violence amongst drug traffickers, which invariably betrays them, became an increasingly easy recourse. The weakness of the institutions responsible for fighting drug trafficking, and the money at the disposal of drug traffickers thanks to the new drug prices in the US market, led to the development of efficient systems to evade justice, and to behave more boldly.

It is not possible to estimate the institutional deterioration that has resulted from what criminologists call the 'over-penalisation' of this industry. The deployment of state force against drug trafficking in the last decade which, taking into account the logic and structure of the international drug market, could never have achieved its objectives, reflects – as well as a political imperative – the institutional cost of maintaining the prohibition policy which has been followed until now. In the last ten years, the authorities responsible for combating drug trafficking, including the army, have had far greater resources than in the 1970s yet their achievements have not been proportional to this increase. It should, of course, be remembered that this is not an exclusively Mexican phenomenon; it is the experience of practically all the countries that increased the scale of their campaigns against drugs.

During the last large-scale campaign against drugs in Mexico, in the latter half of the 1970s, the government, in what at the time constituted a clear militarisation of drug control, assigned 5,000 soldiers and 350 members of the Policía Judicial Federal (PJF) to permanent campaigns aimed at crop eradication, drug seizures and the arrest of traffickers (Craig, 1978). Ten years later, in 1987, the Mexican government had deployed 25,000 soldiers and more than 600 members of the police to the same tasks. One third of the defence budget and over half the budget of the PGR have been spent since then on the same objectives. Under President Salinas, the drug control budget at least quadrupled and the PJF was restructured, giving it around 1,500 new members assigned to anti-narcotic activities.

Despite increased deployment, the number of hectares planted with opium poppy that were eradicated annually with herbicides actually fell between the mid-1970s and the mid-1980s.[9] Something similar happened with drug seizures. Despite the fact that the PGR's main operational sphere was drug control, with the exception of 1984, the quantity of heroin and marijuana that it seized before export to the US market was greater in the 1970s than in the 1980s.   The same, of course, cannot be said for cocaine, given that in the last ten years Mexico has become the most important point of cocaine trafficking in the world.   The amount of cocaine seized by the army and the police multiplied over one hundred times between 1984 and 1990.

Nobody doubts either the intelligence of those who cultivate and export illegal drugs to the USA or the technical difficulties involved in eradicating such a large market.   There will always be a hidden place to begin planting anew; a new way will always be found to set up an airstrip or to drop cocaine in packets from the air.   Consider the use of tunnels that already cross the US-Mexican border and the many other ways in which smuggling between Mexico and the USA is organised.   There are also important legal obstacles to effective drug control.   The Mexican press reports several cases of drug traffickers who are protected, who have legally regained land that has been confiscated by the state, who use false names to protect their goods, and who have been arrested and freed because without a legal identity they cannot be tried by the courts.

The costs in terms of violence and corruption, without doubt the two most important political consequences of the drug trade, are evident although difficult to quantify.   Drug trafficking has been able to pay to have at its service members of the police, armed forces, judiciary, airline companies, media and the legislature.   Although corruption financed by drug trafficking is not a new phenomenon in Mexico, it has increased parallel to the intensification of drug control campaigns in Mexico and the USA, which inevitably increase the earnings of those involved in this business.   In 1984, the authorities were found to be involved in protecting El Búfalo ranch, where thousands of tons of marijuana were being stored (García Ramírez, 1989, p. 34). In 1985, the Dirección Federal de Seguridad (DFS) was found to be so corrupt that it had to be dissolved.[10]

Corruption and violence are often inseparable.   When corruption is unsuccessful, traffickers resort to violence: they intimidate policemen, judges and witnesses; they form private armies; they assassinate police force members and representatives of state justice, of competitors and of enemies.   As with corruption, the violence that typically seems to accompany the investigation of illegal markets accumulated during several decades of drug control policies; but it is also the response to the intensification of the anti-drug campaigns of the 1980s.   Perhaps the most scandalous case was the assassination of US Drug Enforcement Administration (DEA) agent Enrique Camarera in 1985 at the hands of drug traffickers and complicit police.   The case not only uncovered corruption within the police force, but was also one of the first violent incidents involving undercover US agents to be made public in Mexico. Many other violent acts have followed: from the killing of 22 police officers in Veracruz in November 1985 to the murder of Cardinal Posadas, shot dead by drug traffickers in Guadalajara in May 1993.

Historically, the Mexican state has been firmer and more efficient in its fight against the use of violence than against corruption. Nevertheless, in taking on the latter, the government has had recourse to measures such as the dissolution of entire police bodies (like that of the DFS in 1985), prison sentences for those involved,[11] mass police dismissals and, finally, to the practice of supplementing the police force with the army. For many years, the Mexican army has been called upon to participate actively in anti-drug campaigns as the only way to compensate for the multiple inadequacies of the police. The army, which has been the main body in charge of crop eradication since the beginning of the 1980s, has gradually become the 'supreme authority' in some Mexican states, such as Oaxaca, Sinaloa, Jalisco and Guerrero (Doyle, 1993, p. 88), while in others, like Chihuahua, the army has practically assumed leadership of the complete range of anti-narcotic programmes, over and above the Federal Police. The increasing militarisation of anti-drug policy has on occasion resulted in violent clashes between the army and the police, and has led to the armed forces becoming dangerously involved in the pursuit of drug traffickers.

However, if we accept that overpenalisation cannot help but produce these results, then all of the figures which are normally interpreted as Mexico's effort in the fight against drug trafficking can also be read as a measure of the institutional weakness that inevitably results from drug control programmes. Thus, the number of arrests made of those suspected of committing crimes against public health, which have been rising at a considerable rate since 1986, coincide with an increasingly more defiant attitude on the part of drug traffickers in Mexico.

Less studied, but no less important, is the growing difficulty experienced by the state in defending its prerogative, which is by definition exclusive, to administer justice and enforce the law. The US policy of pursuing drug traffickers in other countries, undertaken with unprecedented intensity in the last decade,[12] has become one of the biggest political threats that the Mexican government faces in fighting drug trafficking. The presence within Mexico of a foreign police force like the DEA constitutes, like the *modus operandi* of drug traffickers, the other large threat for state authority, in so far as US police agents (the DEA and recently also the FBI) undertake intelligence and drug control activities on occasions without Mexican government authorisation.

The murder of Camarena exposed the enormous vulnerability of Mexico's police forces to outside intervention. The DEA does not only exchange intelligence with the Mexican police, but also uses undercover agents and Mexican police or ex-police force members to gather intelligence. US intelligence networks are indispensable to the implementation of drug control in Mexico and many other Latin American countries. Cocaine interdiction relies not just on information provided by the DEA but also the FBI and other law enforcement agencies, as well as the Department of Defence which in the wake of the Cold War has become the lead agency in drug interdiction and which runs a sophisticated drug intelligence-gathering network out of US Southern Command (Southcom) in Panama.

Operation Legend, an operation in which the DEA, using any means available, aimed to bring all those presumed responsible for the Camarena kidnapping and murder before US courts, clearly showed that the USA was prepared to expand jurisdiction beyond its borders (Lowenfeld, 1990, p. 713).[13] The Mexican public learned during this period of tension that many local police or ex-police officers in Mexico were working for traffickers or as paid agents of the DEA, and were not following the orders of their own superiors. Lacking full control over both foreign police and local traffickers, the Mexican government found itself 'under siege' as the 1980s came to an end. In this context, the governments of Presidents de la Madrid and Salinas attempted not only to formulate drug control policy that aimed to capture traffickers and seize drugs, but also to limit the activities of US drug law enforcement officers in Mexico (Toro, 1995, p. 66). Anti-drug laws were yet again amended, and the government entered into new bilateral understandings with the USA in an effort to have the US government agree the rules of the game and stick to them.[14]

Conclusions

The expansion of drug trafficking in Mexico, and in other Latin American countries over the course of the last ten years, has been the result of changes in anti-drug policies rather than changes in US drug use.

As with any government policy, what aims to destroy drug trafficking through strict control favours certain types of organisations and hampers others. Although this may seem obvious, it is a point usually avoided in the majority of analyses of drug trafficking in Latin America, which almost always identify drug consumers to the North and rural poverty to the South as the sources of the problem. US drug policy in the 1980s invalidated the Mexican state's efforts to contain drug trafficking within tolerable limits, for both state and society, by causing exorbitant drug price rises in the US market. Those who benefited most from this change in relative prices, which succeeded in dissuading very few users, were the drug traffickers. The biggest loser is, and will continue to be, the Mexican state, which must expend scarce resources on ever-stricter control, while attempting to safeguard the fragile integrity of its criminal justice institutions.

The drug trade can be viewed as an economic phenomenon, a multinational industry experiencing unexpected recent growth. But such a perspective ignores the political and institutional consequences that the expansion of an economic activity, which exploits the weakness of state institutions, has for a country like Mexico. The bribery and subornation of officials, from the lowliest border guard to the most senior government personnel, together with the use of violence, creates a parallel power structure, dedicated to the commission of crimes, which can rival that of the state. To portray drug trafficking as a problem of poverty on the one hand and opulence on the other, or worse still as either a public health problem or a dynamic business driven entirely by consumer preference, does not identify the central problem that the expansion of this illegal trade represents for governments. The boom in drug trafficking in Mexico in the 1980s had political repercussions that were far more important than its economic consequences.

As an internal political problem, what is being confronted is a culture that survives through violence against competitors and persecutors, and through the corruption of the authorities. The money that has been generated by drug trafficking, while it can affect and even distort small economies, is important because it permits drug traffickers to continue their business even against the armed volition of the state. With such incalculable and disproportionate profits, drug traffickers have been able, amongst other things, to buy discretion and complicity, overcome laws and justice, arm peasants and organise the violent defence of illegal plantations and commercial routes. As a dizzying source of wealth and in the light of very serious institutional weaknesses both in the political sphere and in the administration of justice, the drug industry has created a sense of impunity amongst drug traffickers that would otherwise be inexplicable.

In the last decade, drug trafficking has also weakened the ability of some states to defend their exclusive jurisdiction over penal and legal matters in the face of others. The complicity of authorities opened up a vulnerability to the outside that practically no government in Latin America was able to anticipate. US judges, prisons and the DEA constituted a real threat both for smugglers and for governments incapable of containing the violence and corruption related to drug trafficking, a situation that, as in the case of Colombia, the traffickers knew how to exploit, and which in all cases caused strong diplomatic tension. In comparison to this, the economic repercussions of drug trafficking seem less important. If to some extent the interpretation of a problem influences the options for its solution, to begin to reflect on the political price of drug trafficking and the policies that have been established to fight it may mark the start of a change in the prevailing policies that have had such onerous consequences for Mexico.

Notes

* Translated by Simon Webb.

1. It is alleged, in defence of present policies, that drug consumption would be much higher without such programmes. Kleiman provides a detailed discussion of the various regulatory policies and their possible consequences, including the campaigns against cigarettes and alcohol (Kleiman, 1992).

2. Between 1985 and 1990, the number of US users of illicit substances dropped from approximately 23 million people to around 13 million. (Smith, 1992, p. 3).

3. The largest profits are in drug distribution in the US market, a business in which Mexicans have only marginal participation.

4. The volume of cocaine smuggled increased at such a rate that its price began to drop towards the second half of the decade, even though the price differential between the production/export markets in Latin America and the US import market had not significantly changed.

5. Although I have no figures to support this claim, it seems quite likely that this situation changed after 1990. This is suggested by the increasingly profuse evidence of open collaboration between Mexican and Colombian traffickers to transport cocaine to the United States, and by the presence of Mexican groups in Andean countries reported in the press.

6. This is Reuter and Ronfeldt's most conservative estimate based on figures from 1988 (Reuter and Ronfeldt, 1992).

7. This would conform to the lowest estimate, assuming, as Reuter and Ronfeldt do, that earnings from marijuana and opium poppy cultivation in 1988 oscillated between $626 million and $1.4 billion. If we take the highest estimated figure of $1.4 billion, then the annual earnings per family would amount to $28,800.

8. Recent reports from the US Department of State observe that Mexico has become an important money laundering centre, a plausible claim

when we consider that the US government has been combating this illegal activity with increasing determination within its own borders.

9. The amount of marijuana eradicated did, however, increase steadily during the same period from around 6,000 hectares per year in 1975-78 to around 10,000 hectares in 1985-88 (Toro, 1995).

10. The DFS was an important participant in the drug trade throughout the 1960s and 1970s; the Federal Judicial Police and Interpol became implicated in the 1980s (Lupsha, 1992, pp. 177-88). Even the army was sometimes drawn in. The 1991 Tlalixcoyan case involved an incident in Veracruz where soldiers shot dead police officers who were trying to arrest drug traffickers.

11. In 1992, for example, 270 PGR officers and PJF agents were remanded by the authorities for corruption and abuse of authority (US Dept. of State, 1992, p. 4).

12. The best study of the 'internationalisation' of US law enforcement can be found in Nadelmann (1993).

13. The DEA took Mexicans by force to the USA to stand trial for Camarena's murder, the most important cases being those of René Martin Verdugo Urquídez in 1986 and Humberto Alvarez Machaín in 1990. In these cases, the US Supreme Court, reversing previous decisions made by a court of appeal, established that unlawful searches and kidnapping in other countries – with or without US agents' participation, direction or sponsorship – did not necessarily lead to the loss of jurisdiction of a US court over the cases in question. The decision provoked objections on both sides of the US-Mexican border. Mexico protested the violation of its sovereignty, in particular of the 1978 US-Mexico Extradition Treaty (in force since 1980), and there was by no means a US consensus about the legitimacy or legality of such operations (Lowenfeld, 1990, pp. 477-81). In any event, neither case was upheld. It was decided that US courts lacked jurisdiction over Verdugo's case because his abduction violated the 1978 Extradition Treaty; he was repatriated. Alvarez Machaín was found not guilty by a US court in January 1993 (Toro, 1995, p. 86).

14. Mexico proposed new bilateral agreements (in addition to more than 60 that had already been signed during the previous two decades), the most important of which were the Mutual Legal Assistance Treaty (MLAT) which came into force in 1991, modifications to the US-Mexican Extradition Treaty, and the introduction of new guidelines for DEA operations in Mexico (Toro, 1995, p. 66).

PART III

MONEY LAUNDERING AND INTERNATIONAL DRUG CONTROL

CHAPTER 7

OFFSHORE BANKING IN THE CARIBBEAN: THE PANAMANIAN CASE

Anthony P. Maingot

An enterprise as vast as the drug trade takes time to develop. And so it has been in the Caribbean; both time and space have contributed to what is arguably the biggest menace to the survival of law, democracy and simple civil decency in these societies.

The trade in heroin, morphine and cocaine started originally in the 1940s between Medellín, Colombia and Havana, Cuba. The drugs were shipped from Cuba to the USA, Mexico and other Caribbean islands. The trade's clientele tended to be the upper-middle and upper classes, and business was conducted on a relatively small scale. Yet the patterns even back then are the ones evident today: the drug trade was part of an underworld of illegal activities which survived and prospered because of (1) the collaboration of corrupt government officials and members of the private sector, and (2) the complexity of the international connections involved. In Havana, the key intermediary for the trade was Santo Traficante, Jr., an important member of both the US and the Sicilian mafia. Violence was often transnational. Hugh Thomas maintains that the murder of Chicago boss Anastasia was linked to his attempt to capture Meyer Lansky's gambling business in Havana. These were the days when, 'professional gangsters swarmed the new hotels of Havana' (Thomas, 1971, p. 972).

There was no consciousness back then of the threat that the drug trade would eventually represent. In those early days, reminisces one of its earliest Colombian practitioners, drug smuggling 'was still a respectable activity' (Arango and Child, 1987, p. 119). Notably, one of the few countries where a social revulsion against this underworld took place was Cuba. The 1959 Cuban revolution had a strong quotient of moral indignation and, not surprisingly, one of its first acts was to move against the mafia-controlled businesses in Cuba, including casinos and drugs.

Alas, one of the most enduring traits of the Caribbean revealed itself again: what diminishes in one part of the region reappears with renewed vigour in another. After the fall of Batista, the drug trade, as well as a concentration of anti-Castro activities, shifted to Miami and Central America. This shift explains the US Central Intelligence Agency (CIA) links, directly or indirectly, knowingly or unknowingly, with those involved in both anti-communism and drug smuggling to the just then expanding US market, as well as the ease with which Miami-based *lancheros* later engaged in smuggling goods into and drugs out of Castro's Cuba (Henman, 1981, p. 107).

Since those pioneering days, virtually all trends in the Caribbean region, from macroeconomic problems to the war against communist expansion in the region, appear to have favoured the drug trade. It has been twenty years since the US government declared 'war' on drugs. It would require astonishing ignorance or monumental cynicism to claim that that war is being won or even being fought to a stalemate. The general problem is so vast that for the purpose of study it is necessary to divide the drugs business into three conceptually discrete parts: (1) production, (2) distribution, and (3) the utilisation and disposal of the proceeds. The Caribbean Basin is a very small player with regard to (1), and in (2) serves merely as a series of transshipment points, but it is an extremely big player in part (3). Being the site of some of the world's oldest and largest tax-havens or 'offshore' financial centres, the Caribbean has become a major money laundering area. The latter activity will be the focus of this chapter for two reasons: (1) the pursuit of 'dirty money' has become a major strategy in the general war the international community is waging against organised crime; and (2) since developing offshore financial centres is now the region's most important development strategy, it warrants close scrutiny.

Capital Flight, Tax Havens and Money Laundering

Offshore banking is not a subject taught in Caribbean classes on banking and finance, yet the flow of what is now called grey and black market money, seeking safe and anonymous financial havens, caught the attention of a select number of 'forensic' investigators at least two decades ago (Maingot, 1994, pp. 163-82; Maingot, 1995, pp. 1-14). It is not, therefore, an unstudied topic even though it remains a difficult one.[1]

Although the US Department of the Treasury admits that there are no hard-and-fast rules to define a tax haven, it does identify the following common conditions:

1. Relatively low rates of tax or none at all.
2. Tightly-held banking and administrative secrecy laws with heavy penalties if they are breached.
3. A banking and financial centre that is very large relative to the rest of the economy.
4. The availability of modern communications facilities.
5. The absence of currency controls nationally and/or on deposits held in foreign currencies.
6. The country's own promotion of itself as an 'offshore' centre (US Dept. of the Treasury, 1984).

What is widely accepted is that these centres play a critical role in what is called 'money laundering': the process of changing money gained from illegal operations into manageable form (that is, untraceable as to its illicit origins). By far the largest demand for money laundering services comes from the drug trade (President's Commission on Organized Crime, 1984).

There is ample awareness today that the drug trade and the internationalisation of corruption it spawns cannot be discussed in isolation from one of its most cherished privileges: the safe haven for its proceeds, dirty money. If drug trafficking is vilified and punished, the proceeds of this crime – drug money – are welcomed with open arms everywhere. To quote Leon Kellner, ex-US Attorney, Miami: 'The major traffickers may not touch the drugs. But there is one thing they always touch – the money.'[2] The amount is astronomical, perhaps $1 trillion worldwide, of which 40%, or $400 billion, is laundered in the USA. Much of the rest goes into banks offshore. This business is often too good to resist, especially for those societies with few other sources of income.

The vast majority of the cases identified in the criminal investigations of the Internal Revenue Service (IRS) in the late 1970s and early 1980s occurred in the Caribbean. Between 1978-83, there were 464 such cases, of which 45% represented illegal transactions with legal income. Of the other 55%, illegal income was involved (161 cases of which dealt with drug traffic). Of these, 29% involved the Cayman Islands, 28% involved Panama, 22% the Bahamas, and 11% the Dutch Antilles. These four offshore sites alone accounted for 85% of the cases involving transactions with illegal income. The actual movement of large amounts of cash throughout the Caribbean made a mockery of official statistics on the nature of these economies.

The Caribbean, however, was not the only place in the Western Hemisphere where big money was moving. It is critical to an understanding of the growth of Caribbean offshore centres to know that in many ways they are part of a larger financial region of which Florida is an important component. Indeed, by the late 1970s, Florida had become the banking centre for the Caribbean and, perhaps, Latin America. The climate for banking in Florida was clearly propitious: in 1982, Florida banks held 33% of all commercial bank deposits and an extraordinary 51% of all savings and loan deposits in the south-eastern part of the USA. Miami is one of the world's most important money-laundering centres.[3] One Florida banker (William H. Allen, Jr., Chairman of Pan American Bank) calculated that Florida received some $5-6 billion in one year (1982) in flight capital. Another (J.S. Hudson, Executive Vice-President of Flagship Bank) estimated that 'roughly 20%' of the total deposits of his own banks were from non-nationals. A substantial part of this money comes from capital flight. No part of the world exports more capital in this form than does Latin America (see Table 1).

Table 1:
Worldwide Capital Flight (1975-85)

	US $ Billion
Africa	28.5
Asia	18.3
Europe	24.0
Non-oil Middle East	6.2
Western Hemisphere	106.6

Source: IMF, cited in Dornbush (1990, p. 1).

Corruption, in the form of tax evasion, and the under – and over – invoicing of trade flows, are integral parts of this flight. It is a definite form of *laundering* and it creates the avenues, professional expertise and the climate or milieu which accommodates other 'hotter' monies also in flight and looking for safe havens. Clearly, much of the Caribbean continues to be involved in 'capturing' this money through its offshore business. The fact that so much of it takes place in British dependent or colonial territories has concerned the UK's Department of Trade and Industry enough to commission a study of these offshore financial centres in the Caribbean. The Coopers and Lybrand report indicated that there were many grounds for concern, given the virtual absence of local inspection and investigation of financial activities (Gallagher, 1990). Most of the local effort and talent goes into attracting and registering firms. British concern grew over the patently illicit activities of banks in the dependencies of Anguilla and Montserrat. In the latter, two-thirds of the 350 local banks were closed down after à 1989 Scotland Yard investigation, and a moratorium on new banks was mandated in Anguilla in May 1990. By that time, this little island of 7,000 inhabitants had 3,500 registered companies – including 42 banks.

Quite evidently, as we shall note later, this moratorium was not watertight. In the same vein, although Coopers and Lybrand gave the Cayman Islands a relatively clean bill of health, the moratorium did not stop existing banks from accepting massive deposits from Italy and Peru, suspected of being illicitly linked to former Peruvian President Alan García. Despite letters rogatory from Italian and Peruvian courts, and the assistance of the highest paid firm of lawyers in the Cayman Islands (US$360 per hour), the Cayman Supreme Court refused to lift the bank secrecy on the account.   Neither did the investigators receive much cooperation from banks in Miami where the trail had led them.[4] Similarly, 'untraceable Cayman's Corporations' figured prominently in a *New York Times* investigation which attempted to track the millions transferred out of Mexico by Raúl Salinas de Gortari, brother of former Mexican President Carlos Salinas de Gortari. These are some of the reasons why the case of the Cayman Islands contains a significant lesson about the behaviour of offshore centres and the present confusion about what 'sovereignty' means in practice.

Certainly, the Caymans have signed treaties with the USA but the effectiveness of such arrangements is limited by exclusions. For instance, Cayman Islands signed a Mutual Legal Assistance Treaty (MLAT) with the USA, but specifically excluded issues involving the IRS and the Securities and Exchange Commission (SEC). In other words, the Cayman Islands made it clear that it would sign measures combating evident 'dirty money', but not tax evasion monies or flight capital in general.[6] Notwithstanding its formal status as a 'dependent' territory, the Caymans could afford a stubborn position because discussions with the USA are always tripartite: United States-United Kingdom-Cayman.[7]

Despite European efforts, therefore, dirty monies continue to fatten Caribbean banking assets. In the late summer of 1991, two enterprising investigators decided to look into the mechanisms of establishing an offshore network. 'The system', they discovered, 'is shockingly simple and not very expensive to work' (Beaty and Gwynne, 1993, p. 213). For about $1,000 they set up a corporation in a major offshore haven, complete with corporate officers and directors, offshore trusts and bank accounts. This experiment gave the investigators a good insight into how the Bank of Credit and Commerce International (BCCI) managed to pull off what is arguably the most spectacular financial scandal in banking history. The web of cover-ups, bribes and corruption ensnared officials in US administrations and dozens of governments around the world.

A similar approach was taken by a team of undercover agents from the US Drug Enforcement Administration (DEA) in Operation Dinero. They set up their own bank in the British protectorate of Anguilla, and from there ensnared a major band of criminals engaged in money laundering, stolen art and many other illegal activities.[8] The collaboration between Italian and Colombian drug cartels was conclusively proven.[9] These examples illustrate the central argument of this chapter: the most complex part of the drug trade and other forms of international corruption is the disposing and utilisation of the proceeds, money.

It is no surprise that law enforcement agencies are paying greater attention to this fact of criminal enterprise. A recent United Nations conference in Naples on organised crime calculated that some US$750 billion in drug money is laundered every year. The conference recommended hitting the cartels 'where it hurt most: in their wallets'. Professionalism and complexity in money laundering schemes are only two of the reasons why this process is not easily addressed. There is no cohesive and universal political will to tackle the issue.[10] Not surprisingly, everyone condemned lax offshore regulations, but while the Italians mentioned Guernsey and other Channel Islands, the British were quite content to remain silent. In fact, the British press ignored the conference even as the French, German and Belgian press gave it front page headlines. The Belgians seemed most candid in admitting that only 3% of the estimated BFR 21 billion that were laundered through Belgium had been traced and frozen.

This lack of a coordinated effort is also apparent in the Western Hemisphere. Despite impressive declarations, such as those made at the 1992 San Antonio Summit and the Kingston Declaration of the same year, much remains to be done. This became evident at the December 1994 Summit of the Americas in Miami where in the same paragraph it was declared that 'illegal drug and related criminal activities pose grave threats to the societies, free market economies, and democratic institutions of the Hemisphere', and also that any approach to the problem had to include 'respect for national sovereignty'.[11] Despite this important conditionality, the issue created friction with some Caribbean countries, as well as the USA and Canada, 'because of fears that new inter-American rules could conflict with national bank secrecy laws'.[12] The 34 leaders did sign a set of recommendations that emphasised an attack on money laundering (as proposed by Colombia) and on the investigation, prosecution and, where applicable, extradition of corrupt individuals (Venezuela's proposal). Nothwithstanding these reservations, there is a growing awareness that money laundering and the offshore tax havens which facilitate it are major factors in the growth and menace of international drug and crime syndicates. Money is being laundered in virtually all (if not, indeed, *all*) offshore banking centres. And, yet, there is one offshore centre in particular which continues to receive the lion's share of accusation and condemnation: the state of Panama. To illustrate: a search on Panama through the data bank of the University of Miami's North-South Center, Info-South, under three keywords: 'Banks', 'Money' and 'Drugs', yielded 525 items, 75% of which were negative commentaries. Let it be said, however, that even as we focus on Panama that country is hardly the only, or even the largest, of the suspects.

Panama as an 'Offshore' Centre

Allegations that Panama is 'soft' on drugs are certainly not new. Former US Ambassador William Jorden describes how such allegations were used (unsuccessfully) to stop the Panama Canal Treaty in 1978. It was, he said, the accusation which most irritated the then leader Omar Torrijos (Jorden, 1984, p. 523). It continues to irritate Panamanians today.

It is not only the press, however, which gives particular negative attention to Panama. Even after the USA invaded in 1989 to remove General Manuel Antonio Noriega and what was described as his 'narcorepublic', the accusation has continued. In April 1991, US State Department official Michael Kozak told a US House of Representatives panel that drug trafficking and money laundering in Panama had returned to pre-invasion levels.[13] In May 1991 the DEA announced that 'at least' 22 banks in Panama had been used by drug traffickers to launder money.[14] In July 1991 the US General Accounting Office (GAO) stated that drug trafficking and money laundering had increased since the invasion of 1989.[15] In August 1993, Director of the US Office of National Drug Control Policy Lee Brown told a press conference in Panama that Panama should use more forceful measures to get rid of the money launderers.[16] In April 1994, US Assistant Secretary of State for Drug Affairs Robert Gelbard claimed that Panama was again a major centre of drug money laundering.[17] Seeming to sum up all the negative assessments is the US

Department of State's 1996 report which states: 'The GOP [Government of Panama] has yet to successfully prosecute major money launderers in Panama, to tighten up money laundering controls, particularly in the CFZ (Colón Free Zone) or to make functional its new financial analysis unit' (US Dept. of State, 1996, p. 155).

What significance can be drawn from this focus on Panama when, as already noted, money laundering and drug trafficking are transnational enterprises?[18] Is it a well-deserved reputation or is it, as one banker told this author, that Panama is 'an easy target'?[19] The question is not a trivial one. It goes to the heart of two fundamental issues in the study not just of 'offshore' centres but of corruption as a whole. First, can we deal with the development of cases such as that of Panama without understanding the complex historical and geographical contexts which gave rise to contemporary situations? Evidently, only such an understanding can lead to realistic solutions but, equally evidently, such a deep, broad and wide view will mean that responsibilities will be spread more widely.[20]

Second, it is important to ask whether such a 'targeting' of individual countries is conducive to an international consensus on the nature of the problem, a first step towards an international effort to deal with it. In other words, will we continue, as occurred at the Conference in Naples, to blame everyone else even as the general problem escalates?

Both questions have immediate relevance to Panama, one of the oldest offshore banking and service sectors in the Caribbean. From 1855, when the railroad first connected both oceans, Panama's destiny as a mercantile, transit economy was established. Its destiny as such a centre was arguably institutionalised in 1904 when the new republic, hardly a self-determining sovereign state, signed a monetary agreement with the USA (Moreno, 1991). The US dollar was adopted as local currency and Panama agreed not to establish any currency exchange restrictions of any sort. In 1927 Panama took a page from the Delaware and New Jersey corporation laws and passed its first General Corporation Law in order to attract offshore financial business. Aside from providing favourable tax treatment for any capital invested, it also guaranteed confidentiality, and it established that any two people of legal age – whether Panamanian or not, whether resident in Panama or abroad – could establish a corporation. The basic elements of the offshore centre had come into being. Law 18 of 1959 added coded (secret) bank accounts. Both the 1927 and the 1959 legislation were consolidated and amplified by the Banking Law of 1970. Not only did the 1970 law further lower taxes and make the movement of funds free, it also provided complementary legislation in the Criminal Commercial and Labour codes to enforce bank secrecy obligations and guarantees.

The same macroeconomic and geographical reasoning led to the promotion of a free trade zone. Decree Law 18 of 17 July 1948 created the Colón Free Trade Zone (CFTZ). Those who have studied the history and growth of contraband between Colombia and Panama understand that smuggling did not begin with the opening of the free trade zone. The CFTZ merely enlarged and institutionalised smuggling and made the laundering of monies through the zone easier. With the Transoceanic Canal, the international banking centre and the free trade zone, Panama had become the complete 'offshore' service economy and there were no objections. Indeed, the crucial aspect of this 'offshore' development in Panama is that it took place harmoniously with the evolution of Panamanian society proper and this, in turn, with the needs of the major trading countries of the world, particularly the USA.

All this had important social and political consequences. The construction of the railroad and, later, the first effort at building a canal introduced an immigrant element which did not so much integrate into the established society as form a new ethnic enclave. The basic social structure had already been established in the eighteenth century: a white criollo sector (*intramuros*) which lived off trade, and a black and mulatto working class (the *arrobal*). These circumstances hardly changed in the nineteenth century of Colombian domination.

As distinct from the landed and essentially anti-commercial elites of much of Latin America, the Panamanian elite was geared towards the outside world and trade. The absence of any conservative corporativist-type thinking can be attributed to the absence of a landed aristocracy and the predominance of trade. Panama has always been 'a relatively open urban society in which commercial, liberal values thrived.' (Ropp, 1985, p. 602).

With the US building of the canal and the commercial activity to which it gave rise, new *barraca* neighbourhoods emerged: El Chorillo, Marañon, California. These *rentals* gave the old elites a new source of income.[21] The very growth of Panama City guaranteed the income of this rentier class. Between 1900 and 1920, the city doubled in size; between 1930 and 1960 it quadrupled.

During this period, Panamanian politics was dominated by what Marco Gandásegui calls the 'separatist aristocrats' (Gandásegui, 1989, p. 141). After 1960, this group lost its grip on state power. After 1960, admits Gandásegui: '*En Panamá no existe lo que podría llamarse aristocracia*'. Those who are direct descendants from the colonial aristocracy, '*se encuentran divididos y alejados del poder económico y del poder político*'. (Gandásegui, 1989, p. 149).

Like many other Latin American countries, Panama experienced the stirrings of nationalism and populism. What began was the era of Torrijos, which, contrary to the interpretations of Marxist and *dependentista* scholars, was also the real beginning of modern 'offshore' Panama. The common interpretation that the military *coup d'état* in 1968 responded to a crisis in the 'liberal' or 'capitalist' project is quite erroneous. Overarching theories about the 'hegemonic crisis' never called for a clearer definition of what the *burguesía nacional* really was. Very often this term was used interchangeably with *capital financiero* and *clase dependiente* (also called *clase entreguista* – 'hand-over' class). Similarly erroneous was the thesis that the 1968 *coup d'état* resulted from a Panamanian 'crisis in hegemony' as well as a hemisphere-wide (even world-wide) crisis in 'dependent capitalism'.[22]

A fundamental problem with these still-utilised theses is that they mystify the nature of the changes wrought by the 1968 coup. Talk of 'radical and significant changes in the country's political and economic life' (Priesly, 1986, p. 1) miss the point. Changes were occurring but they were hardly what the literature of the 1970s and 1980s was describing, that is, the incorporation of urban workers, peasants, students and intellectuals into the decision-making processes of Panamanian social, economic and political life.

What had occurred was that Torrijos's populist regime had increased social expenditures in a redistributive manner rather than a new productive one. This gave impetus to a state-led development which became the dominant factor in internal demand. Between 1968 and 1987 the number of schools increased from 1,851 to 4,171 although expansion in education could still hardly keep pace with the increase in enrolments (from 273,184 in 1965 to 632,336 in 1987). University enrolments grew from 7,091 to 56,506. Illiteracy fell from 21.7% in 1960 to 12.2% in 1980. Another area in which the Torrijos reforms brought about significant changes was public health. The percentage of population covered by Social Security grew from 28.9% in 1972 to 56.5% in 1981; the infant mortality rate (per 1,000 live births) fell from 36.8 in 1976 to 19.4 in 1986. The Torrijos regime invested heavily in housing for various social classes with very generous terms offered by a number of state institutions. Mortgages of up to 80% were provided for commercial properties and 90% for private houses. The state financed 78% of all construction between 1973 and 1980.

Not surprisingly, this was the period when, as Table 5 shows, the expanding banking sector fattened its loan portofolios. A building boom physically modernised Panama City's growing financial sector, a point to which we shall return. Table 2 clearly shows the dramatic shift in ownership patterns, one consequence of this state involvement in construction financing. This populism had a significant political consequence: it eliminated the rents which were a major source of income for the old bourgeoisie. Their children had to turn to the service sectors for employment.

Table 2:
Type of Occupancy

	1930		1950	1960	1970	1980	
	%	Units	%	%	%	%	Units
Owned	9.5%	2,066	17.0%	26.5%	40.2%	60.1%	83,900
Rented	90.5	19,789	79.2	70.3	52.4	33.0	46,015
Other	---	---	3.8	3.1	7.4	6.9	9,610

Source: Uribe (1989).

Table 3:
Government Expenditure (as percentage of total)

	1977	1980	1983	1986
Debt Service	23.3	32.6	42.7	55.5
Education	19.8	15.3	12.7	11.0

Source: Dirección de Estadística y Censo de la Contraloría General de la República (Castro et al, 1989, p. 27).

There were two other consequences of this populist agenda. First, the state heavily indebted itself and eventually had to curtail expenditure on social services (see Table 3). Second, and critically, since expenditures were not in primary production but rather in consumption, the very nature of the economy changed radically. Only 10.8% of the loans made by the Panamanian banking system went to *Sectores Productivos*; 'personal consumption' took 41.2%, *Empresas Financieras y de Seguros* 26.7% (Castro et al, 1989). The secular trend towards a subsidised society based on a service economy, evident before 1968, now became manifest (see Table 4). One must conclude, therefore, that far from radicalising the Panamanian social structure, the Torrijos reforms provided the working class with subsidies, and urban middle and upper classes with the capacity to participate in the enormous expansion of the 'offshore' sector.

Table 4:
Economic Structure (as percentage of GDP)

Economic Sector	1962	1970	1978	1986
Primary	24.2	18.3	15.7	9.8
Secondary	17.3	23.2	17.6	13.5
Tertiary	58.4	58.5	66.7	76.7

Source: Panamá en Cifras.

The basic pragmatism that had traditionally characterised the Panamanian middle classes did not disappear during this 'revolution'. Relations with the USA had always underpinned Panamanian nationalism and nationalism had been at the core of Panamanian politics. Central to that, in turn, was the issue of the Canal. The bloody riots of 1959 and 1964 demonstrated the intensity of Panamanian feelings about the Canal. Equally true is that anti-US sentiments of one sort or another are shared by Panamanians across social classes. In a 1963 survey, only 13% of upper and upper-middle class students agreed with the assertion: 'Essentially the United States and this country [Panama] are good friends.' In Costa Rica a similar sample gave a 51% affirmative response (Goldrich, 1966, p. 110).

Interestingly, however, Goldrich found Panamanian anti-US feeling tempered by some hard-core economic realism. The majority of students indicated that they would like to work for a US company, opposed the nationalisation of the Canal and did not believe Panamanians could run the Canal without US help. Even the United Fruit Company – abhored in the rest of the Caribbean – was seen as 'beneficial' to Panama by 79% of the students.

Rather than the heavily ideological interpretations of Panamanian attitudes,[23] one should take note of the open, trade-oriented nature of the society and, after the 1960s, the predominance of the service sector in its economy. Torrijos's reforms were far from antagonistic to the expansion of the most advanced form of capitalism: an offshore financial system.   If anything, the open, trade-oriented nature of the society and its political culture was strengthened.

The Explosive Growth of the Panamanian Banking Sector

The growth of the banking sector under military rule is indisputable. The reforms established by Decree 238 of 2 July 1970 liberalised banking legislation, and growth was explosive from that point. In 1970, there were twenty banks with assets of US$854 million and hiring 2,881 employees; in 1982, there were 122 banks with US$49 billion in capital and 8,726 employees (Moreno, 1991, pp. 23, 50).

Once again, other circumstances played their part. Panamanians are the first to admit that while their service sector was not designed or intended for illegal practices, it did serve them quite well. *'Esta capacidad bancaria'*, states a spokesman for the banking community, *'se desarrolla precisamente, en la década en que el tráfico de drogas alcanza niveles sin precedentes'* (Moreno, 1991, p. 79). As a report published by the US Embassy in Panama in January 1989 notes, 'Panama's banking sector has flourished in part because certain banks are actively involved in the laundering of drug money, primarily Colombian drug money'.

Panama did make some efforts to improve its image as an offshore centre. In 1984, the Asociación Bancaria created a *Código de Conducta* and *Comisión de Vigilancia*. Law 23 of 30 December 1986 provided the first definition of 'money laundering' and recognised crimes committed abroad as a basis for action in Panamá. It does not appear, however, that such legislation made much difference to the money launderers; Panama continued to be a favourite destination.

A series of US undercover and 'sting' operations (Operation Piscis in 1987, Operation Calibre Chase in 1988, Operation Polar Cap in 1989) all showed Panama to be a major player in money laundering. But Panama had become more than that: it had become one of the major centres for criminal activity. When the Cuban government wished to circumvent the US embargo, it established the CIMEX Corporation in Panama, a country which provided it, and many others, with all offshore facilities. Panama and its *de facto* ruler, General Manuel Antonio Noriega, were in business. Citizenship papers, passports, visas were all for sale. It was later revealed by the director of the newly reorganised Policía Técnica Judicial (PTJ) that 75% of the criminals sought by Interpol had entered or settled in Panama at some point.[24]   Panama's role in the arms trade that serviced both ideological combatants and criminal groups was evident.

The discovery on 6 January 1989 of a container in the port of Kingston, Jamaica, with US$8 million in arms illustrated that the problem had wider ramifications. Of West German manufacture, the weapons were shipped from Portugal on a Panamanian registered ship and were destined for an unspecified group in Colombia. It took a joint effort by Jamaican, British, US and Colombian intelligence to break the Jamaican link of what was called 'an international network of drug traffickers and terrorists'. The Panamanian ship was owned by Bluewater Ship Management Inc. of Panama, and both the company and its British (naturalised Panamanian) president had previously been linked to illegal arms shipments, cocaine distribution and the laundering of drug-related monies (Gómez, 1989).

Several trends put Panama in the eye of the storm and then brought down its dictator and his clique. First, Noriega simply stopped being geopolitically useful to the USA and, indeed, might have turned against the very agencies with which he had been involved (Kempe, 1990; Dinges, 1990). Second, internal US pressures forced the government to take a stronger stance against corrupt offshore centres in general and Panama in particular.

Money laundering had an impact on the USA in several ways: it funded criminal enterprises, it deprived the government of legitimate tax revenues and it undermined the societies of its allies. As tends to be the case in democratic societies, legislation was bound to follow. In response to the apparent inefficiency of the *Bank Secrecy Act* as a mechanism to impose criminal liability on money launderers, Congress enacted the *Money Laundering Control Act of 1986*. Additionally, the reach of the *Racketeer Influenced and Corrupt Organizations Law of 1970* (RICO), originally intended to combat organised crime, was expanded to a wide range of white collar crimes, including securities and commodities fraud, and money laundering.

Table 5:
Balance Sheet of Banks Operating in Panama (US$ millions)

	1985	1988	1992	1993
Total Assets	38,236	14,817	23,522	26,658
Loans				
Local	3,933	3,669	3,400	3,900
Foreign	19,412	5,983	10,707	12,908

Source: Peat Marwick (1993).

Noriega's indictment by a Miami Grand Jury and the ensuing political crisis finally led to the flight of some banks and money from Panama. Many – not all, according to the US Embassy – of the big laundering banks and their capital left. The figures in Table 5 illustrate just how much of the money deposited in Panama was scared off by the country's bad reputation and the pressures applied by the USA against Noriega, two years before the actual invasion. However, only five 'general licence' and two 'international licence' banks abandoned Panama during that period. The money – electronically transferred – went to other offshore centres in the Caribbean. Following an historical Caribbean pattern, Panama's troubles were other islands' gains. It appears that the British Virgin Islands were the big winners this time.

Political Repercussions

Despite the dramatic impact on its most important economic sector, the Panamanian political elite remained unconcerned about money laundering. The constant flow of accusations from the international press and the US government were met with a defensiveness bordering on disingenuousness.

In March 1993, the director of the Panamanian Banking Commissions took note of his country's bad reputation but claimed that it was unjust; money laundering, he said, was 'insignificant' in Panamá.[25] One year later, President Guillermo Endara said he would lodge a protest against the US government's accusation that his country was a major launderer of money.[26] Panamanians tended to interpret US actions as the result of frustration with its own failed efforts to control domestic drug trafficking and money laundering. 'Panama bashing' was perceived as a cheap substitute for US action.[27]

This Panamanian defensiveness only aggravated the situation. As Stephen Labaton of *The New York Times* (6 February 1990, p. 1) pointed out, official Panamanian reticence was due to the fact that 'It is difficult to find any senior officials here who do not have important ties to banks'. Indeed, both the President and the second Vice-President were said to have had ties with banks linked to the laundering of Colombian drug money.[28] These accusations raise an extremely contentious issue, one not often broached in Panama: what, if any, are the links between the drug trade, money laundering and the political system?

If Panamanians of all stripes are today ready to acknowledge the involvement of dirty money in the case of previous military regimes and in particular that of General Noriega, they are less forthcoming about the post-Noriega system. One of the truly noteworthy and sociologically important facets of contemporary Panama is that it is virtually impossible to find anyone in a position of responsibility who believes that there is drug-related corruption in the political system.[29] This elite refusal to question the integrity of politicians and political institutions distinguishes Panama from the rest of the Caribbean Basin, where accusations about drug-related corruption permeate virtually all political processes. There were no partisan accusations about dirty money during the 1994 electoral campaign. It would be two years later that the new editor of *La Prensa*, Gustavo Gorriti, would reveal that drug monies had been used in the campaign of President Pérez Balladares. After some public discussion of the issue, however, the matter disappeared from the headlines.[30]

As paradoxical as this apparent indifference might seem, it may have fairly simple sociological explanations. It would seem that the change appears to be more a modification of governance style than any structural change in the realities of the Panamanian underground economy. The new style is one of reserve and discretion at all levels, a collective effort to change the image of the country. The reasons for this are not hard to find. First, the depths of private and public depravation to which General Noriega carried Panama and its international reputation weigh heavily on today's elites of all persuasions but perhaps most gravely on those of Noriega's party, including President Pérez Balladares himself. They have tried to eradicate the ostentatious, vulgar style of the Noriega period. Noriega's imprisonment in a federal jail in Florida is a constant reminder of this national shame. Second, and perhaps most importantly in terms of explaining this new demeanour, Panamanians have had to ponder the causes and consequences of the massive flight of capital which started in 1988 (see Table 5). As the statistics reveal, and as officials of Peat Marwick Mitchell in Panama confirmed,[31] some $10 billion of the money that fled from international licence banks never returned.

One argument is that Panama should welcome the flight of what were in all probability the 'dirtiest' of monies, whose owners were unwilling to face a US probe into the Panamanian 'offshore' system. There is another opinion, however, that these were 'legitimate' offshore monies fleeing from Panama's bad reputation.[32] As such, Panama is perceived as having lost a comparative advantage *vis-à-vis* the many other offshore centres around the world but especially in the Caribbean. This is, in fact, the official position of the Asociación Bancaria de Panamá. Admitting that no one could deny that funds originating in illegal activities have passed through the banks of Panama, the Asociación notes the dangers of notoriety: 'Nothing is more

Table 6:
Panama: Legislating the New National Image

	Legislation
15 July 1991	National Assembly ratifies the Mutual Legal Assistance Treaty (MLAT) with the USA.
12 December 1993	National Assembly ratifies the Vienna Convention.
19 September 1994	Executive Decree No. 468 orders all *Agentes Residentes* to identify their clients.
27 September 1994	Decreto Ejecutivo No. 473: creates Comisión Presidencial to establish a national policy on the laundering of drug profits.
30 November 1994	*Código de Etica de la Zona Libre de Colón.*
1995	The Pérez Balladares government establishes the Financial Analysis Unit, the first of its promised money laundering controls. Office of 'drug czar' created.
	The US-Panamanian MLAT ratified in 1991 comes into effect. Five letters of agreement for counternarcotics cooperation signed with the USA.
	Public Statements
5 January 1994	'Efforts to Combat Money Laundering in Panama' (Article Prepared by the Panama Banking Association).
June 1994:	'Money Laundering: Position of the Panama Banking Association'
15 July 1994:	'Aspectos Económicos de los Delitos de Drogas' (Asociación Bancaria de Panamá).
Sept.-Oct. 1994:	Julio Antelo S., 'El Uso Indebido de la Banca vs. el Secreto Bancario' (*Centro Financiero*).

remote to banking than the limelight. Nothing is more foreign to banking than noise, uproar, or the front page' (Panama Banking Association, 1993, p. 2). The Asociación elaborated further on the need for a change of style:

Los depósitos *externos no bancarios* de todo el Centro panameño crecieron en sólo US$783 millones en los últimos cuatro años, lo cual es un indicador de la pérdida de interés internacional en la plaza local y una señal de que las normas del negocio bancario en Panamá y la imagen del país deben revisarse a fondo si se quiere mantener la importancia de la actividad financiera en el país' (Asociación Bancaria de Panamá, 1994).

This call for a new national decorum seems to be the product of a consensus evident from the rash of new legislation and declarations by banking officials (see Table 6). Obviously, legislation and rhetoric do not necessarily translate into action. They are, however, necessary preconditions for action. The best predictor of whether Panamanians will move from a change in attitudes to a change in behaviour is not international pressure *per se,* but rather their perceptions about national honour and the nature of their economic future both of which, of course, are heavily dependent on international reputation.

Conclusions

It might very well be that the pressures emanating from Washington contribute to this heightened sense of alarm about the consequences of attracting dirty money. More important, however, appears to be a rational Panamanian calculation premised on two realities. First, that with virtually the whole world dollarising and liberalising economies, Panama's relative geographical advantages as an 'offshore' centre, while losing some comparative advantage through increased competition, are still viable. Second, factors other than geography, such as technical skills and reputation, remain important. There will be enormous advantages to having a reputation as a respectable banking country offering an expert and respectable set of offshore services. In this, they are doing what Switzerland and the Cayman Islands, for instance, are attempting: cleaning up their reputations. This latter calculation and goal is based on solid empirical macroeconomic grounds: Panama today depends on a healthy banking sector for its very existence.

The real benefits of the banking sector in the 1990s are not in terms of direct total employment (2% of the labour force) nor in direct contribution to GDP (only 6.5% even in the 1980s). Rather, banking has a comprehensive and complex relationship with the entire Panamanian economy and is, therefore, an important factor in Panamanian politics. Luis Moreno states it clearly:

> Panamá, por su economía abierta, por su sistema monetario sin restricciones [dolarizado], ha sido y es un país con un déficit tradicional de magnitud considerable en la cuenta corriente de su Balanza de Pagos. *En la casi automática compensación* de esta deficiencia, el sistema bancario panameño juega papel estelar, por medio del ingreso neto de capitales....compensa alrededor del 30% del déficit en la Cuenta Corriente (Moreno, 1991, pp. 72-3).

Beyond this vital macroeconomic function, capital in the international banks also contributes to the ready availability of credit at relatively low rates (compared with both the rest of Latin America and even the USA). This has allowed the political system to continue the momentum of popular economic participation begun by the Torrijos 'revolution'. There are simply no substitute sources of such capital in Panama and, given the open political competition that electoral democracy involves, it is not logical to expect any rational Panamanian political aspirant to do anything structurally damaging to the sources of capital.

All this appears to be the background to the important Panamanian attempt to 'come clean' through new legislation and rhetoric (see Table 6). The most important initiative in this new trend was Executive Decree 473 (September 1994). A Presidential Commission was assigned the task of creating a *Política Nacional Contra el Lavado del Dinero Producto del Narcotráfico* – a national policy against the laundering of drug money.

The Commission's first report states that Panama's open economic system makes it potentially a 'vulnerable victim' of international crime. The basis of the Commission's recommendations, it appears, will be the recommendations contained in the 1988 United Nations Convention Against the Illicit Traffic in Narcotics (the Vienna Convention). Panama's legislature has already ratified that convention. For the first time, Panama is represented at the various meetings of the Financial Action Task Force (FATF), a multilateral organisation based at the headquarters of the Organisation for Economic Cooperation and Development (OECD) in

Paris, which is geared towards assisting individual countries to combat money laundering. Panama's attorney-general was the president of CFATF (the Caribbean branch of the FATF) in 1995.

Panama has also established a special (though more discreet) commission to study drug trafficking and money laundering through the CFTZ where trade in 1993 was over US$10 billion. Because only 200 of the nearly 1,000 operatives in the CFTZ are formally members of the association, this area will be much more difficult to police than the banks. Panama appears to be making a rational choice in taking on the offshore banking system first.

Whatever the recommendations of these commissions might be, they will have to take into account two serious lacunae in any country's arsenal against financial fraud in general, and money laundering specifically: (1) the absence of international-level expertise in any specialised and centralised national agency they might establish for the analysis of financial data; and (2) control over the operations of non-banking agencies that are major sources of money laundering. Beyond the reach of Panamanian authorities are Casas de Cambio, Compañías Financieras, Cooperativas de Ahorro y Crédito, and Empresas de Transferencia de Dinero. The *Casinos Nacionales* are national and supervised. Finally, with cash payments now accounting for nearly 25% of all transactions in the CFTZ, policing the money and the movement of merchandise in and out of Colón remains an enormous challenge. This will become an even more intractable problem when the port for container transshipments is completed.

Closing these gaps will challenge both the political will and the administrative/technical capacity of the nation. It will require much more than a change of style. Panama, it appears, has little choice but to bite the bullet. It either cleans up its own house or others (with 'offshore' agendas of their own) will make loud noises about doing it for them, even as their own 'offshore' centres continue to prosper. Paradoxically, the very magnitude of the problem might force the Panamanians to modernise their state apparatus. This will be necessary if they are to cope with the extraordinarily complex economy which history, geography, imperialism and the choices of their own elites has bequeathed to today's generation.

Notes:

1. To Ingo Walters, for instance, the flow of monies to tax havens is a topic of enormous qualitative and quantitative importance. He laments,

therefore, that there is so little hard evidence available on the subject. According to Walters, the reason for this secrecy is that the offshore tax haven business is 'of great value to some, yet positively bad for others'. An additional obstacle to its study is that the business thrives on schemes of 'almost diabolical complexity', a complexity made possible by sophisticated technology. As the Chief Executive Officer of one of Canada's largest banks told a Canadian Senate committee: 'I can hide money in the twinkle of an eye from all the bloodhounds that could be put on the case, and I would be so far ahead of them that there would never be a hope of unravelling the trail'. The secret, he concluded, was electronics.

2. Associated Press Report, 7 May 1987.

3. According to Charles Intrago, former US Federal Prosecutor and now publisher of *Money Laundering Alert* which specialises in reporting money-laundering cases: 'Miami has all the banking facilities you need, it has all the nonbanking facilities you need, it has all the trades and businesses necessary for laundering money.' To Intrago, Miami provides 'one-stop shopping for the money launderer' (Ackerman, 1994; Maingot, 1988, pp. 167-88).

4. See the Peruvian magazine *Caretas*, 21 July 1994, pp.12-17; 14 July 1994, pp.12-17; 4 August 1994, pp. 20-21.

5. *The New York Times*, 5 June 1996, pp. 1, 8.

6. Despite the fact that there were 18,952 tax exempted corporations in the Cayman Islands, employing 1,300 and providing US$26 million in licence fees, there is serious question about their capacity, or, indeed, their determination, to hold dirty money at bay. In May 1995, the BBC aired a story on the Caymans which revealed that there is only one banking regulator and a police force untrained in bank fraud, to monitor the transactions of some 520 banks.

7. As the Attorney General of the Cayman Islands informed his island's legislature on the MLAT negotiations:

> We, the Government of the Cayman Islands, have a specific, categorical undertaking from our *Sovereign Mother*, the United Kingdom, that there will be no further offence added to this list, even though the United Kingdom and the United States both agree, without the specific consent, Sir, of the Government of the Cayman Islands. *We have the say so. They cannot do it without us.*

Michael Bradley, Attorney General, Cayman Islands, September 1986 (Gilmore, 1990, p. 383).

8. This section draws heavily from Maingot (1994), pp. 163-82 and Maingot (1995), pp. 1-14.
9. See *New York Times* 17 December 1994, pp. 1, 6.
10. As James Morgan of the *Financial Times* noted, in this issue of offshore banking, 'everyone finds someone else to blame for crime'. See *Financial Times*, 26 November 1994, p. xxiv.
11. See *Summit of the Americas: Declaration of Principles*, Final Revised Draft, 11-9-94, p. 15.
12. See *Financial Times*, 10-11 December 1994, p. 30.
13. See *The Miami Herald*, 18 April 1991, p. 9.
14. See *El Nuevo Herald*, 29 May 1991, p. 3.
15. See *Washington Post*, 28 July 1991, p. 1C.
16. See *La Prensa* (Panamá), 12 August 1993, p. 2.
17. See *La Prensa* (Panamá), 14 April 1994, p. 1.
18. Is it any wonder that John le Carré should have decided that the proper location for his 1996 post-Cold War *roman à clef* (*The Tailor of Panama*) should be Panama, which 'is not a country. It's a business'? See John le Carré, 'Quel Panamá', *The New York Times Magazine*, 13 October 1996, pp. 52-5.
19. Interview with former senior official of BCCI, Miami, Florida, 4 December 1994.
20. While it is self-evident that no nation voluntarily shares in historical guilt, the researcher need not participate in such denials. John le Carré shows admirable historical and moral sensibility when he notes: 'The odd thing is, Panama is not half the mess it might be after being mauled and abused and corrupted by a succession of colonial exploiters' (Le Carré, 1996, p. 55).
21. For a summary of the literature, see Raúl Leis (1987).
22. See Memorias, VI Congreso Nacional de Sociología, *Revista Panameña de Sociología*, No. 5 (1989).
23. The tendency is to interpret any pro-US attitudes as resulting from '*dependencia*'. See Soler (1974), pp. 25-8.
24. See *El Nuevo Herald*, 30 December 1990, p. 2.
25. See *La Prensa* (Panamá), 28 March 1993, p. 17.
26. See *La Prensa* (Panamá), 6 April 1994, p. 1.
27. See *La Prensa* (Panamá), 24 September 1993, p. 11.
28. See also similar accusations of ex-Fiscal Rogelio Miranda in *El Nuevo Herald*, 21 September 1990, p. 3.
29. Interviews with 19 Panamanian leaders, 4-10 December 1994.
30. Interview with Gustavo Gorriti, Miami, Florida, 15 July 1996. See also *The Miami Herald*, 10, 13, 17 and 20 June 1996. Gorriti is a Peruvian,

well-known as an investigative journalist in his native land.

31. Interviews with officials of Peat Marwick, Panama, 8 December 1994.
32. Interviews, Panama, 4-10 December 1994.

CHAPTER 8

COCAINE TRAFFICKING AND BRITISH FOREIGN POLICY

Elizabeth Joyce

In 1985, the House of Commons Home Affairs Committee, in its interim report on the Misuse of Hard Drugs, described the prospect of Latin American cocaine exporters targeting the British market as 'the most serious peacetime threat to our national well-being'.[1] The seriousness of this assessment shows at least one group of British policy-makers conceiving of the problem in much the same security terms as their counterparts in the USA. The similarity to the US response is no coincidence. In 1985, Britain and its European neighbours were first becoming aware of a potential cocaine threat as a result of US warnings. Their perceptions of the production, trafficking and consumption of cocaine were almost entirely drawn from US experience. Given the lack of knowledge and experience of cocaine in Europe, the US view of the Andean countries as the root of the global drug problem became, in the late 1980s and early 1990s, the global view. More than ten years later, it is appropriate to ask whether this threat has been realised and, crucially, whether we would know if it had.

Cocaine in Britain is a curious phenomenon. The most curious fact of all is that police and customs regularly seize far more cocaine than any other drug. Heroin remains the hard drug of choice for most habitual British users, yet in the first half of the 1990s British police and customs seized twice as much cocaine as heroin. In 1994, cocaine seizures (2,261 kilos) were more than three times those of heroin (744 kilos) (Home Office Research and Statistics Department, 1995). In 1995, it took an 80% increase in the amount of heroin seized to make the two totals roughly equal.[2] British customs or police regularly make single seizures of more than half a tonne of cocaine. In 1994, Italy made one seizure of six tonnes, Europe's largest-ever single cocaine haul (IRELA, 1995). This influx is recent. Fewer than 1,400 kilos were seized in the whole of western Europe in 1986. Five years before that, cocaine seizures throughout Europe were negligible.

There were warnings that this would happen. Towards the end of the 1980s, the US Drug Enforcement Administration (DEA) was predicting that Latin American drug traffickers, having saturated the USA with cocaine, were targeting Europe in an effort to widen their market base. Whether a drug market can reach saturation point in the way they estimated is open to question. Nevertheless, European policymakers heeded the DEA's predictions. By 1989, British Home Secretary Douglas Hurd was convening a meeting of Council of Europe ministers to tell them that crack-cocaine was 'the spectre hanging over Europe'.[3] US urban communities were on the verge of collapse under an avalanche of cocaine; Europe would be next. The main area of contention was about the time-scale, whether the process would take three years (the DEA), five years (the House of Commons Home Affairs Committee) or seven years (US diplomats in Europe). Yet the threatened social breakdown has not occurred. The reasons why can tell us much about the weakness of perceiving the drug trade through a prism of powerful metaphors, and about the drawbacks of applying the lessons learned in one country to another.

It is difficult to make any reliable estimates on drug use in Britain. The UK has no equivalent of the US National Survey on Drug Abuse, and the lack of data makes it difficult to produce a reliable national overview of drug consumption. Britain is typical of European countries in producing no detailed national survey of drug use. As Reuter notes in Chapter 1 in this volume, the data collected in other large European Union (EU) member states are often sparse. However, the need to produce responses in the absence of data can influence perceptions and the formulation of policy, with the consequence that official responses to drug supply have, in the past, been somewhat susceptible to external influence. Nowhere has this been more clearly demonstrated than in Britain's initial response to cocaine trafficking. Rather less is known about the supply and use of cocaine than the other Class A illicit drugs.[4] As one study noted: 'Much has been written in the press about the alleged growth of cocaine consumption. There does not, however, appear to have been any substantial research on the subject at all in the UK.[5] Elsewhere, the available data have been described as 'extremely patchy and incomplete' (Shapiro, 1993, p. 12).

In part, less is known about cocaine because the drug has not traditionally been particularly popular or readily available in Britain. Yet it has historically played, and continues to play, an idiosyncratic role in the formulation of UK drug policy. In attempting to shed more light on the European-Latin American trafficking nexus, this chapter will focus on the place of cocaine in British drug trafficking. The UK is considered here as an example of what is known about the cocaine trafficking that takes place in Europe generally.

The British Cocaine Market

Judging from seizures alone, the volume of cocaine reaching the United Kingdom appears to be far greater than the volume of heroin. Yet very little is known about its destination or use once it arrives. There are few instances of seizures in larger quantities once the drug has entered the country. Evidence of some growth in crack use does not yet begin to account for the growth in cocaine imports. [6] Cocaine use is not linked to crime in the way associated with heroin and cannabis use, and this denies the police a valuable source of intelligence about distribution. Similarly, cocaine users do not present themselves in any numbers at drug agencies and hospitals, denying workers in these fields a large enough sample from which to draw reliable conclusions about use.

Two of the possible explanations for the increase are concerned with the organisation of European trafficking and control rather than consumption. First, police believe that some cocaine arriving in the UK is in transit to other countries.[7] Drugs move around Europe with alarming ease. New markets are emerging in Central and Eastern Europe which both absorb drugs from EU countries and produce them for use in Britain and elsewhere. US foreign policy on drugs might neatly divide the world into producers (like Bolivia, Thailand, Myanmar), transit countries (Brazil, Mexico, Nigeria) and markets (the USA, Canada, Australia and Europe), but the reality is not so clear-cut. As Pérez Gómez demonstrates in Chapter 2, there appears to be a significant market for illicit drugs in Latin America. The USA is one of the largest producers of marijuana. Britain – like the Netherlands, Italy, Spain, Portugal and Ireland – is a transit country. Nevertheless, this unquantifiable factor alone is unlikely to account for the large volume of seizures. Second, it is possible that a greater concentration by customs on cocaine intelligence has resulted in a greater proportion of imports being seized, but this still would not explain the discrepancy between seizures for heroin (whose import and distribution networks are relatively well-known) and cocaine.

Of the main illicit drug markets in Britain – heroin, cannabis and cocaine – the heroin market has been the most studied and its effects the easiest to assess. Notwithstanding the analytical problems presented by the UK's patchy and unreliable data base, it is possible to say with some certainty that, in the UK, heroin is consumed with greater regularity and with more serious social consequences than cocaine. According to the Institute for the Study of Drug Dependence, under 1% of people surveyed on drug use report *ever* using heroin, cocaine and crack. Samples of inner city inhabitants aged 16-25 suggest that 1% may have used crack-cocaine,

2% heroin and 4% cocaine (United Kingdom, 1994, p. 84). In any one year, at least 6% of the population take an illegal drug (some three million people). Cannabis is the most widely used; some 14% of people between the ages of 12 and 59 report experience of the drug.[8]

Among 16-19 year olds, surveys show that 11% have tried amphetamines, 9% Ecstasy and 8% LSD (United Kingdom, 1994, p. 84). At least one researcher has attributed cocaine's relative lack of success in the UK drug market to the competition it faces from the well-established local amphetamine industry (Bean, 1993a, p. 74). Amphetamines have a long tradition of use in the UK. Their effect as a stimulant is close enough to cocaine to suggest that the two drugs might attract the same potential users. However, unlike cocaine, they tend to be produced locally in large quantities, and are always readily available. They are also substantially cheaper, which might put cocaine at a competitive disadvantage.[9] However, seizures of amphetamines by both police and customs amounted to 569 kilos in 1992, little more than a quarter of the volume of cocaine seized.

Historically, the linchpin of drug control policy in the UK has been the so-called 'British System' whereby the supply of addictive drugs is controlled by the medical profession. Any doctor who attends a patient they suspect, or know, to be addicted to certain drugs must notify the Home Office. Notifiable drugs comprise 13 opiates/opioids (including heroin, methadone and opium) and cocaine.[10] Over 25,000 addicts in England were notified to the Home Office in 1993, with a male:female ratio of 3:1 (United Kingdom, 1994, p. 84). More data are becoming available with the introduction of drug misuse databases. The first English national report was published by the Department of Health in 1994, limited to the six months between 1 October 1992 and 31 March 1993 (United Kingdom, 1994, p. 86). This showed that 17,800 individuals started treatment either for the first time or after a six-month gap. Only 3% reported cocaine as their primary drug.[11] Similarly, every year between 1985 and 1994, only 2% of drug-related convictions and cautions involved cocaine (Home Office Research and Statistics Department, 1995, p. 46).

The 'British System' dates from the findings of the Rolleston Committee (the Departmental Committee on Morphine and Heroin Addiction) in 1924-26.[12] A register of addicts collected by the Home Office has been available since 1934. The existence of a supply line independent of medical practitioners was considered unlikely in the 1920s. Addicts were not considered to have the drive, intelligence or initiative to make their own arrangements through illegal channels.

Cocaine played a critical role in the original development of British drug control policy. Regulation 40B of the *Defence of the Realm Act 1914* made it an offence for anyone other than authorised persons (retail pharmacists, doctors etc) or persons who had received the drug on a doctor's prescription to possess cocaine or preparations containing more than 0.1% cocaine. The regulation was prompted by concern that an epidemic of cocaine use had broken out among prostitutes and Canadian soldiers. The fear resulting from highly publicised instances of excessive cocaine use at the turn of the century led a *Chemist and Druggist* editorial to comment in 1921: 'Of all the horrors that have been created during the past twenty years, cocaine-taking is probably the worst'(Spear and Mott, 1993, p. 30). At this point, supplies of cocaine in Britain were legitimately acquired from Germany (the main manufacturer), France, Switzerland, the Netherlands and the USA. Then, as now, stories appeared in the press pointing to isolated instances of excessive consumption. These were used to characterise a threatening problem. The notion that social stability was being threatened by the consequences of cocaine use appears to have been totally false. In 1917, a police report to the Home Office disclosed that there was no evidence of cocaine abuse among either soldiers or civilians outside London.

The restrictions of Regulation 40B were extended to morphine under the *Dangerous Drugs Act 1920*. The government also had at this time honoured its obligations under the *International Opium Convention of 1912* (the Hague Convention), the international agreement to limit the use of opium, morphine and cocaine to 'legitimate purposes'. Despite this early emphasis on extensive cocaine abuse, the prescribing of cocaine to addicts was not included in the Rolleston Committee's terms of reference in the 1920s and did not arise during their enquiry. For over fifty years, between 1930 and 1985, there was no evidence of extensive cocaine use in Britain (Spear and Mott, 1993).

Although London has a large Colombian community of around 50,000, there is little evidence that immigrant Colombians, most of whom work in low-paid jobs, are involved at the British end of the drug supply chain. Latin American communities remain small relative to other ethnic groups and their members still encounter difficulty in passing unremarked in the UK, even in London. In contrast, the ethnic heterogeneity of large US cities like New York and Los Angeles have long provided cover for illicit commerce and the frequent travel needed to effect it. Cocaine trafficking in New York developed rapidly through massive, long-established Hispanic communities that retained strong social and family links with Latin America.

In Britain, British citizens tend to provide cocaine for British users, engaging in *ad hoc* trade with foreign contacts where needed and maintaining external trade links.[13] The indigenous character of British trafficking undermines assumptions, based on the US model, that a multinational Colombian 'mafia' is controlling cocaine imports to the UK. A more homely picture emerges of British criminal entrepreneurs finding another highly-profitable scheme on which to focus their energies. Some conduct their arrangements through European intermediaries, while others appear to have direct contact with Latin American suppliers.

Writing in 1985, Roger Lewis describes the London drugs market – specifically heroin – as 'neither as established nor as violent as that of New York. Business throughout the system...appears to be conducted in a more amateurish fashion.' (Lewis, 1985, p. 47). A more recent and comprehensive study tends to confirm this assumption that the British drug markets do not form a neat hierarchical structure controlled by foreign cartels (Dorn, Murji and South, 1992). British trafficking was found to be fragmented and fluid, containing many simple structures rather than few fixed ones, with stable trafficking organisations containing one or two people, rarely more than five or six, regardless of the amount traded.

Indeed, there is little evidence to suggest that international organised crime has much role in the British case. One particularly strong indicator of this absence has been the fact that almost all the cocaine reaching Britain and much that reaches end-users is of a remarkable purity. Seizures of around 75-90% purity were common in the early 1990s. This fact alone suggests that importers had a direct link with Latin American suppliers and indicated further the absence of an extended supply chain inside Britain.

If cocaine trafficking appears largely to be controlled by British criminals, the same cannot be said of crack. The traffic in crack that takes place within the United Kingdom has become increasingly associated with Jamaicans, a view augmented by often lurid press articles which detail the activities of violent gangs. A wave of ill-informed media articles about its effects and the scale of consumption, strongly influenced by the tone the US media used to discuss crack, started to appear in Britain.[14] Trafficking aside, the use of crack is strongly associated with violence and loss of social control. Heroin use, by contrast, is not. Jamaican traffickers were regarded as having the necessary contacts in the Western Hemisphere to facilitate drugs shipments, combined with links to the British Afro-Caribbean community. In addition, they share a common language with their British contacts and can pass unnoticed in London, for example, in a way that is not possible for Latin Americans, North Americans or most other Europeans.

Much of British intelligence in relation to the Jamaican gangs has been acquired from US sources. In several cases, the same traffickers operate in both countries.[15] With regard to intelligence and surveillance operations, the Metropolitan (London) Police placed considerable emphasis on the role of Afro-Caribbean networks within London's crack distribution system in the late 1980s and early 1990s. In 1987, the police launched a surveillance operation known as Operation Lucy to investigate the existence of Afro-Caribbean involvement in drugs. The officer in charge had spent three months studying organised crime at the Federal Bureau of Investigation (FBI) academy in Washington. The team worked closely with US law enforcement agencies to gain intelligence on which kind of firearms the Jamaicans favoured and the illegal use of passports. In the late 1980s and early 1990s, other regional police forces in Britain also called on US intelligence on crack markets and advice on policing the effects of its use (Silverman, 1994, pp. 196-8).

Yet the number of crack seizures in Britain remains relatively small. In 1994, the police made 2,992 cocaine seizures of which 1,320 involved crack (Home Office Research and Statistics Department, 1995). One indication of how small the market may be came from one senior police officer in the north of England who suspected that undercover police operations to buy crack in one of his areas, in effect, created the main market for the drug. The supply of crack increased in response to demand from police undercover buyers and diminished when the operations was over.[16] Fears that immigrant Jamaican 'mafias' would create a violent, volatile crack market in Britain similar to that existing in New York have not yet been realised. Evidence of some growth in crack use does not fully account for the growth in cocaine imports.

Since the late 1980s, there has been an increasing trend in Britain towards national intelligence-gathering. Britain's local police forces have traditionally had a high degree of autonomy, being formally accountable to local Police Committees of their city or county. The creation of the National Criminal Intelligence Service (NCIS) in 1992 resulted specifically from a recognition of the need to centralise the collation and analysis of data on drugs. Thus, in the UK, the need for law enforcement agencies to tackle the problem of drug trafficking has, to some extent, stimulated the modernisation of policing, particularly with regard to intelligence and financial investigation. Even prior to Operation Lucy, the NCIS's precursor, the National Drugs Intelligence Unit (NDIU), was undertaking such work. NCIS, however, is restricted to the collection, analysis and dissemination of intelligence; individual police services, regional crime squads and customs carry out the operational work.

The current move towards intelligence-gathering favours increased concentration on international links. The commitment to a significant shift in drug policy towards a concentration on intelligence mechanisms was demonstrated in the November 1994 budget, when the government announced that 4,000 jobs would be lost in Customs & Excise (16% of the entire workforce), including 600 'frontline' officers. Several provincial airports no longer have a permanent customs presence and are covered by rapid-response teams operating from regional offices and acting on central intelligence.[17]   Law enforcement in Britain is increasingly focused on strategic targeting of large shipments of drugs and on the detection of organised crime rather than on the detection and arrest of minor dealers. There is more emphasis on such activities as the gathering of information from 'controlled deliveries' where drug shipments are allowed to pass into the country to gain intelligence on their movements and the people involved. Money laundering and the confiscation of assets, particularly appropriate to London's position as a financial centre, have also become priorities. In this regard, Britain shares the current international priorities on drug control.[18]

The interesting development in these policy changes was the increasing focus on cocaine. In effect, the official reaction to the threat of cocaine – particularly in the form of crack – helped stimulate some of these changes. The fact that in the late 1980s cocaine was seen as a potential rather than a realised threat and that it had not been traditionally used much in Britain stimulated the need for policymakers to look abroad for advice on how to deal with its effects. When awareness of cocaine increased in the 1980s, fears that crack use would lead to violence gave the need to prevent widespread consumption a particular urgency.

By 1989, British law enforcement was already displaying some concern about cocaine imports. However, in April 1989, Robert Stutman, who was then head of the New York branch of the DEA, arrived in Britain with apocalyptic warnings.[19]   Speaking at a meeting of the Association of Chief Police Officers, he warned that crack-cocaine had devastated New York's social fabric and that its use had led to a massive rise in social deprivation, violence and murder. He counselled British law enforcement agencies to learn from the mistakes of US policymakers in other US cities who had initially tried to ignore New York's crack problem and were now facing the consequences, and he guaranteed that within two years British cities would suffer the same social consequences of crack use that had afflicted US cities.

The speech was simply the most publicised version of a warning that was repeatedly issued in Europe at this time.[20] Stutman's message was not particularly new to the British establishment. Police officers and politicians had been visiting the USA for several years and had received similar messages that US drug problems would be replicated in Europe. This had, for example, led the House of Commons Home Affairs Committee to warn as far back as 1985: 'We believe, from all that we saw and heard, that as the American market becomes saturated the flood of hard drugs will cross the Atlantic.'

One month after the Stutman speech, Home Secretary Douglas Hurd convened an extraordinary meeting of ministers who sit on the Pompidou Group of the Council of Europe to warn them of the cocaine threat. On 24 July, he made a similar speech to the Action on Addiction Conference. Later that month, he made another speech as chairman of the Ministerial Group on the Misuse of Drugs, confirming a promise to host a major international summit in London on ways of reducing demand for drugs, particularly cocaine. This eventually took place in collaboration with the Colombian government and the United Nations in April 1990.

The police agencies were similarly active. Two senior police officers were sent on a tour of New York, Washington, DC, and Boston. Their report recommended that Britain was indeed in a position to learn from US mistakes. US police told them they regretted not putting in place soon enough effective 'intelligence machinery' which could drive arrest and seizure operations. The two officers recommended that such intelligence machinery should be created in the UK.

By the end of 1989, a joint police-customs unit – the Crack Intelligence Co-ordinating Unit – had been established specifically to gather information on crack and cocaine. It was not an operational unit like Operation Lucy. Its purpose was to gather as much data as possible about a drug about which British police realised they knew very little. At this point, police officers admitted they did not even know what crack looked like, let alone how it was traded (Silverman, 1994, p. 112). Stutman's speech did not itself result in a major policy shift. Hurd's recommendations in 1989 on confiscation of assets, increased support for the United Nations work on drugs and aid for law enforcement in Latin America were mechanisms that were either in place or already recommended. Nevertheless, it helped crystallise the importance of the 'cocaine threat'.

It quickly became apparent that cocaine and crack did not pose quite the problems that were anticipated at first and, by August 1990, the Crack Unit had been wound down. Fears of a British crack-cocaine epidemic in the early 1990s have been described as a media-inspired panic created out of hearsay (Bean, 1993, p. 59). Yet, given the increase in seizures, it was not altogether clear at the time that cocaine was not a threat. Moreover, if fears of a British crack epidemic in the late 1980s are characterised as a temporary panic, then it was one naturally reported by the media but not created by them. The media were reporting a strong government response. In addition, given the lack of information available to the British law enforcement agencies, their reaction was rather conscientious and in harmony with their counterparts in Europe. Other governments in Europe and the European Commission were demonstrating similar concern. In 1990, Commission officials opted, as part of the nascent foreign drug policy, to tackle the 'cocaine threat' by offering aid to Colombia and preferential trade access to European markets to all the Andean countries. Other European countries were reacting in a similar way. Italy was also exploring ways of cooperating with the Andean countries (Sciacchitano, 1991).

The effect of this period demonstrates the influence that US perceptions of drug control can have on other governments in a number of areas that include the analysis of drug markets, law enforcement intelligence-gathering and policing methods when governments have to draw on US advice and data for lack of their own. In the 1980s, the USA was seen to prosecute its highly publicised war on drugs, specifically against cocaine. Once the premise was accepted that cocaine was an imminent problem in Europe, it was reasonable for other governments, in the short-term, to witness the social problems occurring in US inner cities and become concerned that this could occur in their own. The USA had extensive experience in implementing specifically anti-cocaine supply reduction policies (whether those policies were successful is not at issue here), which the European governments lacked. That the European governments would call on US expertise was, at least initially, inevitable. Thus, the US perception of cocaine became other countries' perception. Indeed, to some extent, the US view of the Andean countries as the root of the global drug problem became, in the late 1980s and early 1990s, the global view. When President Virgilio Barco came to Europe in 1990 to solicit help for Colombia's fight against drug trafficking, he found many responsive audiences. The European Parliament passed an ambitious resolution calling on the Commission to provide 'sufficient aid and financial resources to enable it [Colombia] to make good the damage which might be caused to the nation' (European Parliament, 1989).

The USA, experiencing a growing awareness that its efforts alone in the Andean countries were not enough to eradicate the drug problem, tried to encourage the participation of other countries. If Europe was to be a major destination for cocaine, it was argued, it was only reasonable to expect a helping hand from European governments in the implementation of supply reduction programmes in the Andes. In 1990, a report to the US

House of Representatives Committee on Foreign Affairs expressed concern that the USA had failed to form a programme to 'sell' the US Andean Strategy to the European Community (EC) and its member states (United States, 1990). President Bush had launched the Andean Initiative in 1989 as the centrepiece of US foreign drug policy. Its objective was to reduce the amount of Latin American cocaine reaching the United States by 60% over a period of 10 years, to be effected by a combination of development programmes, eradication operations and interdiction.[21]   Originally, Washington envisaged that its initial five-year $2.2 billion foreign assistance package would be matched by a similar amount contributed by the countries of Europe. There is no evidence that the European countries either individually or collectively ever seriously considered offering support to the Western Hemisphere on this scale.

Britain's Relations with the Andean Countries on Drugs

British concern about cocaine led the government to look at the Andean region and assess whether there was a need and scope for action there. During the incumbency of Prime Minister Margaret Thatcher, Britain had temporarily turned its attention to political matters in Latin America, as a result of the war with Argentina over the Falkland/Malvinas Islands. Although this was an isolated incident in British-Latin American relations, it nevertheless stimulated the interest of the British government in Latin American affairs – particularly with regard to security matters.

The British response to concerns about cocaine trafficking, however, was directed largely towards Colombia. In the late 1980s, a conjunction of circumstances produced this focus. In the main, the British government perceived drug control in Latin America as a trafficking problem and was less concerned with the complexities of drug production. Like its European counterparts, it did not share the US enthusiasm for 'going to the source', reducing trafficking by means of eradicating coca cultivation. Although not opposed in principle, Britain never intended to become so closely involved with Latin American drug control that such massive projects would become an important concern. Nor was it primarily concerned – as were Germany, Sweden and Norway – with a development response to drug production. Although Britain contributed development funds to the United Nations International Drug Control Programme (UNDCP) for Bolivia, the British government saw bilateral drug-related aid largely in terms of law enforcement cooperation aimed at reducing trafficking rather than drug production. This was demonstrated by the fact that in the late 1980s and early 1990s the lead agency on affairs related to international trafficking was the Home Office. Given that cocaine trafficking from Latin America to Europe was largely being undertaken by Colombians, Colombia's drug problems aroused more interest in London than those of Peru and Bolivia. There were also disincentives for initiating cooperation with Peru and Bolivia. The British government disapproved of Peruvian President Alan García. His decision to withhold repayments on Peruvian foreign debt in the 1980s did not endear him to London.[22] Moreover, like the EC, London did not judge Peru to be an ideal country with which to initiate cooperation on drugs. The granting of assistance was complicated by Peru's increasing tendency to conflate counter-insurgency campaigns and anti-drug operations and the involvement of the military in each (see Chapter 5). With regard to development projects, the presence of *Sendero Luminoso* guerrillas in coca production zones in the Upper Huallaga Valley who were extremely hostile to a foreign presence made such areas dangerous for foreigners. Programmes could not be effectively monitored and evaluated (procedures the British were particularly keen on) if personnel could not even reach them.

Bolivia was seen as a country that required drug-related development aid, and Britain contributed to the UNDCP's alternative development programme, but the strengthening of bilateral relations was seen to be hindered by the parlous state of the Bolivian economy; Britain was less interested in fomenting close bilateral relations with a country that it saw primarily as a destination for development aid. Moreover, Bolivian President Jaime Paz Zamora was cooperating closely with the USA but, internationally, had launched his 'coca diplomacy' initiative in a bid to have coca removed from the list of proscribed substances in the 1961 UN Convention. This bid won Bolivia the rhetorical support of Spanish Prime Minister Felipe González, but did not win approval from the Conservative British government. Had Britain been planning to establish a large and comprehensive anti-drug cooperation strategy in Latin America or one that was more focused on development policies as a means of reducing drug production, Paz's initiative would not have proved much of an hindrance. For a country looking to be useful in small and experimental ways in the field of conventional law enforcement, it was not conducive to cooperation.

Britain's decision to help Colombia, in particular, was also motivated by a wish to support the USA on drugs. During this period, Colombian-US relations on drug policy were close, characterised by a 'convergence of policy perceptions' (Tokatlian, 1988, pp. 143-4). Although they perennially struggled over whether Colombian traffickers could be extradited to the USA, Colombia was increasingly compliant with US wishes on this and other issues and was paying a heavy price in terms of drug-related violence perpetrated by the Medellín cartel, its reward being warm US approval for its willingness to confront drug trafficking (see Chapter 3). British support to Colombia during this period was almost synonymous with support to the USA, at a time when London and Washington's 'special relationship' was at its most intense.

British willingness to be seen assisting the USA in Colombia was not simply an altruistic gesture of support from a sympathetic friend. It had the advantage of helping in a small way to smooth any ruffled US feathers over Britain's stance on drugs and money laundering in its Caribbean dependencies. British-US relations on drug policy in the Western Hemisphere were not confined to concerns about cocaine. As Maingot shows in Chapter 7, for much of the 1980s the two countries were locked in legal and diplomatic disputes and negotiations about extraterritoriality in the Caribbean. Indeed, this was the most important matter in bilateral relations on drugs.[23] By supporting Colombia, Britain could reinforce support for the USA on hemispheric drug control, while strengthening its position in matters related to international drug control.

Britain was not intending to act as a mediator in relations between Colombia and the USA. Such a role would have required a far greater commitment than Britain intended to give. When relations between Colombia and the USA soured after the 1994 election of President Ernesto Samper, neither Britain nor any one of its European counterparts was in a position to mediate individually, although the European Parliament passed a resolution condemning Colombia's decertification in 1996.

Colombia itself was an attractive partner for Britain at this time. Relations between the two countries were warm but, in the words of one British diplomat, 'not full of content'.[24] There was, however, a perceived potential for improvement in trade, although Colombia was not a trading priority for Britain in comparison with other countries in Latin America. In the late 1980s, many potential British investors appeared to be deterred from greater involvement by the violent climate. In 1989, four planned British trade missions were all cancelled owing to lack of interest. Nevertheless, Colombia's traditionally cautious and independent management of economic policy, relative to many of its Latin American neighbours, was a reassuring factor for Britain in relations with Bogotá.

Britain appeared to regard Colombia, notwithstanding its many political problems and social inequities, as fundamentally a decent and democratic state. When Foreign Secretary Geoffrey Howe met President Barco for a working lunch during a visit to Colombia in 1987, he described Colombian democracy as a model for other countries of the region.[25] In addition, Colombia had been the only Latin American country to criticise Argentina for the invasion of the Falkland/Malvinas Islands in 1982 (Ramírez, 1991). This position produced no immediate strengthening in Colombian-British relations but, according to Foreign Office officials, the British prime minister had not forgotten; Colombia's support made her sympathetic to a request for help.[26] The timing was right for cooperation with Colombia because Britain knew and trusted President Barco, who had previously served as ambassador in London. The British considered Barco to be weak on foreign policy. Nevertheless, aware of the degree to which the traffickers had corrupted Colombian politics, the British government judged the President and his immediate advisers to be benign and, crucially, clean.

Colombia had also won the respect of a British government that liked to regard itself as muscular in matters of law and order by its willingness to confront the traffickers. Like Italy, Britain could identify with some of Colombia's domestic political problems. Italy's domestic experience of transnational crime and trafficking made it particularly receptive to the problems faced by the Latin American governments with regard to the containment of politically powerful international criminals. Similarly, Britain had some twenty years experience of combating terrorism and political violence in Northern Ireland, of holding in check domestic forces that threatened state security.[27] The Colombian government faced not only the violence of the drug traffickers, but also the activities of the FARC and ELN guerrilla groups. President Belisario Betancur (1982-86) had attempted to negotiate a peace process and draw the terrorist groups into the mainstream of political life, a strategy with which the British government was sympathetic even if, in the late 1980s, the British public was not in a position to understand the extent of this sympathy.[28] When Colombia later attempted to negotiate with the drug traffickers, Britain could further sympathise with the pragmatism of the approach. Certainly, such negotiations were unlikely to attract opprobrium in London as they had in Washington.

In 1987, Foreign Secretary Geoffrey Howe visited Colombia and told the government there that Britain was willing to supply training and equipment for the fight against drugs. At around the same time, Germany and the Netherlands made similar promises (Ramírez, 1991, p. 60). President Barco's meeting with the British Prime Minister in 1990 was a conspicuous success. The Colombian President had been carefully briefed for the encounter and Thatcher agreed that British bilateral help, promised by Howe, would be immediately forthcoming. On 28 September 1989, Britain announced a package of aid for Colombia worth £11 million to be disbursed over a period of five years. This included money for police training and equipment for the following matters: personal protection, bomb disposal, telecommunications, criminal investigation, customs advice, the creation of a computer database and prison construction. The Royal Navy frigate HMS *Alacrity* – the Navy's Caribbean guard ship – was sent to Cartagena in October and November 1989 to discuss future coordinated efforts with Colombia. Later, a group of Special Air Service (SAS) personnel were temporarily based in Colombia to assist with training.

This level of aid was not forthcoming for either Bolivia or Peru. In the period 1989-91, Britain contributed alternative development funds to Bolivia *via* the UNDCP and made some bilateral aid donations for law enforcement equipment and training. Bilateral drug-related aid to Peru was negligible, and Britain did not contribute to UNDCP programmes in Peru during the period 1989-91. Most of Britain's donations to the UNDCP, however, were being spent in Latin America rather than in other parts of the world. This was a consequence of the UNDCP's interest in Latin America as well as British interest in cocaine trafficking.[29]

Although this was a period of experimentation, there was never a suggestion that Britain would play anything more than a support role in Latin American drug control. When visiting US officials questioned their counterparts on Britain's support for the US Andean Strategy, they were told that Britain would welcome any 'lessons learnt' from the USA before proceeding further (United States, 1990, p. 10). There was no strategic aid plan for drug control; Britain decided that it would respond to specific requests from the Andean governments. In the late 1980s and early 1990s, the Foreign and Commonwealth Office wrote to the British posts in the Andean region at the beginning of every financial year to remind them that bilateral drug-related cooperation funds were available and to ask them to contact local law enforcement agencies to find out what they needed and inform London. The initiative would, therefore, come from Latin America. The British government tended to look for counterparts with which it could work effectively in a practical way, both in police operations and in support for Latin American national drug programmes. Here, there is a clear parallel with the European Commission. The Commission also acted in Latin America on drugs largely at the behest of the Latin American governments and European Non-Governmental Organisations (NGOs), and sought projects with partners with which it could work effectively.

This *ad hoc* bilateral response had certain advantages. Policy could be responsive to changing circumstances and was a useful balance to Britain's contribution to co-ordinating multilateral organisations *via* the EC, the UNDCP, the Council of Europe and the Dublin Group. Latin American governments, however, tended to regard *ad hoc* aid as a sign of a lack of commitment. In as much as British aid was not intended to be much more than a token gesture of support, this perception was correct. However, Foreign Ministry officials in Colombia, Bolivia and Peru tended to believe that more frequent formal contact with the Europeans might have acted as an engine of increased cooperation, which was less likely.

The lack of a strategic plan was in keeping with the view that Britain was in no position to offer much more than a gesture of solidarity with both the USA and the Andean governments on drug control. At no point was it ever thought that Britain would do more than offer a small but effective contribution and some political influence. It was not envisioned that the high level of aid to Colombia would be permanent, although a more enduring form of cooperation was not ruled out, dependent on results. There was a balance to be struck between the experimental nature of the cooperation and the knowledge, from the start, that Britain as an independent actor would not expend the resources to take a leading role in Andean drug control.

On an international level, Britain organised the World Ministerial Summit to Reduce Demand for Drugs and to Combat the Cocaine Threat which took place in London on 9-11 April 1990. Colombia played a prominent role. The opening speeches were made by the British Prime Minister, UN Secretary-General Javier Pérez de Cuéllar and President Barco. The conference was intended to provide encouragement to Colombia and the other Latin American governments. The US delegation did not take a prominent position. Moreover, the conference concentrated on demand reduction, thus responding to calls from the Latin American countries and the UN that developed countries take seriously their own responsibility for consumption. The unusually specific summit title addresses two matters that appear at first glance to be incongruous: policies that reduce the demand for all illicit drugs; and discussion of how trafficking in one particular drug (cocaine) from a specific area of the world may be addressed. The juxtaposition of these two themes, however, is an important indicator of concerns in 1989-90, neatly encapsulating US-inspired concern about Latin American cocaine, and the fact that the rhetoric of shared responsibility and the importance of demand reduction had become important.

Conclusions

Britain, like France and its other European counterparts, was receptive to

US warnings about the possibility of an influx of cocaine to Europe largely because little was known about the drug in Europe either in terms of its consumption or trafficking. US perceptions of cocaine trafficking in the Andes were extremely influential in the late 1980s and early 1990s when Britain was first taking decisions about how to react to an incipient cocaine threat. By 1995, however, it had become apparent that US circumstances would not be replicated in Europe.

Like the European Commission, and other EU member states, Britain saw drug cooperation with the Andean countries as an experimental initiation into global drug cooperation. Britain's bilateral response was partly responsive to US and UN attempts to call attention to the need for greater international cooperation among states to stem trafficking. It was also, however, a way of improving British influence on international drug control generally, and a means of ensuring that Britain was in a position to influence the direction taken at international drug control meetings. Moreover, unlike the European Commission, Britain was motivated as much by a willingness to be seen supporting the USA, the principal actor in international drug control, as by a willingness to assist the Latin American governments. Although sharing many of the attitudes of EU member states, in its bilateral relations with the Andean countries Britain largely saw itself as an independent actor, and was not much concerned about contributing to a European position.

Britain gave more drug-related aid to Colombia than to other Andean countries and, although willing in principle to make it permanent if results were satisfactory, never really anticipated that it would be much more than a symbolic gesture of moral support for Colombia and for the USA. Even though Britain was sympathetic to the US view of drug control – and at times the political rhetoric mirrored US rhetoric very closely indeed – Britain had an attitude towards Andean drug control that was fundamentally European, in seeing cooperation as largely a matter for law enforcement and development rather than as a major security threat. Britain and the other European countries that offered bilateral drug-related aid to Colombia and the other Andean countries were untrammelled by the sort of powerful domestic political imperatives that conditioned the US approach.

Notes

1. Quoted in Wagstaff and Maynard (1988), p. 1.
2. *The Guardian*, 19 March 1996, p. 5.
3. Quoted in Silverman (1994), p. 109.

4. Illicit drugs are classed under the *Misuse of Drugs Act* 1971 as Class A, Class B, or Class C. Conviction for possession and use of Class A drugs carry higher sentences than the other categories and, as well as cocaine, they include heroin, other opiates, LSD and MDMA, also known as Ecstasy. Class B drugs include cannabis (marijuana), barbiturates and most amphetamines.

5. Wagstaff and Maynard (1988), p. 83. This study found that the 'fundamental problem facing the Government in its deliberation on drug control measures is the paucity of information on the subject'.

6. Crack is a smokable form of cocaine, created with the addition of an alkali, such as sodium bicarbonate (baking powder), ammonia or caustic soda. It should not be confused with *basuco*, smoked in Latin America, which is essentially a low-quality coca paste that has not completed the manufacturing process that would transform it into cocaine hydrochloride. The smoking of crack, also known as freebasing, has only become prevalent since the late 1980s.

7. Interviews, 1995.

8. The only national estimates on cannabis consumption derived from regularly collected data are those of the British Crime Survey (BSC). This survey is conducted on a face-to-face interview basis and the questions on use are posed in the context of a survey on offences; it is not, therefore, considered a reliable basis for estimating the number of drug users (Wagstaff and Maynard, 1988).

9. Bean notes that in 1991 the UK price of cocaine was £80 ($120) per gram offering an effect that lasted 20-30 minutes, while the price of amphetamines was £12-15 ($18-23) per gram, offering an effect that lasted three to four hours (Bean, 1993, p. 74).

10. In practice, notification data refer almost exclusively to opiate/opioid addicts. Studies in London have estimated that only one in five daily opiate users is notified. Whether this multiplier can be applied nationally is unknown.

11. Heroin was the primary drug of approximately half of the total number of clients. Some 15% reported methadone as the primary drug; 11% amphetamines; 7% cannabis; 4% benzodiazepines; and just 3% cocaine.

12. This section draws on a more detailed account of cocaine's historical role in British drug policy in Spear and Mott (1993).

13. In July 1990, Eddie Richardson, a notorious South London gangland villain of the 1960s, was convicted of attempting to smuggle 153 kilos of cocaine through Southampton docks, at the time the largest cocaine haul ever made in Britain (Silverman, 1994, pp. 211-18). In

November 1995, two British men received 30-year jail sentences after they shipped almost 800 kilos of cocaine to London from Venezuela (*The Guardian*, 25 November 1995). A Manchester man, Joseph Kasser, was jailed for 24 years in 1994 for a similar operation after he set up an import/export company in Caracas, Venezuela, as a front for his operation. A Midlands man involved in the same case reportedly aroused suspicion when it was noticed that he was running a Bentley, a Rolls Royce, two private jets and a deep-sea diving boat while selling second-hand cars from a forecourt in Middlesborough (*The Sunday Times*, 16 January 1994).

14. During 1994, *The Sunday Times* regularly printed arresting stories under such headlines as 'Drug trials stopped by Yardie rule of terror' (17 April) and 'Babies born addicted to crack as epidemic sweeps Britain' (10 July).

15. See Silverman's account of Jamaican involvement in British cocaine trafficking, and its links with US trafficking (Silverman, 1994).

16. Interview, 1995.

17. *The Independent*, 30 November 1994, p. 12.

18. The legislation implements the provisions of the 1988 Vienna Convention and the 1990 Council of Europe Convention on Laundering, Search, Seizure and Confiscation of Proceeds from Crime. Under the *Drug Trafficking Offences Act 1986*, the Crown Court is required to impose a confiscation order on every person convicted of a drug trafficking offence who has received any payment or reward in connection with drug trafficking at any time. The Act also provides powers to enable the assets of traffickers to be traced and restrained. Money laundering is criminalised under this Act and the *Criminal Justice (International Co-operation) Act 1990*, which also permits the forfeiture of drug trafficking money being imported or exported from the United Kingdom. The *Criminal Justice Act 1993* strengthens these confiscation procedures and creates a range of new drug money laundering offences designed to enable the United Kingdom to implement fully the 1991 EC Money Laundering Directive.

19. For a more detailed account of the consequences of Stutman's visit, see Bean (1993), pp. 59-75.

20. The speech was reportedly dismissed by one criminologist as 'one of the most ill-informed and irresponsible pieces of writing on the subject' (Silverman, 1994, p. 118).

21. The USA would provide $1.1 billion in economic aid and $1.04 billion in military and law enforcement aid to the governments of

Bolivia, Colombia and Peru for the 1990-94 period, thus increasing US economic support to the Andean region on an unprecedented scale.

22. Interview, Foreign and Commonwealth Office, London, October 1992.

23. In the 1980s, the emergence of British dependencies like the Cayman Islands as prime centres for the laundering of drug profits created friction between London and Washington. The tension was only partly resolved through the successful negotiation in 1984 of a *Mutual Legal Assistance Treaty* (MLAT) for the Cayman Islands, the first MLAT that Britain had ever signed, and limited (at Britain's demand) to drug-related cases (Gilmore, 1990a; Nadelmann, 1993, pp. 356-67). However, the complex legal and diplomatic demands of extraterritoriality, of balancing the US need to gain access to evidence held in another country for its own drug investigations against Britain's duty to protect the sovereignty of its dependencies' laws, ensured that US-British relations on drug control in the Caribbean remained an abiding source of potential friction.

24. Interview, Foreign and Commonwealth Office, London, October 1992.

25. *El Espectador*, 4 April 1987.

26. Interviews, Foreign and Commonwealth Office, London, September/October, 1992.

27. British officials were not the only Europeans to cite counter-terrorism as an experience they shared with Colombia: one French drug control officer reportedly cited his own country's experience in Algeria as a point of reference in its relations with Colombia (Sauloy and Le Bonniec, 1994, p. 142).

28. According to former Irish Prime Minister Garret Fitzgerald, successive British governments from 1971 negotiated secretly with the Irish Republican Army (IRA) and Sinn Fein (*The Independent*, 13 July 1996, p. 17).

29. For UNDCP projects ongoing in 1994, Britain had contributed $11.5 for Latin America, $1.3 million for Africa and $2.3 million for Asia (United Nations, 1995).

CHAPTER 9

CONCLUSIONS

Elizabeth Joyce

In recent years, those involved in international illicit drug production and trafficking have been described variously as entrepreneurs in a vast multinational business or as a security threat, opponents in a drug war waged by the community of nations and led by the USA.[1] Such labels matter. They help define perceptions and determine policy. They have their limitations, however, as the chapters in this book amply demonstrate.

The term 'drug war' as a description of policies aimed at suppressing the trade in drugs became common currency in the 1980s when US President Ronald Reagan (1980-89) undertook to tackle a perceived drug abuse epidemic in the USA and declared drug trafficking a national security issue.[2] Few metaphors better describe official recognition of an urgent problem that threatens law and order and government's willingness to assume responsibility for dealing with it. It was not only in the USA that drug policy in the 1980s was discussed in the emotive terms of combat. The European Union (EU) donated drug-related aid to Latin America as part of a *Campaign* against Drug Abuse. Former Colombian President Virgilio Barco (1988-90) launched a *lucha contra la droga* in 1989 in response to the assassination by drug traffickers of presidential candidate Luis Carlos Galán. The British government organised a summit with the United Nations in 1990 to discuss how governments and Non-Governmental Organisations (NGOs) might best *combat* the cocaine threat. Governments routinely, and in many different contexts, have talked of the *fight* against drugs.

For the United States, recent extensive deployment of the military in drug control has made the drug war appear less an analogy and rather a literal description of policy. By 1996, the Department of Defense (DoD) had spent more than $7 billion on counter-narcotics operations since 1989, when Congress formally ordered the participation of the military in drug control, a change that had been resisted by the DoD for much of the 1980s. Most of these operations have been carried out within the USA, raising questions about the extent to which the military can become involved in domestic law enforcement without violating one of the basic tenets of US civil-military relations, the constitutional prohibition on army participation in domestic arrests, searches and seizures enshrined in the *Posse Comitatus Act* of 1878.

The USA has also actively encouraged the participation of Latin American armed forces in drug control. Contrary to popular perception, military spending on drug control increased dramatically during President Clinton's first term in office (1993-97). The DoD's budget for counter-drug operations in 1997 was more than double its 1989 level.[3] President Clinton also appointed the first military man, a retired four-star general, to the civilian post of 'drug czar', director of the administration's Office of National Drug Control Policy.

The 'drug war', officially used to embrace all aspects of drug policy, implicitly emphasises policies designed to suppress the supply of illicit drugs. However, those who would reduce drug use must address a far more complex set of policies than the military strategies implied by a drug war. The drug war analogy is a crude representation of what drug policy actually involves. Such metaphors are also at odds with the thinking of those who stress priorities in drug control other than a strict emphasis on arresting traffickers and seizing drug supplies. The notion of a state-sponsored war, even a metaphorical one, can be incongruous in the context of the complex social circumstances produced by drug cultivation and consumption, and the benefits of considering official opposition to any transnational criminal phenomenon as a war are largely limited to quick-fix rhetoric. Perhaps the greatest logical error that can be produced by conceiving of drug control as a 'war' is to raise the expectation that there is a finite goal in prospect, that of victory, whether over drug consumption itself or over the individuals who facilitate it. Recent studies that weigh the costs and benefits of international drug policy to the USA stress broadly the need to think in terms of incremental and marginal adjustment to existing regulations (Riley, 1996; Stares, 1996).

Also inconsistent with the waging of war is an increasing awareness that international responsibility for drug trafficking must be shared among nations; that while the effects of drug trafficking may vary from country to country, states are fundamentally interdependent in the way they have to implement international controls of that traffic. There is more concern about the ease with which traffickers can transfer their profits around the international financial system and a new concentration on means to oppose this. Since the Vienna Convention entered into force in 1990, states have implemented more measures to increase international policy coordination in their attempts to control such complex facets of the drug business as money laundering. They have also become concerned about the criminal manipulation of otherwise legitimate economic activities for the purpose of drug production and trafficking. International controls have been introduced to monitor the global trade in the licit chemicals that are required to process the raw materials of drug production.

Given these circumstances, there are several advantages in thinking of the global traffic in illicit drugs as a multinational trade and in discussing the characteristics in economic terms rather than in the security terms implied by the use of the term 'drug war'. Drug trafficking is, quite literally, a multinational trade. To consider it thus is simply to use an accurate descriptive term, without implying any particular policy response. It is appropriate to contemporary considerations of economic globalisation and liberal trade regimes and emphasises the importance of transnational non-state actors. It gives due prominence to the fact that the vast profits that accrue from illegal drug trafficking present a valuable resource in other forms of transnational crime. Thinking of drug cartels in terms analogous to consideration of multinational enterprises (MNEs) can be useful when it helps policymakers focus more clearly on the financial aspects of drug control, when it assists understanding of economic considerations in the drug trade and when it underscores the complexity of the operations involved.

Successful traffickers have undoubted financial expertise and are skilled at arranging product distribution and marketing. The analogy can be furthered. Why not describe the Fuerzas Armadas Revolucionarias de Colombia (FARC) guerrilla movement as a sub-contractor in certain circumstances if such a description provides insight in analysis? It might even be useful to discuss Latin American penetration of the European drug market in terms of corporate clusters, networks, joint ventures and marketing agreements. It is essential, however, not to lose sight of the limitations of such exercises. No other multinational trade has consequences as broad and profound for the Latin American countries considered here as the illicit drug business. Moreover, the effects of efforts to *control* illicit drug production and trafficking are also important.[4]

Latin American concerns as expressed in the foregoing chapters can be divided into two broad categories. First, there are the primary effects of the drug trade; the threat it poses to institutional integrity, security, stability, international prestige, public health and moral values. Second, there are concerns about policy and the effect that drug control has on Latin Americans, including the distorting effect on policy of foreign pressure, although it is not always accurate to attempt to draw a clear line between the effects of the drug trade and those of drug control. The authors in this volume point out the negative effects of both the drug trade and anti-drug policies.

Latin American Concerns

Although the illicit drug trade poses for Latin American governments many problems similar to those addressed by their US and European counterparts, their drug concerns are not coterminous. The drug trade poses a literal threat to security, as well as to social and political stability, in several Latin American countries. There are also incentives to control the drug trade other than as a response to US pressure. Some countries' international political standing depends partly on their ability to convince foreign counterparts that they are not hostages to violent organised crime. Moves to more market-oriented economies have made it more vital to assure foreign investors of the integrity of the governments they deal with and the safety of their investments and personnel. Increasing intra-regional trade and the mechanics of regional integration mean the countries must convince their partners that the drug problem will not be exported. Governments and citizens of the countries within the Andean region and Mexico, and various sectors of society within those countries, react in dissimilar ways and with varying degrees of intensity to the disparate consequences of drug production and trafficking. Bolivia's role in the drug trade is significantly different from that of Panama or Colombia, as are the official policies formulated to address it. As Atkins (Chapter 4) and Lerner (Chapter 5) demonstrate, many of the problems coca production generates in Bolivia are unlike those created by its production in Peru. Public reaction to these activities can depend to a great extent on the geographical and political context. Yet in light of these inevitable variations, the most striking feature of these studies is the similarity between the consequences of drug production and trafficking in each of these countries.

What emerges from the studies here is that the most damaging threat that the drug trade poses in many Latin American countries is to the integrity of state institutions. Damage results directly from the widespread corruption of state employees, bribed or threatened to act in ways conducive to the exercise of the trade. The judiciary, the police and the military are vulnerable, but the legislature and the executive can also be dangerously corrupted.[5] Such corruption of individuals occurs in all societies. Yet in countries like Colombia, drug traffickers, potentially the country's 'dominant economic group' (Thoumi, 1992, p. 70), have the capacity to wreak havoc in the political system. As Atkins (Chapter 4), Toro (Chapter 6) and Maingot (Chapter 7) make clear, such destructive capacity from the cumulative effect of an extremely high number of acts of corruption also exists in Bolivia, Mexico and the Caribbean. Even when allegations are untrue, the mere perception of corruption is hazardous, since it can weaken government legitimacy and undermine real achievements in institution-building. Political activity in all the countries studied here has been profoundly affected by the drug problem. Drug-related corruption of the legislature occurs. And, corruption aside, as Atkins points out in the case of Bolivia, the indirect repercussions arising from drug-related scandals in countries in which the drug trade and its control is a dominant political theme can include damaging intra-party schism, and political cleavage so fierce that it can impede and even prevent normal political and legislative business.

The sheer volume of criminal activity generated by the drug trade has threatened to overwhelm already weak state institutions in all the countries analysed here. In the case of Mexico, Toro argues, one of the most damaging effects of the drug trade has been the undermining of an already weak criminal justice system. Melo in Chapter 3 makes a similar point with regard to Colombia: a criminal justice system that was already incapable of operating efficiently in the 1950s and 1960s was all but destroyed by the burden of investigating and prosecuting drug-related crime. Such deterioration affects the institution's capacity to operate in other areas and has the secondary damaging effect of reducing public confidence in the institution's credibility. The diversion of valuable resources from other sectors further weakens state capacity. The inevitable result is an erosion of civil rights. Military institutions and the police are also placed *in extremis* by the overwhelming demands of drug control.[6] The corruption that afflicts other state institutions infects them also; and, in addition, deployment of these institutions has, in numerous well-documented incidents, eroded citizens' civil and human rights. Illegal violence perpetrated by state institutions as well as by drug traffickers and their paramilitary groups has been the result.

The threat to public life analysed in these chapters is linked to perceptions of the drug trade's legitimacy during a period of extremely rapid social change, particularly in the 1980s. In Chapter 3, Melo describes the changes that the success of the drug trade has wrought in the social attitudes and moral values of many Colombians. Atkins in Chapter 4 notes how drug control operations in Bolivia have created a division between government and population in a country where the cultivation of coca is a traditional occupation and where coca growers enjoy a certain amount of popular support. The debt crisis of the 1980s and the collapse of international commodity prices, particularly for tin and coffee, helped stimulate the Latin American drug trade. By 1990, 40% of the population in Latin America was living in poverty (IRELA, 1993, p. 13). The impact of economic stabilisation and adjustment programmes provided a ready labour supply for the drug trade as GDP stagnated and incomes fell. In several countries, Peru and Bolivia in particular, the drug trade acted as an economic buffer, providing alternative sources of income when other options were foreclosed. The debt crisis led governments to reduce already limited social services. Hyperinflation attacked the salaries of public sector workers, leaving them vulnerable to corruption by traffickers. Moreover, the 1980s considerably worsened income distribution in most Latin American countries, fomenting general disillusionment with social and political systems and severely undermining state legitimacy. This has often made involvement in the drug trade seem less an exercise in lawlessness and more a rational form of self-help.

The second set of perceptions about the drug trade that Latin Americans share centre on resentment of the US role. Toro, in Chapter 6, argues that one of the main objectives of Mexican drug policy has been to minimise US interference in this regard. This resentment is based on awareness that the main aim of US foreign drug policy is to prevent a supply of illicit drugs reaching the US market and that, in furtherance of this aim, the Latin American governments are subject to serious pressure to pursue anti-drug policies that might not always be the most appropriate responses to the problems that the drug trade creates for the Latin American countries. The social consequences of illicit drug abuse in the USA and Europe are not the overriding concerns of Latin American governments.

The US Role in Western Hemisphere Drug Control

Several of the authors in this volume analysed illicit drug production, trafficking, and control in terms of their effects on the countries of Latin America, rather than in terms of the success or failure of drug control as part of US foreign policy. They have also demonstrated that Latin American drug control policies can never be fully disaggregated from those of their northern neighbour. The drug trade in Latin America is fuelled by US demand for cocaine; drug control in Latin America is largely driven by the imperative that cocaine must be prevented from penetrating US borders. US policies, strategies, and even perceptions tend to prevail in Western Hemisphere drug control,[7] and it is worth examining here the framework which defines this approach.

The countries of Latin America – principally Bolivia, Colombia, and Peru – supply most of the world's cocaine and this fact helps define their relations with the world's largest consumer of cocaine, the USA.[8] Despite the fact that European cocaine seizures soared in the early 1990s, Europe remains a relatively small market for cocaine (see Chapter 1). Although concern among European policymakers and law enforcement agencies during the last ten years has increased and there is a certain willingness to offer assistance to the Latin American countries, EU countries do not regard the Latin American drug problem as their main priority, given the greater predilection among European consumers for other drugs produced elsewhere in the world. In terms of international drug control, the need for EU law enforcement agencies to tackle transnational criminal links with Eastern and Central Europe is a vital new challenge, and European countries will increasingly invest resources in assistance to those countries. The USA will remain, therefore, by far the single most important foreign actor in Latin American drug control.

The 'grand strategy' of US drug policy has been that drugs must be prevented from reaching consumers in the USA (Walker, 1995, p. 300). This principle has twin pillars: control at the source of production and interdiction. Interdiction in the Caribbean and at the borders has not succeeded in preventing drugs from entering the USA. In Chapter 6, Toro argues that US interdiction efforts may have *encouraged* trafficking and increased the net amount successfully smuggled by removing smaller competing operators from the drug trade. While US law enforcement was occupied with capturing the less efficient traffickers, those willing to invest greater resources (and thus expecting greater profits) were operating at a lower risk. Although such assertions are hard to prove, their plausibility, given the other known conditions of the Latin American drug trade, demonstrates the need to look at the wider picture.

In addition to interdiction within and at its own borders and in international waters, the USA attempts to reduce the flow of illicit drugs reaching US consumers through cooperation with countries where drugs are produced or traded in large quantities. This influence is intended to maximise the ability of those countries to prevent the production and export of drugs. Pressure is effected by a panoply of bilateral means ranging from the unreservedly positive (the promise of aid, diplomatic support and other benefits) to the negative (the threat of trade sanctions, aid withheld and international opprobrium). A supporting pillar of US drug diplomacy, which helps give the impression that a strong state is not bullying some weaker states, has been the promotion of multilateral drug control regimes and institutions, particularly the Vienna Convention.

The US Certification Process

Some ten years have elapsed since the USA introduced the practice of judging annually the effectiveness of other countries' drug control efforts and making US relations with those countries conditional upon the results. Over this decade, the 'certification' ritual has become an established means of persuading countries to conform to US drug control criteria and the process lends an annual rhythm to international drug control. Countries regarded by the USA as major drug producing or transit countries are examined for their efficiency in drug control during the previous year. If their efforts are judged to have been unsatisfactory, the offending countries are 'decertified'. This may render them ineligible for US aid and invoke a US boycott on loans from multilateral institutions such as the International Monetary Fund (IMF) and the Inter-American Development Bank (IDB).[9] Each March, the State Department publishes with the certification results its annual *International Narcotics Control Strategy Report*, a 500-page document which summarises on a country-by-country basis what has been gathered from the various US agencies involved in foreign drug control about the state of illicit drug production, trafficking and control in almost every country in the world, regardless of whether they are under scrutiny for certification. The outcome of the US certification procedure is awaited with far more attention worldwide than the deliberations of the UN's International Narcotics Control Board (INCB), whose annual report provides a more disinterested summary of global drug control.

The criteria for certification as set out in the presidential memorandum that accompanies the report is for those countries that 'have cooperated fully with the United States, or taken adequate steps on their own, to achieve full compliance with the goals and objectives of the [UN Vienna Convention]' (US Dept. of State, 1996, p. xii). The impression that the USA is acting as a self-appointed global drugs officer is deceptive. The decision to invoke the Vienna Convention rather than US standards of drug control was made some time after the certification procedure had been designed and was intended to give a veneer of multilateralism to a procedure that essentially responded to domestic US political demands, so that it might then be more attractive to the international community.[10] Notwithstanding the reference to the international regimes of drug control, success is measured by the degree to which a certified country works with the USA on US policy objectives, that is, reduction of the supply of illicit drugs to the US market.

This concern with US drug control objectives explains why the certification procedure weighs more heavily on the Latin American countries than on drug-producing countries in other regions; the Andean countries and Mexico, in particular, are judged to be the main external providers of illicit drugs to the USA and, therefore, in terms of US drug supply, the principal security threat. The degree and quality of 'leverage' – the ability to influence the formulation and implementation of other governments' drug policy – is the direct measure of success. As one senior US official told a House of Representatives Select Committee:

> The Colombian system is sophisticated enough so that putting money into military assistance, the army, the air force of Colombia, we could hope to leverage those institutions who are sometimes reluctant, not used to fighting narcotics traffickers, leverage those institutions into moving against narcotics traffickers...We have helped to leverage, move the Colombian military into acting against the narcotics industry.[11]

The perceived power of certification has also become far greater over time for the countries of Latin America because, since 1995, there has been the real possibility that they might fail to meet the criteria. The threat became immediate after March 1995 when Bolivia, Colombia and Peru were subject to the intermediate classification of being conditionally certified only on grounds of US national interest. One year later, Colombia was completely decertified.

Despite the rhetoric of the procedure, certification has not made drug control the main determinant in the USA's bilateral relations with other countries. Drug control is hardly ever the greatest priority in US relations with other countries (Colombia is perhaps the one exception in this regard). The decision to decertify does not usually depend on the perceived quality of a country's drug control alone. All aspects of a country's relations with the USA condition the decision. Drug control quality is seldom the deciding factor. Decertified countries tend already to have poor relations with the USA, often having pariah or near-pariah status independent of their relative indifference to drug control. In 1995, the decertified countries were Afghanistan, Burma, Iran, Nigeria and Syria (US Dept. of State, 1996). Countries of major importance for reasons other than drug control are usually certified and, in 1995, they included China, Taiwan, Vietnam, Mexico, Panama and Brazil. Countries that are decertified have often been ineffective and indifferent to drug control over a sustained period, but this need not be the case. Judged solely in terms of drug control, Colombia had one of the best records of cooperation on drugs with the USA yet was decertified in 1996. Iran, also decertified, takes a draconian line on drug control.[12] Conversely, many regularly certified countries have, by US criteria, remarkably low-quality drug control.

There are no standard criteria for judging the countries; each case for certification is judged on its own merits. A country stands a better chance of certification if there are other facets to its relations with the USA, which might include important trade ties, the potentially destabilising effect a negative outcome might have on the country concerned, or the need to strengthen general relations, support an unstable regime, or avoid further 'muddying the waters' of a complex but important bilateral relationship. Russia, for example, does not appear on the list of certifiable countries, even though criminal groups there rapidly became heavily involved in the drug trade in the early 1990s, establishing Moscow as an important money-laundering centre and the region as a transhipment point for drugs being shipped to both the USA and Europe (Galeotti, 1995).[13] There are self-evidently more important aspects to US-Russian relations than drug control, but this serves to reinforce the central anomaly in the certification procedure: in its relations with those countries where drug production and trafficking is prevalent, the USA holds the quality of drug control to be the primary feature of bilateral relations only in the absence of other, more important concerns. This occurs in apparent contradiction of the procedure itself which purports to make drug control the overriding consideration in bilateral relations with certifiable countries.

Even in relations with countries where it might be expected that there are fewer other major issues in relations and where it might be expected that drug control would be among the most important, there are other considerations which can prove decisive to certification. In some cases, the certification decision makes this linkage of drug control to other political considerations explicit. In 1996, Paraguay was approved because it was argued that 'a denial of certification could undermine the transition to democracy and weaken support for President Wasmosy's reform process' (US Dept. of State, 1996, p. xlviii). In the same year, the State Department argued that despite the fact that Peru's 'central role as the largest coca producer in the world' expanded in the previous year, 'a denial...would result in a significant disruption of the US roles as one of the guarantors of the Peru-Ecuador peace process, would impede the economic restructuring currently underway in Peru, and reduce US influence in ensuring progress on human rights cooperation' (US Dept. of State, 1996, p. 1). The risks associated with denying certification were judged to be greater than the risks associated with Peru's failure to cooperate fully with the USA to reduce coca cultivation.

Another aspect of the process is that the decisions on all the countries that are judged are linked. The certification procedure is itself a discrete entity, a package that the administration presents to Congress for approval. A decision to certify one country can be influenced by the decision taken on another, although unsurprisingly this linkage is not explicit in the rubric of the decision. In 1996, Colombia's chances of being decertified were closely linked to those of Mexico. Mexico's certification was governed by several important factors other than the quality of its drug control. The quality of drug control in both Mexico and Colombia was causing concern in Washington. US relations with the government of President Samper in Colombia had been strained since he took office in 1994. Drug trafficking across the US-Mexican border had increased rapidly and evidence had emerged of official collusion with drug traffickers at high political levels.[14] In advance of the 1996 presidential elections, the Republican-dominated Congress accused President Clinton of being 'soft' on drugs and the administration needed to be seen taking a hard line on foreign drug control policy in Latin America.[15]

Mexico and Colombia were the two countries that were causing most concern in Congress. Although both had cooperated closely with the USA on drug control over the years, both were facing drug-related political scandals at a high level. The Colombian administration was accused of receiving drug money to fund its election campaign. Mexico had endured a series of complex political scandals that involved, among other things, schism within the ruling party and allegations that senior politicians were linked closely to major Mexican traffickers, the assassination of a presidential candidate, the arrest of the brother of former President Carlos Salinas and alleged corruption in the Attorney-General's office, the institution charged with the investigation of drug trafficking. However, the US administration had to avoid the decertification of Mexico at all costs. Sceptics of the North American Free Trade Agreement (NAFTA) were already critical of policy towards Mexico with regard to the multi-billion dollar US rescue of the Mexican peso in February 1995, and relations with Mexico were a potentially controversial electoral issue on which the administration feared it would be open to criticism. Yet Congress's concern over drugs was such that it would have been impossible to win full congressional approval for both countries and full decertification of Colombia was recommended partly in the hope that this would allow for the full certification of Mexico (US Congressional Research Service, 1996, pp. 23-4).[16]

Approval by Congress naturally depends more on the exigencies of domestic politics than on objective criteria for the judgement of foreign drug control. Such negotiations demonstrate the way in which the mechanics of domestic politics can influence US foreign policy decisions on drugs. However, it should not be understood from this type of bargaining that the various US institutions – Congress and the executive, in particular – are in fundamental disagreement over the basic principles of certification, or about the countries that are decertified. There is a high level of agreement that pressure must be exerted on foreign countries to cooperate on US drug control objectives.[17] Colombia's decertification is a particular case. Unusually, drug control *is* the principal issue in relations between Colombia and the USA. The very fact that there were no other features of US-Colombian relations as important as drug cooperation meant that there was little to save Colombia from US sanctions.

To summarise, the certification process encapsulates US foreign relations on drugs in several ways. It is an indication of the pressure that the USA is prepared to exercise in order to persuade other countries to comply with its drug control objectives. The procedure is intended to serve as a warning to countries Washington judges are liable to control drugs with anything less than the commitment the USA considers appropriate, that they will be subject to sanctions. However, certification never overrides other foreign policy considerations, and the quality of drug cooperation is only the principal determinant of certification in the absence of other more important issues. Decertification occurs in two discrete circumstances: either as part of a foreign policy package of sanctions against a pariah country, in which the quality of drug control can be almost irrelevant, or where other aspects of US relations with the certifiable country are of little importance.

With the certification procedure the USA places itself at the centre of international cooperation on drugs. Invocation of the Vienna Convention is little more than rhetoric, but the procedure has become one of the focal points of global drug control. The procedure is generally unpopular outside the USA. It creates resentment in those countries subjected to its strictures, for which it is 'the sword of Damocles' (APEP, 1990) in 'societies that do not understand why supposedly cooperative endeavors should be judged unilaterally by the country that created the entire problem in the first place' (Toro, 1992, p. 318). The certification procedure may be effective in that it induces other governments to cooperate more with the USA than they would otherwise have done. However, in as much as such actions are only a means to an end, success can only be judged in terms of the achievement of those objectives, that is, whether a reduction has been effected in the supply of illicit drugs to the US market and whether this, in turn, has reduced demand. Reuter concludes in Chapter 1 that this is unlikely and that any reduction in demand is unlikely to have been the result of foreign drug control efforts to reduce supply.

The Challenge of Transnational Crime

All over the world, fundamental changes in the way nations trade, combined with advances in transport and communications, have helped provide greater opportunities for the smuggling of drugs and other forms of transnational crimes. Already this has changed how drug trafficking and transnational crime are perceived. Latin America began, in the late 1980s, to reevaluate the borders between the public and private sectors and search for ways to generate a trade surplus that would accommodate debt service payments. The policy was to replace inward-looking development by export-led growth and state intervention by market forces (Bulmer-Thomas, 1996, p. 10). The changes were consistent with other moves towards trade liberalisation elsewhere in the world, combined with rapid technological advances in communications which made financial services an important feature of many economies, facilitating the speed and efficiency of global money transfers.[18] The transition to more liberal, market-oriented economies, combined with democratisation in Latin America, may have made drug control in the Western Hemisphere more efficient by stimulating international cooperation. But these changes have improved opportunities for drug producers and traffickers as well as for legitimate enterprise: countries with liberal economies trade more with their neighbours, providing more cover for illicit commerce. Communications that allow a high volume of rapid international financial transactions enhance the efficiency of the drug trade.

In the Western Hemisphere, the implementation of NAFTA in the USA, Canada and Mexico has made cross-border trafficking far easier and has enhanced access to the US drug market. As Toro notes in Chapter 6, air interdiction efforts in the Caribbean led traffickers in the early 1990s to increase the flow of drugs from the Andes to the USA *via* Mexico. A second reason that Mexico became a preferred transit route was that the increasing flow of goods across the US border provides excellent cover for illicit flows. Every day, some 1,700 commercial vehicles cross the border from Ciudad Juárez alone (IRELA, 1996). US law enforcement agencies are unable to cope with the growth in commercial traffic. NAFTA has resulted in a 50% increase in the number of trucks crossing the frontier. However, in the early 1990s, even prior to NAFTA, US Customs only had the capacity to inspect a maximum of 15% of vehicles coming from Mexico.[19]

Awareness of the importance of such changes has already provided much of the inspiration for the creation of a set of international regimes that would allow greater international cooperation in drug policy. To some extent, there has been limited international consensus on the need for cooperation on drug control since the turn of the century (Walker, 1996). For the last decade, governments and NGOs have argued that there should be 'shared responsibility' among nations for addressing the related problems of illicit drug production, transnational drug trafficking and consumption. Latin American governments have been particularly prominent in this regard. The effort has produced more than rhetoric. The UN Vienna Convention which, when first proposed by Venezuela, many thought impossible to draft let alone implement, has resulted in real progress in operations against drug trafficking and related crime.[20]

The challenge is how to encourage licit transnational commerce while maintaining some control over transnational crime. US officials often discuss the 'restoration' of borders as a means to offering protection against transnational crime (Andreas, 1996, p. 53). The USA's border to the south has never traditionally offered protection against transnational crime, drug-related or otherwise. If NAFTA expands and deepens, transnational crime in the Western Hemisphere will inevitably expand, even if, as Reuter suggests, the boom period in the Latin American cocaine industry is over. The question is how perceptions of this growth shape US policy towards Latin America. Effective regulation in these circumstances may have to involve a more cooperative and collaborative relationship on drug control between the USA and its neighbours inspired by necessity. This will involve the reevaluation of transnational crime as something from which no region can be entirely protected.

Notes:

1. The community of nations consists of all the signatories to the 1988 *UN Convention against Illicit Traffic in Narcotics and Psychotropic Substances* (the Vienna Convention).
2. The link between security and US drug policy is not new. The connection between drug trafficking and national security can be traced back to the 1930s and the ambition of Harry J. Anslinger, head of the Federal Bureau of Narcotics (FBN) to find for the FBN a support role in the struggle against Communism (Nadelmann, 1993). The first US

'war on drugs' was declared by President Richard Nixon in 1968 and resulted in, among other things, the establishment of several offices for drug policy coordination and enforcement, including the Drug Enforcement Administration (DEA) in 1973. President Reagan issued National Security Decision Directive No. 221 on 8 April 1986, which defined drug production and trafficking as a threat to US national security and the security of the Western Hemisphere in general.

3. In 1989, the DoD's counter-drug appropriation was $438 million; for fiscal year 1997, Congress granted $947 million, a 16% increase on the previous year. See: *The Washington Post*, 29 Nov. 1996, p. A30.

4. The two ideas were conveniently embodied in the way in which the two best known Latin American trafficking cartels were popularly described in the late 1980s and early 1990s: the Medellín cartel posed a violent threat to the Colombian state and warranted the waging of a war to control its actions while later the Cali cartel was seen as having a reputation for discretion, financial acumen, organisational efficiency as an international business operation, eligible for the title of MNE. From this perspective, the Cali cartel was interpreted as being another Coca-Cola or IBM. Like the war metaphors, these images draw their power from the fact that they can, in some ways, be applied literally as well as analogously.

5. It is worth noting in this discussion of such matters in Latin America that no country is immune to the potential corruption of state employees by the drug trade. In June 1995, the USA announced the indictment of 59 individuals allegedly in the pay of the Cali cartel, including a former US Assistant Attorney General, two former federal prosecutors and the ex-chief of the Office of International Affairs at the US Department of Justice (IRELA, 1995, pp. 4-5).

6. Like the US military, the Latin American armed forces were initially reluctant to become involved in drug control arguing, *inter alia*, that it distracted them from counter-insurgency operations (WOLA, 1991).

7. Chapter 8 argues that this can also be the case in Europe.

8. Although marijuana and opium poppy are also cultivated in Latin America, particularly in Mexico, Colombia and Guatemala, cocaine remains the principal export drug. There is concern among law enforcement agencies about the spread of drug trafficking to countries where hitherto drug production and trafficking were less prevalent. This trend suggests that countries other than those in the Andes and Mexico will increasingly be forced to spend limited state resources on implementing drug control policies. Illicit drugs have long been shipped through Mexico, Central America and the Caribbean to the

USA, but other countries, including Brazil, Chile and Venezuela, are experiencing a rise in drug trafficking.

9. Decertification has three compulsory consequences. They are: 1) the suppression of 50% of bilateral aid, with the exception of some humanitarian and drug control aid; 2) a negative vote for loans in six international financial bodies, including the IDB and the World Bank; and 3) denial to US exporters of access to Export-Import Bank credits to finance sales to the country in question, and refusal to investors of access to Overseas Private Investment Corporation (OPIC) credit (IRELA, 1996, p. 38).

10. As one senior Congressional aide notes: 'Several years ago we shifted the certification process in favour of tying certifications to 1988 UN Convention so that it would be less US-oriented' (US Congressional Research Service, 1996, p. 9).

11. Comments of Deputy Assistant Secretary of State for Inter-American Affairs Michael Skol (United States, 1989, p. 9).

12. Arguing that the government of Iran maintains 'extremely vigorous' drug control policies that include massive forcible eradication of illicit crops, large seizures of drugs, the execution of drug traffickers and the arrest of drug users, one analyst told a US Senate hearing that the USA 'decertified Iran because basically we don't like the country's leadership; we don't like their policies'. A former senior State Department official agreed 'that there is a tendency to focus on countries like Iran. It's easy. You up your quota of decertification by adding countries that don't matter anyway and everybody hates' (US Congressional Research Service, 1996, pp. 12, 21).

13. Galeotti quotes the chair of Russia's parliamentary Security Committee's estimate that organised crime controls 55% of capital in Russia, 80% of all voting stock, and 15-25% of the nation's banks.

14. As the US decision approving Mexico at the beginning of 1996 made clear, drug-related corruption was causing concern: the brother of former President Salinas had been arrested and was under investigation for a variety of drug-related charges; other charges had been made against current or former officials; and 19 federal police officers were arrested for complicity in a multi-ton shipment in Baja California.

15. The notion of being 'soft' on drugs refers to what Congress perceived as unacceptably high federal spending on demand reduction policies and community policing programmes within the USA, which President Clinton had championed. To many Republican members of Congress not only was this evidence of an insufficiently tough approach to drug control, it also smacked of the 'Big Government' they had committed

themselves to eliminating. Demand reduction programmes presented for approval to Congress were consistently cut in the preceding year, eventually making untenable the position of former New York police commissioner Lee Brown as head of the Office of National Drug Control Policy. He was replaced in February 1996 by General Barry McCaffrey, former commander of Southcom and the first military official to occupy the post of 'drug czar'. Thus did the President seek to assuage Congress. This effort was also extended to foreign drug policy: a hard-line approach to foreign drug control would assuage the demands of Congress at little cost to the administration.

16. The US administration again recommended Mexico's full certification in 1997, despite the arrest just 10 days before the decision, of the country's top counter-narcotics official, General Jesús Gutiérrez Rebollo, on charges that he had accepted bribes from Amado Carrillo Fuentes, a Mexican trafficker. Colombia was decertified in 1997 for the second time.

17. The exception was the country desk officers at the State Department for whom any such dispute is, to some degree, a failure for those charged with the task of maintaining good relations with foreign governments.

18. The growth of the Eurodollar market – an electronically integrated international system which guarantees anonymity and instant transfers using computer technology – has benefited those charged with laundering the profits of illicit drug transactions (Andelman, 1994).

19. The US government has responded with Operation Hard-line, announced in February 1995, which aims to increase surveillance of drug shipments in commercial traffic. The measures included an additional 80 customs agents and new surveillance devices. These measures will probably not be sufficient to resolve the problem.

20. The Vienna Convention, which refers to measures designed to restrict trafficking, is one of the three international drug control treaties designed to prevent the use of drugs for non-medical purposes. The 1961 *Single Convention on Narcotic Drugs* incorporated earlier national and international measures to control the production and distribution of drugs, ensuring that they would be available for medical and scientific purposes, and preventing their diversion to licit channels. The 1971 *Convention of Psychotropic Substances* expanded the scope of control by including many synthetic drugs. Neither the 1961 nor the 1971 convention was designed specifically to address illicit drug trafficking, hence the Vienna Convention.

BIBLIOGRAPHY

Abel, C. (1993) 'Colombia and the Drugs Barons: Conflict and Containment', *World Today*, Vol. 49, No. 5, pp. 96-100

Ackerman, E. (1994) 'A Dictator's Guide to Miami', *The New Times*, 8-14 December

Alcalá Afanador, P. (1990) 'Características de los consultantes a UDAF, 1988-1989', *Archivos venezolanos de psiquiatría y neurología*, Vol. 36, No. 75, pp. 65-71

Arango, M. and J. Child (1987) *Narcotráfico: imperio de la coca*, Mexico City: Edivisión

Americas Watch (1992) *Peru under Fire*, New Haven, Conn.: Yale University Press

Andelman, D.A. (1994) 'The Drug Money Maze', *Foreign Affairs*, Vol. 73, No. 4 (July/August), pp. 94-108

Anderson, M. (1993) 'The British Perspective on the Internationalization of Police Cooperation in Western Europe', in C. Fijnaut (ed.), *The Internationalization of Police Cooperation in Western Europe*, Deventer: Kluwer, pp. 19-40

Andreas, P. and Youngers, C. (1989) 'US Drug Policy and the Andean Cocaine Industry', *World Policy Journal*, Vol. VI, No. 3, pp. 529-62

Andreas, P. and Boyle, K. (1994) 'The Drug War is Dead', *Hemisphere* Vol. 6, No. 2, pp. 34-7

Asociación Bancaria de Panamá (1994) *Boletín Económico*, Vol. 1, No. 4 (October-November)

Asociación Peruana de Estudios e Investigación para la Paz (1990) *Cocaína: Problemas y soluciones andinas*, Lima: Asociación Peruana de Estudios e Investigación para la Paz

Arango, M. and J. Child (1986) *Coca-Coca: Historia, manejo política y mafia de la cocaína*, Madrid: Dos Mundos

Arrieta, C.A., L.J. Orjuela, E. Sarmiento and J.G. Tokatlian (1990) *Narcotráfico en Colombia: Dimensiones políticas, económicas, jurídicas e internacionales*, Bogotá: Tercer Mundo Editores/Ediciones Uniandes

Bagley, B. (1988) 'Colombia and the War on Drugs', *Foreign Affairs*, Vol. 67, No. 1, pp. 70-92

Bagley, B. (1988a) 'The New Hundred Years War? US National Security and the War on Drugs in Latin America', *Journal of Interamerican Studies and World Affairs*, Vol. 30, No. 1, pp. 161-82

Bagley, B. (1988b): 'US Foreign Policy and the War on Drugs: Analysis of a Policy Failure', *Journal of Interamerican Studies and World Affairs*, Vol. 30, Nos. 2 & 3 (Summer/Fall), pp. 189-211

Bagley, B. (1992) 'After San Antonio', *Journal of Interamerican Studies and World Affairs*, Vol. 34, No. 3, pp. 1-12

Bagley, B. (1992a) 'Myths of Militarization: Enlisting Armed Forces in the War on Drugs', in P.H. Smith (ed.), *Drug Policy in the Americas*, Boulder, Colo.: Westview, pp. 129-50

Bagley, B. and J.G. Tokatlian (1985) 'Colombian Foreign Policy in the 1980s: The Search for Leverage', *Journal of Interamerican Studies and World Affairs*, Vol. 27, No. 3, pp. 27-62

Bagley, B. and J.G. Tokatlian (eds.) (1990) *Economía y política del narcotráfico*, Bogotá: CEREC/Ediciones Uniandes

Bahamón Dussán, A. (1992) *Mi guerra en Medellín*, Third edition, Bogotá: Intermedio Editores

Bassiouni, M.C. (1990) 'Critical Reflections on International and National Control of Drugs', *Denver Journal of International Law*, Vol. 18, No. 3, pp. 311-37

Baum, R.J. (1992) 'Stopping Airborne Drug Traffickers', *Hemisphere* Vol. IV, No. 3 (Summer)

Bean, P. (ed.) (1993) *Cocaine and Crack: Supply and Use*, Basingstoke: Macmillan

Bean, P. (1993a) 'Cocaine and Crack: The Promotion of an Epidemic', in P. Bean (ed.), *Cocaine and Crack: Supply and Use*, Basingtoke: Macmillan, pp. 59-75

Beaty, J. and S.C. Gwynne (1993) *The Outlaw Bank: A Wild Ride into the Secret Heart of BCCI*, New York: Random House

Betancourt, D. and M.L. García (1994) *Contrabandistas, marimberos y mafiosos: Historia social de la mafia colombiana (1965-1992)*, Bogotá: Tercer Mundo Editores

Bieleman, B. et al (1993) *Lines Across Europe: Nature and Extent of Cocaine Use in Barcelona, Rotterdam and Turin*, Amsterdam: Swets and Zeitlinger

Blom, T. and H. van Mastrigt (1994) 'The Future of the Dutch Model in the Context of the War on Drugs', in E. Leuw and I. Haen Marshall (eds.), *Between Prohibition and Legalization: the Dutch Experiment in Drug Policy*, Amsterdam: Kugler, pp. 255-81

Bolivia (1995) *Programa Boliviano de lucha contra las drogas*, La Paz: Ministerio de Gobierno, Secretaría Nacional de Defensa Social

BOTEC Analysis Corporation (1993) *A Heroin Situation Assessment*, Cambridge, Mass.: BOTEC

Brackelaire, V. (1992) Coca, Développement et Coopération Internationale en Bolivie, *Revue Tiers-Monde*, No. 131, pp. 673-89

Bulmer-Thomas, V. (ed.) (1996) *The New Economic Model in Latin America and its Impact on Income Distribution and Poverty*, Basingstoke: Macmillan/ILAS

Bustos Ramirez, J. (1990) *Coca-cocaína: entre el derecho y la guerra política criminal de la droga en los países andinos*, Barcelona: Promociones y Publicaciones Universitarias

Cabrera Solís, C. et al (1992) *Epidemiología del abuso de drogas en la República Mexicana: panorama comparativo con los Estados Unidos de América*, Mexico City: Centros de Integración Juvenil

Campodónico, H. (1989) 'La política de avestruz', in D. García-Sayán (ed.), *Coca, cocaína y narcotráfico: laberinto en los Andes*, Lima: Comisión Andina de Juristas

Campodónico, H. (1996) 'Drug Trafficking, Laundering and Neo-Liberal Economics: Perverse Effects for a Developing Country', in N. Dorn, J. Jepsen and E. Savona (eds.), *European Drug Policies and Enforcement*, Basingstoke: Macmillan

Carter, W. and M. Mamani (1986) *Coca en Bolivia*, La Paz: Juventud

Castillo, F. (1987) *Los jinetes de la cocaína*, Bogotá: Editorial Documentos Periodísticos

Castillo, F. (1991) *La coca nostra*, Bogotá: Editorial Documentos Periodísticos

Castro, G. et al (1989) 'Crisis y políticas sociales en Panamá: los años 80', *Cuadernos nacionales*, No. 2, pp. 7-64

Castro Aguilar, C and A. Hernández (1991) *Conocimientos, actitudes y prácticas sobre drogas y drogadicción en población general entre 15 y 54 años del área metropolitana de San Salvador*, San Salvador: Fundasalva

Catholic Institute for International Relations (CIIR) (1994) *European Drug-Control Policy and the Andean Region*, London: CIIR

CEDRO (1993) *Opiniones sobre drogas en el Perú: población urbana*, Lima: CEDRO

CEDRO (1993a) *Drogas y control de la información*, Buenos Aires: Ediciones Tres Tiempos

Clutterbuck, R. (1990) *Terrorism, Drugs and Crime in Europe after 1992*, London: Routledge

Comisión Andina de Juristas (1994) *Drogas y control penal en los Andes*, Lima: CAJ

Comisión Andina de Juristas (1995) *Andean Region: Jan-June 1995. Semester Progress Report*, Lima: CAJ

214   *Latin America and the Multinational Drug Trade*

Council of Europe (1992) *The Incidence of 'Crack' in North American and European Cities*, Strasbourg: Council of Europe

Coyuntura Social (1990) 'Justicia y criminalidad', *Coyuntura Social*, No. 2 (May), pp. 20-37

Craig, R.B. (1978) 'La Campaña Permanente: Mexico's Anti-Drug Campaign', *Journal of Interamerican Studies and World Affairs*, Vol. 20, No. 2 (May), pp. 107-131

Craig, R.B. (1980) 'Operation Condor: Mexico's Antidrug Campaign Enters a New Era, *Journal of Interamerican Studies and World Affairs*, Vol. 22, No. 3 (August), pp. 345-63

Craig, R.B. (1985) 'Illicit Drug Traffic and US-Latin American Relations', *Washington Quarterly*, Vol. 8, No. 4

Cuánto (1994) *El impacto de la coca en el Perú*, Lima: Cuánto

Daniel, B. and R.L. Miller (1991) *Undoing Drugs: Beyond Legalization*, New York: Basic Books

Deas, M.D. and C. Ossa (eds.) (1994) *El gobierno Barco: Política, economía y desarrollo social en Colombia: 1986-1990*, Bogotá: Fedesarrollo/Fondo Cultural Cafetero

DeFeo, M.A. (1990) 'Depriving International Narcotics Traffickers and Other Organized Criminals of Illegal Proceeds and Combatting Money Laundering', *Denver Journal of International Law*, Vol. 18, No. 3, pp. 405-15

De Rementería, I. (1992) 'Economía y drogas', *Colombia Internacional* No. 20 (Oct-Dec), pp. 9-16

De Rementería, I. (1995) *The Drugs Trade and the Environment*, London: CIIR

De La Quintana, M. (ed.) (1992) *Estudio sobre el consumo de sustancias psicoactivas y la salud mental*, La Paz: Fundación San Gabriel

Del Olmo, R. (1990) 'La Convención de Viena y el derecho interno', *Boletín Comisión Andina de Juristas*, No. 25 (June), pp. 37-55

De Soto, Hernando (1987) *El otro sendero*, Lima: Editorial el Barranco

Dinges, J. (1990) *Our Man in Panama: How General Noriega Used the US and Made Millions in Drugs and Arms*, New York: Random House

Dominguez Solís, C. (1994): *Los carteles sudamericanos de narcotráfico*. Lima: Grafal

Donnelly, J. (1992) 'The United Nations and the Global Drug Control Regime', in P.H. Smith (ed.), *Drug Policy in the Americas*, Boulder, Colo.: Westview, pp. 282-304

Dorn, N., J. Jepsen and E. Savona (eds.) (1996) *European Drug Policies and Enforcement*, Basingstoke: Macmillan

Dorn, N., K. Murji and N. South (1992) *Traffickers: Drug Markets and Law*

Enforcement, London: Routledge

Dornbush, R. (1990) *Capital Flight: Theory, Measurement, and Policy Issues*, Washington, D.C.: Inter-American Development Bank

Doyle, K. (1993) 'The Militarization of the Drug War in Mexico', *Current History*, Vol. 92, No. 571, pp. 83-7

Duke, S.B. and A.C. Gross (1993) *America's Longest War: Rethinking our Tragic Crusade against Drugs*, New York: Putnam

Duzán, M.J. (1994) *Death Beat: A Colombian Journalist's Life inside the Cocaine Wars*, New York: Harper Collins

Economist Intelligence Unit (1994) *Bolivia: Country Profile 1994-95*, London: EIU

Economist Intelligence Unit (1994a) *Bolivia and Peru Country Report, 1st Quarter 1994*, London: EIU

Economist Intelligence Unit (1995) *Bolivia Country Report, 1st Quarter 1995*, London: EIU

Escohotado, A. (1989) *Historia de las drogas*, 3 volumes, Madrid: Alianza Editorial

European Commission (1993) *Inventory of EC (Legal) Texts on Drugs*, Luxembourg: European Commission

European Parliament (1986) *Report of the Committee of Inquiry into the Drugs Problem in the Member States of the Community*, Brussels: European Parliament

European Parliament (1989) *Resolution on the Fight against Drug Trafficking and the Grave Situation in Colombia*, No. OJ C256/113, 9 October, Brussels: European Parliament

European Parliament (1992) *Report on the Spread of Organized Crime Linked to Drugs Trafficking in the Member States of the European Community*, PE 152.380/fin, Brussels: European Parliament

European Parliament (1995) *Report by the European Parliament Committee in Civil Liberties and Internal Affairs, on 'The Communication from the Commission to the Council and the European Parliament on a European Union Action Plan to Combat Drugs'*, PE 211.498/fin, Brussels, June 1995

Everingham, S. and P. Rydell (1994) *Modeling the Demand for Cocaine*, Santa Monica, Calif.: Rand

Falco, M. (1995) 'Passing Grades: Branding Nations Won't Resolve the US Drug Problem', *Foreign Affairs* (Sept/Oct), pp. 15-20

Ferrando, D. (1988) 'Segunda encuesta de opinión pública sobre drogas: principales resultados', *Psicoactiva*, Vol. 2, No. 2, pp. 5-56

Ferrando, D. (1989) 'Conciencia social del problema de la pasta en el Perú', in F. León and R. Castro de la Mata (eds.), *Pasta básica de cocaína: un estudio multidisciplinario*, Lima: CEDRO

Ferrando, D. (1989a) 'Encuesta de evaluación de la Segunda Campaña Audiovisual de CEDRO', *Psicoactiva*, Vol. 3, No. 1, pp. 75-114

Ferrando, D. (1989b) *Estudio de percepciones sobre drogas de la población urbana del Perú*, Lima: CEDRO

Ferrando, D. (1990) *Uso de drogas en las ciudades del Perú: encuesta de hogares 1988*, Lima: CEDRO

Ferrando, D. (1991) *Opiniones y actitudes de los líderes Peruanos sobre drogas: encuesta en seis ciudades*, Lima: CEDRO

Ferrando, D. (1992) *Los jóvenes en el Perú: opiniones, actitudes y valores: encuesta nacional de hogares 1991*, Lima: CEDRO

Ferrando, D. et al (1993) *Drogas en el Perú urbano: estudio epidemiológico 1992*, Lima: CEDRO

Ferrando, D. (1993) *Conocimiento y uso de drogas en los colegios de secundaria: encuesta nacional 1992*, Lima: COPUID

Ferrando, D. and R. Lerner (1991) 'Encuesta de evaluación de la tercera campaña masiva audiovisual de CEDRO "Acepta Vivir"', *Psicoactiva*, Vol. 5, No. 8, pp. 15-54

Franks, J. (1991) 'La economía de la coca en Bolivia: ¿Plaga o salvación?', *Informe Confidencial*, No. 64 (June), La Paz: Muller Associates

Gallagher, R. (1990) *Survey of Offshore Finance Sectors in the Caribbean Dependent Territories*, London: HMSO

Gamarra, E.A. (1994) *Entre la droga y la democracia*, La Paz: ILDIS/Friedrich Ebert Stiftung

Gandásegui, M.A. (1989) *La democracia en Panamá*, Mexico City: Editorial Mestiza

García Ramírez, S. (1989) *El narcotráfico: un punto de vista mexicano*, Mexico City: Miguel Angel Porrúa

García-Sayan, D. (ed.) (1989) *Coca, cocaína y narcotráfico: el laberinto en los Andes*, Lima: Comisión Andina de Juristas

George, S. (1992) *The Debt Boomerang*, London: Pluto

Gfroerer, J. and M. Brodsky (1992) 'The Incidence of Drug Use in the United States', *British Journal of Addiction*, Vol. 87, No. 9, pp. 1345-52

Gilmore, W.C. (ed.) (1990) *International Efforts to Combat Money Laundering*, Cambridge: Grotius/Research Centre for International Law

Gilmore, W.C. (1990a) 'International Law Against Drug Trafficking: Trends in United Kingdom Law and Practice', *The International Lawyer*, Vol. 24, No. 2 (Summer), pp. 365-92

Goldrich, D, (1966) *Sons of the Establishment Elite Youth in Panama and Costa Rica*, Chicago, Ill.: Rand McNally

Gómez, H.J. (1990) 'El tamaño del narcotráfico y su impacto económico',

Economía Colombiana, No. 226-27 (March)

Gómez, H.J. (1990) 'La economía ilegal en Colombia: tamaño, evolución, características e impacto económico', in J.G. Tokatlian and B.M. Bagley (eds.), *Economía y política del narcotráfico*, Bogotá: CEREC

Gómez, I. (1989) *El complot del 'Copacabana'*, Bogotá: Editorial Retina

González, G. (1989) *El narcotráfico como un problema de seguridad regional*, Santiago: Comisión Sudamericana de Paz

González, G. and M. Tienda (eds.) (1989) *The Drug Connection in US-Mexican Relations*, San Diego, Calif.: Center for US-Mexican Studies, University of California, San Diego

Gonzales, J. (1994) *The Peruvian Promise*, New York: Credit Lyonnais

Gorriti, G. (1990) *Sendero Luminoso: historia de la guerra milenaria en el Perú*, Lima: Apoyo

Gugliotta, G. (1992) 'The Colombian Cartels and How to Stop Them', in P.H. Smith (ed.), *Drug Policy in the Americas*, Boulder, Colo: Westview, pp. 111-28

Haaga, J.G. and P. Reuter (1990) *The Limits of the Czar's Ukase: Drug Policy at the Local Level*, Santa Monica, Calif.: Rand

Hargreaves, C. (1992) *Snowfields: The War on Cocaine in the Andes*, London: Zed

Hauge, R. (1985) 'Trends in Drug Use in Norway', *Journal of Drug Issues*, Vol. 15, pp. 321-31

Healy, K. (1991) 'Political Ascent of Bolivia's Peasant Coca Leaf Producers', *Journal of Interamerican Studies and World Affairs*, Vol. 33, No. 1 (Spring), pp. 87-121

Henman, A. (1979) *Mama Coca*, London: Hassle Free Press

Henman, A. (1981) *Mama Coca*, Bogotá: Editorial Oveja Negra

Henman, A. (1993) *La coca: panorama actual. II Forum Internacional por la Revalorización de la Hoja de Coca*, Lima: ENACO

Home Office Research and Statistics Department (1995) *Statistics of Drugs Seizures and Offenders Dealt With, United Kingdom, 1994*, London: Government Statistical Service

Hyatt, R. and W. Rhodes (1992) *Price and Purity of Cocaine: The Relationship to Emergency Room Visits and Deaths, and to Drug Use Among Arrestees*, Washington, D.C.: Office of National Drug Control Policy

IEPALA (1982) *Narcotráfico y política: militarismo y mafia en Bolivia*, Madrid: IEPALA

Instituto Latinoamericano de Investigaciones Sociales (ILDIS)/Centro de Documentación e Información – Bolivia (CEDIB) (1992) *Coca-cronología. Bolivia: 1986-1992*, La Paz/Cochabamba: ILDIS/CEDIB

Institute for European-Latin American Relations (IRELA) (1993) *Latin America, Europe and the Environment: The Greening of Biregional Relations*, Madrid: IRELA

Institute for European-Latin American Relations (IRELA) (1995) *Cooperation in the Fight against Drugs: European and Latin American Initiatives*, Madrid: IRELA

Institute for European-Latin American Relations (IRELA) (1996) *Colombia: The Challenge to Governability*, Madrid: IRELA

Inter-American Commission on Drug Policy (1991) *Seizing Opportunities: Report of the Inter-American Commission on Drug Policy*, La Jolla, Calif.: Institute of the Americas/Center for Iberian and Latin American Studies, UCSD

Jamieson, A. (ed.) (1994) *Terrorism and Drug Trafficking in the 1990s* Dartmouth: Research Institute for the Study of Conflict and Terrorism

Johnston, L., J. Bachman and P. O'Malley (annual) *Monitoring the Future*, Ann Arbor, Mich.: Institute for Social Research, University of Michigan

Jorden, W.J. (1984) *Panama Odyssey*, Austin, Tex.: University of Texas Press

Joyce, E. (1996) 'Narcocassettes Jeopardise a President', *World Today*, Vol. 52, No. 5, pp. 122-4

Justiniano, J.G. (1992) 'The Power of Coca Producers', in P.H. Smith (ed.), *Drug Policy in the Americas*, Boulder, Colo.: Westview, pp. 99-104

Jutkowitz, J. et al (1987) *Uso y abuso de drogas en el Perú*, Lima: CEDRO

Kalmanovitz, S. (1994) 'Análisis macroeconómico del narcotráfico en la economía colombiana', in R. Vargas (ed.), *Drogas, poder y región en Colombia*, Bogotá: CINEP

Kaufman Purcell, S. and F. Simon (eds.) (1995) *Europe and Latin America in the World Economy*, Boulder, Colo.: Lynne Rienner

Kempe, F. (1990) *Divorcing the Dictator: America's Bungled Affair with Noriega*, New York: Putnam

Kleiman, M.A.R. (1989) *Marijuana: Costs of Abuse, Costs of Control*, Boulder, Colo.: Greenwood

Kleiman, M.A.R. (1992) *Against Excess: Drug Policy for Results*, New York: Basic Books

Krauthausen, C. and L.F. Sarmiento (1993) *Cocaína & Co.: Un mercado ilegal por dentro*, Bogotá: Tercer Mundo Editores

Le Carré, J. (1996) 'Quel Panama?', *The New York Times Magazine*, 13 October, pp. 52-5

Leal Buitrago, F. (1994) *El oficio de la guerra: La seguridad nacional en Colombia*, Bogotá: Tercer Mundo Editores

Leal Buitrago, F. (1995) *Defensa y seguridad nacional en Colombia, 1958-*

1993, in F. Leal Buitrago and J.G. Tokatlian (eds.), *Orden mundial y seguridad*, Bogotá: Tercer Mundo Editores, pp. 131-72

Leal Buitrago, F. and J.G. Tokatlian (eds.) (1994) *Orden mundial y seguridad: Nuevos desafíos para Colombia y América Latina*, Bogotá: Tercer Mundo Editores ·

Leal Buitrago, F. and L. Zamocs (eds.) (1990) *Al filo del caos: Crisis política en la Colombia de los años 80*, Bogotá: Tercer Mundo Editores

Lee, R.W. (1985-86) 'The Latin American Drug Connection', *Foreign Policy* No. 61 (Winter), pp. 142-60

Lee, R.W. (1988) 'Dimensions of the South American Cocaine Industry', *Journal of Interamerican Studies and World Affairs*, Vol. 30, Nos. 2 & 3 (Summer/Fall), pp. 87-126

Lee, R.W. (1989) *White Labyrinth: Cocaine and Political Power*, New Brunswick, NJ: Transaction

Lee, R.W. and S.B. MacDonald (1993) 'Drugs in the East', *Foreign Policy* No. 90 (Spring), pp. 89-107

Leis, R. (1987) 'Ciudad y movimientos sociales urbanos', *Revista panameña de sociología*, No. 3, pp. 9-26

Lerner, R. (1987) 'Asociaciones libres al término "Droga" en dos grupos de estudiantes universitarios', *Psicoactiva*, Vol. 1, No. 1, pp. 55-64

Lerner, R. (1987a) 'Balance de una campaña masiva', *Psicoactiva*, Vol. 1, No. 2, pp. 139-46

Lerner, R. (1989) 'Reflexiones en torno a la prevención como práctica global', in F. León and R. Castro de la Mata (eds.), *Pasta básica de cocaína: Un estudio multidisciplinario*, Lima: CEDRO

Lerner, R. (1991) *Drugs in Peru: Reality and Representations*, Doctoral thesis, Amsterdam: Catholic University of Nijmegen

Lerner, R. (1992) 'Drug Abuse Prevention in Latin America', in P.H. Smith (ed.), *Drug Policy in the Americas*, Boulder, Colo.: Westview, pp. 207-16

Lerner, R. and D. Ferrando (1987) 'Acerca de un estudio epidemiológico sobre uso y abuso de drogas en el Perú urbano', *Psicoactiva*, Vol. 1, No. 1, pp. 89-108

Lerner, R. and D. Ferrando (1995) 'Inhalant Abuse in Peru', in National Institute of Drug Abuse (NIDA), *Epidemiology of Inhalant Abuse: An International Perspective*, Rockville, Md.: NIDA

Lewis, R. (1985) 'Serious Business – The Global Heroin Economy', in A. Henman, R. Lewis and T. Malyon (eds.), *Big Deal: The Politics of the Illicit Drugs Business*, London: Pluto

Linowitz, S.M. (1988/89) 'Latin America: The President's Agenda', *Foreign Affairs* Vol. 67, No. 2 (Winter), pp. 45-62

Lowenfeld, A.F. (1990) 'US Law Enforcement Abroad: The Constitution and International Law, Continued', *American Journal of International Law*, Vol. 84, No. 2, p. 444

Lowenfeld, A.F. (1990a) 'Kidnapping by Government Order: A Follow-up Correspondence', *American Journal of International Law*, Vol. 84, No. 3, p. 712

Lowenfeld, A.F. (1990b) 'Still More on Kidnapping', *American Journal of International Law*, Vol. 85, No. 4, pp. 655-61

Lowenthal, A.F. and G.F. Treverton (eds.) (1994) *Latin America and the United States in a New World*, Boulder, Colo.: Westview

Lupsha, P.A. (1992) 'Drug Lords and Narco-Corruption: The Players Change but the Game Continues', in A.W. McCoy and A.A. Block (eds.), *War on Drugs: Studies in the Failure of US Narcotics Policy*, Boulder, Colo.: Westview, pp. 177-95

MacCoun, R.J., A.J. Saiger, J.P. Kahan and P. Reuter (1993) 'Drug Policies and Problems: The Promise and Pitfalls of Cross-national Comparison', in N. Heather, A. Wodak, E. Nadelmann and P. O'Hare (eds.), *Psychoactive Drugs and Harm Reduction: From Faith to Science*, London: Whurr, pp. 103-17

MacDonald, S.B. (1988) *Dancing on a Volcano: The Latin American Drug Trade*, New York: Praeger

MacDonald, S.B. (1989) *Mountain High, White Avalanche: Cocaine and Power in the Andean States and Panama*, New York: Praeger

Machiado, F. (1992) 'Coca Production in Bolivia', in P.H. Smith (ed.), *Drug Policy in the Americas*, Boulder, Colo.: Westview, pp. 88-104

MacKenzie, D.L. and C.D. Uchida (1994) *Drugs and Crime: Evaluating Public Policy Initiatives*, Newbury Park, Calif.: Sage

MacNamara, D.E.J. and P.J. Stead (eds.) (1982) *New Dimensions in Transnational Crime*, New York: John Jay Press

Maingot, A.P. (1988) 'Laundering the Gains of the Drug Trade: Miami and Caribbean Tax Havens, *Journal of Interamerican Studies and World Affairs*, Vol. 30, Nos. 2 & 3 (Summer/Fall), pp. 167-87

Maingot, A.P. (1994) *The United States and the Caribbean*, Basingstoke: Macmillan

Maingot, A.P. (1995) 'Offshore Secrecy Centers and the Necessary Role of States' *Journal of Interamerican Studies and World Affairs*, Vol. 37, No. 4 (Winter), pp. 1-14

Malamud-Goti, J. (1992) *Smoke and Mirrors: The Paradox of the Drugs Wars*, Boulder, Colo.: Westview

Martin, L.M. (1992) 'Foundations for International Cooperation', in P.H. Smith (ed.), *Drug Policy in the Americas*, Boulder, Colo.: Westview, pp.

249-64

Martin, J.M. and A.T. Romano (1992) *Multinational Crime: Terrorism, Espionage, Drug and Arms Trafficking*, Newbury Park, Calif./London: Sage

Martínez Lanz, P. and E. Alfaro Murillo (1988) *Prevalencia del consumo de drogas en Costa Rica*, San José, Costa Rica: Instituto sobre Alcoholismo y Farmacodependencia/OMS

Martz, J.D. (1994) 'Colombia: Democracy, Development and Drugs', *Current History*, Vol. 93, No. 581, pp. 134-7

Matayas Camargo, E. (1990) 'Narco paramilitarismo y derechos humanos en Colombia', *Boletín Comisión Andina de Juristas*, No. 25 (June), pp. 9-15

Matos, J. (1988) *Desborde popular y crisis del estado*, Lima: Concytec

McClintock, C. (1988) 'The War on Drugs: The Peruvian Case', *Journal of Interamerican Studies and World Affairs*, Vol. 30, Nos. 2 & 3 (Summer/Fall), pp. 127-41

McKenna, T.K. (1992), *Food of the Gods*, London: Rider

Melo, J.G. and J. Bermúdez (1994) 'La lucha contra el narcotráfico: éxitos y frustaciones', in M. Deas and C. Ossa (eds.), *El gobierno Barco: Política, economía y desarrollo social en Colombia: 1986-1990*, Bogotá: Fedesarrollo/Fondo Cultural Cafetero

Menzel, S.H. (1994) 'Southcom in the Andes', *Hemisphere* (Summer), pp. 38-41

Míguez, H., M.C. Pecci and A. Carrizosa (1992) 'Epidemiología del abuso de alcohol y las drogas en el Paraguay', *Acta Psiquiátrica y Psicológica de América Latina*, Vol. 38, No. 1, pp. 19-29

Ministerio de Salud (1993) *El consumo de drogas en Colombia*, Bogotá: Ministerio de Salud

Morales, E. (1989) *Cocaine: White Gold Rush in Peru*, Tucson, Ariz.: University of Arizona Press

Moreno, Jr., L.H. (1991) *Panamá: una vocación de servicio*, Panamá: Banco Nacional de Panamá

Mott, J. and C. Mirrlees-Black (1993) 'Self-Reported Drug Misuse in England and Wales from the 1992 British Crime Survey', in Home Office Research and Statistics Department, *Research Findings*, London: Home Office

Musto, D. (1973) *The American Disease*, New Haven, Conn.: Yale University Press

Nadelmann, E.A. (1985) 'Negotiations in Criminal Law Assistance Treaties', *American Journal of Comparative Law*, No. 33, pp. 467-504

Nadelmann, E.A. (1985a) 'International Drug Trafficking and US Foreign Policy', *Washington Quarterly*, Vol. 8, No. 4, pp. 87-104

Nadelmann, E.A. (1986) 'Unlaundering Dirty Money Abroad: US Foreign Policy and Financial Secrecy Restrictions', *University of Miami Interamerican Law Review*, No. 18, pp. 33-82

Nadelmann, E.A. (1987-8) 'The DEA in Latin America: Dealing with Institutionalized Corruption', *Journal of Interamerican Studies and World Affairs*, Vol. 29, No. 4, pp. 1-39

Nadelmann, E.A. (1988) 'US Drug Policy: A Bad Export', *Foreign Policy*, No. 70, pp. 97-108

Nadelmann, E.A. (1990) 'Global Prohibition Regimes: The Evolution of Norms in International Society', *International Organization*, No. 44, pp. 479-526

Nadelmann, E.A. (1993) *Cops Across Borders: The Internationalization of US Criminal Law Enforcement*, University Park, Penn: Pennsylvania State University Press

Nadelmann, E.A. (1993a) 'Harmonization of Criminal Justice Systems', in P.H. Smith (ed.), *The Challenge of Integration: Europe and the Americas*, New Brunswick, N.J.: Transaction, pp. 247-77

National Narcotics Intelligence Consumers Committee (NNICC) (annual) *Narcotics Intelligence Estimate*, Washington, D.C.: NNICC

National Institute of Justice (annual) *Drug Use Forecasting: Annual Report on Adult Arrestees*, Washington, D.C.: National Institute of Justice

Office of National Drug Control Policy (1993) *Crop Substitution in the Andes*, Washington, D.C.: ONDCP

Office of National Drug Control Policy (1994) *National Drug Control Strategy Budget Summary*, Washington, D.C.: ONDCP

Office of National Drug Control Policy (1995) *National Drug Control Strategy*, Washington, D.C.: ONDCP

Painter, J. (1994) *Bolivia and Coca: A Study in Dependency*, Boulder, Colo.: Lynne Rienner

Panama Banking Association (1993) *A Guide for the Prevention of the Wrongful Use of Banking Services*, Second Edition, Panama City: Panama Banking Association

Pardo, R. (1995) 'The Issue of Drug Traffic in Colombian-US Relations: Cooperation as an Imperative', *Journal of Interamerican Studies and World Affairs*, Vol. 37, No. 1 (Spring), pp. 101-11

Pardo, R. and J.G. Tokatlian (1989) *Política exterior Colombiana*, Bogotá: Tercer Mundo Editores/Ediciones Uniandes

Paternostro, S. (1995) 'Mexico as a Narco-democracy', *World Policy Journal* (Summer), pp. 41-7

Pearce, F. and M. Woodiwiss (eds.) (1993) *Global Crime Connections: Dynamics and Control*, Basingstoke: Macmillan

Pearson, G., H.S. Mirza and S. Phillips (1993) 'Cocaine in Context: Findings from a South London Inner-City Drug Survey', in P. Bean (ed.), *Cocaine and Crack: Supply and Use*, Basingstoke: Macmillan, pp. 99-129

Peat Marwick (1993), *Balances de situación de bancos que operan en Panamá*, Panama: Peat Marwick

Pérez Gómez, A. (ed.) (1994) *Sustancias psicoactivas: historia del consumo en Colombia*, Bogotá: Presencia

Pérez Gómez, A., L. Aja and E. Correa (1993) 'Qué consumen los colombianos? Bogotá 1988-1992', *Adicciones*, Vol. 5, No. 3, pp. 247-56

Pérez Gómez, A., E. Correa and L. Aja (1993) *El consumo de sustancias psicoactivas en Santa Fé de Bogotá*, Bogotá: Alcaldía Mayor/UCPI

Pérez Gómez, A. and A. Escallón Emiliani (1990) 'El consumo de drogas en América Latina: una perspectiva desde el ojo del huracán', *Comunidad y drogas*, Vol. 15, pp. 37-50

Perl, R.F. (1988) 'Congress, International Narcotics Policy, and the Anti-Drug Abuse Act of 1988', *Journal of Interamerican Studies and World Affairs*, Vol. 30, Nos. 2 & 3 (Summer/Fall), pp. 19-51

Perl, R.F. (1993-4) 'Clinton's Foreign Drug Policy', *Journal of Interamerican Studies and World Affairs*, Vol. 35, No. 4 (Winter), pp. 143-52

Pettersson, B. and L. Mackay (1993) *Human Rights Violations Stemming from the 'War on Drugs' in Bolivia*, Cochabamba: Andean Information Network

Posada-Carbó, E. (ed.) (1997), *Colombia: The Politics of Reforming the State*, Basingstoke: Mcmillan/ILAS

President's Commission on Organized Crime (1984) *The Cash Connection: Organized Crime, Financial Institutions and Money Laundering*, Washington, DC: President's Commission on Organized Crime

Priesly, G. (1986) *Military Government and Popular Participation in Panama*, Boulder, Colo.: Westview

Quiroga, J.A. (1990) *Coca/cocaína: una visión Boliviana*, La Paz: AIPE/PROCOM – CEDLA – CID

Ramírez, J.L. (1991) 'Las relaciones internacionales de Colombia con la CEE', in J.L. Ramírez, M.J. Osorio, A. Fuentes, M.C. Rueda and K-P Schutt, *Colombia y América Latina Frente a Europa 1992*, Bogotá: Fundación Friedrich Ebert de Colombia, pp. 13-74

Reuter, P. (1985) 'Eternal Hope: America's Quest for Narcotics Control', *The Public Interest*, No. 79 (Spring), pp. 79-95.

Reuter, P. (1985a) *The Organization of Illegal Markets: An Economic Analysis*, Washington, D.C.: GPO

Reuter, P. (1988) *Can the Borders be Sealed: The Effects of Increased Military Participation in Drug Interdiction*, Santa Monica, Calif.: Rand

Reuter, P. (1989) *Quantity Illusion and Paradoxes of Drug Interdiction*, Santa Monica, Calif.: Rand

Reuter, P., G. Crawford and J. Cave (1988) *Sealing the Borders: The Effects of Increased Military Involvement in Drug Interdiction*, Santa Monica, Calif.: Rand

Reuter, P., P. Ebener and D. McCaffrey (1994) 'Patterns of Drug Use', in D.J. Besharov (ed.), *When Drug Addicts Have Children*, Washington, D.C.: American Enterprise Institute

Reuter, P., M. Falco and R. MacCoun (1993) *Comparing Western European and North American Drug Policies*, Santa Monica, Calif.: Rand

Reuter, P. and J. Haaga (1989) *The Organization of High – Level Drug Markets: An Exploratory Study*, Santa Monica, Calif.: Rand

Reuter, P., R. MacCoun and P. Murphy (1990) *Money from Crime: A Study of the Economics of Drug Dealing in Washington DC*, Santa Monica, Calif.: Rand

Reuter, P. and D. Ronfeldt (1992) 'Quest for Integrity: The Mexican-US Drug Issue in the 1990s', *Journal of Interamerican Studies and World Affairs*, Vol. 34, No. 3, pp. 89-154

Reyes Posada, A. (1992) *La violencia y la expansión territorial del narcotráfico*, Bogota: CSV

Revista Panameña de Sociología, (1989) 'Memoria, VI Congreso Nacional de Sociología', *Revista Panameña de Sociología*, No. 5

Riley, K.J. (1995) *Snow Job? The War against International Cocaine Trafficking*, New Brunswick, N.J.: Transaction

Rodríguez, O., L.F. Duque and J. Rodríguez (1993) *Encuesta nacional sobre el consumo de drogas en Colombia*, Bogotá: Ministerio de Justicia/DNE

Ropp, S. (1985) 'Panama Domestic Power Structure and the Canal: History and Future', in H.J. Wiarda and H.F. Kline (eds.), *Latin American Politics and Development*, Second Edition, Boulder, Colo.: Westview

Rubio, M. (1994) *Legislación Peruana sobre drogas, 1920-1993*, Lima: CEDRO

Ruggiero, V. and N. South (1995) *Eurodrugs: Drug Use, Markets and Trafficking in Europe*, London: UCL Press

Ruiz Cabañas, M. (1989) 'México: participación en las incautaciones mundiales de droga', in G. González and M. Tienda (eds.), *México y Estados Unidos en la cadena internacional del narcotráfico*, Mexico City: Fondo de Cultura Económica

Ruiz Cabañas, M. (1989a) 'Oferta internacional de estupefacientes ilícitos: indicadores de su evolución reciente', in G. González and M. Tienda (eds.), *México y Estados Unidos en la cadena internacional del narcotráfico*, Mexico City: Fondo de Cultura Económica

Ruiz Cabañas, M. (1989b) 'La oferta de drogas ilícitas hacia Estados Unidos: el papel fluctuante de México', in G. González and M. Tienda (eds.), *México y Estados Unidos en la cadena internacional del narcotráfico*, Mexico City: Fondo de Cultura Económica

Salazar, A. and A.M. Jaramillo (1992) *Medellín: Las subculturas del narcotráfico*, Bogotá: CINEP

Sauloy, M. and Y. Le Bonniec (1994) *¿A quién beneficia la cocaína?* Bogotá: Tercer Mundo Editores

Sciacchitano, G. (1991) 'Possible Cooperation between Italy and the Andean Countries in Substituting Coca Plantations and Repressing Drug Trafficking', in F. Bruno (ed.), *Cocaine Today: Its Effects on the Individual and Society*, Rome: UNICRI, pp. 219-22.

Scott Palmer, D. (1992) 'Peru, the Drug Business, and Shining Path: Between Scylla and Charybdis?', *Journal of Interamerican Studies and World Affairs*, Vol. 34, No. 3 (Fall), pp. 65-88

Seward, V. (1993) *Combating Drugs Trafficking and Abuse: the Challenge to Europe*, London: HMSO

Shapiro, H. (1993) 'Where Does All the Snow Go? – The Prevalence and Pattern of Cocaine and Crack Use in Britain', in P. Bean (ed.), *Cocaine and Crack: Supply and Use*, Basingstoke: Macmillan, pp. 11-28

Sharpe, K.E. (1988) 'The Drug War: Going After Supply', *Journal of Interamerican Studies and World Affairs*, Vol. 30, Nos. 2 & 3 (Summer/Fall), pp. 77-85

Silverman, J. (1994) *Crack of Doom*, London: Headline

Smith, P.H. (ed.) (1992) *Drug Policy in the Americas*, Boulder, Colo.: Westview

Smith, P.H. (1992a) 'The Political Economy of Drugs: Conceptual Issues and Policy Options', in P. H. Smith (ed.) *Drug Policy in the Americas*, Boulder, Colo.: Westview, pp. 1-21

Soberón, R. (1992) 'Efectos jurídicos de la ratificación de la Convención de Viena hecha por el Perú', *Boletín Comisión Andina de Juristas*, No. 25 (June), pp. 37-47

Soler, R. (ed.) (1974) *Dependencia y liberación*, San José: Editorial Universitaria

Spear, H.B. and J. Mott (1993) 'Cocaine and Crack within the 'British System': A History of Control', in P. Bean (ed.) *Cocaine and Crack*, Basingstoke: Macmillan, pp. 29-58

Stares, P.B. (1996) *Global Habit: The Drug Problem in a Borderless World*, Washington, D.C.: Brookings Institution

Stewart, D.P. (1990) 'Internationalizing the War on Drugs: The UN Convention against Illicit Traffic in Narcotic Drugs and Psychotropic

Substances', *Denver Journal of International Law*, Vol. 18, No. 3, pp. 387-404

Strong, S. (1995) *Whitewash: Pablo Escobar and the Cocaine Wars*, Basingstoke: Macmillan

Swedish National Institute of Public Health (1993) *A Restrictive Drug Policy: The Swedish Experience*, Stockholm: Swedish National Institute of Public Health

Tarazona-Sevillano, G. and J.B. Reuter (1990) *Sendero Luminoso and the Threat of Narcoterrorism*, New York: CSIS/Praeger

Thomas, H. (1971) *Cuba*, New York: Harper and Row

Thoumi, F.E. (1987) 'Some Implications of the Growth of the Underground Economy in Colombia', *Journal of Interamerican Studies and World Affairs*, Vol. 29, No. 2, pp. 35-53

Thoumi, F.E. (1992) 'The Economic Impact of Narcotics in Colombia', in P.H. Smith (ed.), *Drug Policy in the Americas*, Boulder, Colo.: Westview, pp. 57-71

Thoumi, F.E. (1992) 'Why the Illegal Psychoactive Drugs Industry Grew in Colombia', *Journal of Interamerican Studies and World Affairs*, Vol. 34, No. 3, pp. 37-64

Thoumi, F.E. (1994) *Economía, política y narcotráfico*, Bogotá: Tercer Mundo Editores

Tokatlian, J.G. (1988) 'National Security and Drugs: Their Impact on Colombian-US Relations', *Journal of Interamerican Studies and World Affairs*, Vol. 30, No. 1, pp. 133-59

Tokatlian, J.G. (1989) *Drogas y seguridad nacional: ¿la amenaza de la intervencion?*, Santiago: Comisión Sudamericana de Paz

Tokatlian, J.G. (1993) 'El desafío de la amapola en las relaciones entre Colombia y Estados Unidos', *Colombia Internacional*, No. 21 (Jan-Mar), pp. 3-10

Tokatlian, J.G. (1994) 'The Miami Summit and Drugs: A Placid, Innocuous Conference?', *Journal of Interamerican Studies and World Affairs*, Vol. 36, No. 3, pp. 75-91

Tokatlian, J.G. (1994a) 'Seguridad y drogas: una cruzada militar prohibicionista', in F. Leal Buitrago and J.G. Tokatlian (eds.), *Orden mundial y seguridad*, Bogotá: Tercer Mundo Editores, pp. 77-118.

Tokatlian, J.G. (1995) *Drogas, dilemas y dogmas: Estados Unidos y la narcocriminalidad organizada en Colombia*, Bogotá: Tercer Mundo Editores

Tokatlian, J.G. and B.M. Bagley (eds.) (1990) *Economía y política del narcotráfico*, Bogotá: CEREC

Toro, M.C. (1992) *Are Mexican Drug Control Policies Exacerbating or*

Addressing the Country's Drug Problem?, Paper presented at LASA meeting, Los Angeles, Calif, September (mimeo)

Toro, M.C. (1995) *Mexico's War on Drugs: Causes and Consequences*, Boulder, Colo.: Lynne Rienner

Trebach, A. and J. Inciardi, (1993) *Legalize It?*, Washington, D.C.: American University Press

Treverton, G.F. (1989) *Combatting Cocaine in the Supplying Countries: Challenges and Strategies*, Boston, Mass.: World Peace Foundation

UNDCP (1995) *Drugs and Development*, Discussion paper for World Summit for Social Development, Copenhagen, Denmark, 6-12 March 1995 (mimeo)

United Kingdom (1994) *Tackling Drugs Together: A Consultation Document on a Strategy for England 1995-98*, London: HMSO

United Nations (1995) *Proposed Revised Budget for the Biennium 1994-1995 and Proposed Outline for the Biennium 1996-1997 for the Fund of the UNDCP. Compendium of Ongoing Projects during the Biennium 1994-1995*, E/CN.7/1995/CRP.1, Vienna: United Nations

United States (1989) *Cocaine Production in the Andes*, Hearing before the Select Committee on Narcotics Abuse and Control, House of Representatives, 101st Congress, 1st Session. June 7. Washington, D.C.: US GPO

United States (1990) *European Integration, The United States, and Narcotics Control: Rhetoric and Reality*, Report of a Staff Study Mission to Great Britain, Italy, Portugal, Spain, and Kenya, 8-26 January, 1990 to the Committee on Foreign Affairs, US House of Representatives, March 1990. 101st Congress, 2nd Session. Washington, D.C.: US GPO

United States (1990a) *Operation Snowcap: Past, Present and Future*, Hearing before the Committee on Foreign Affairs, US House of Representatives, 101st Congress, 2nd Session, 23 May. Washington, D.C.: US GPO

United States (1990b) *United States Government Anti-Narcotics Activities in the Andean Region of South America*, Report made by the Permanent Subcommittee on Investigations of the Committee on Governmental Affairs, United States Senate. Washington, D.C.: US GPO

Uprimny, R. (1990) 'Relatoria de las discusiones sobre el problema del narcotráfico en Colombia', *Boletín Comisión Andina de Juristas*, No. 25 (June), pp. 56-72

Uribe, A. (1989) *La ciudad fragmentada*, Panama City: CELA

Urrutia, M. (1990) 'Análisis costo beneficio del tráfico de drogas para la economía colombiana', *Coyuntura económica*, Vol. 20, No. 3, pp. 115-26

US Drug Enforcement Administration (1994) *Colombian Economic Reform: The Impact on Drug Money Laundering within the Colombian Economy*, Washington, D.C.: Drug Enforcement Administration

US Department of Health and Human Services (annual) *National Household Survey on Drug Abuse: Main Findings*, Washington, D.C.: Department of Health and Human Services

US Department of Health and Human Services (annual) *Drug Abuse Warning Network*, Washington, D.C.: Department of Health

US Department of State, Bureau of International Narcotics Matters (1992) *International Narcotics Control Strategy Report*, Washington, D.C.: Department of State

US Department of State, Bureau of International Narcotics Matters (1994) *International Narcotics Control Strategy Report, Executive Summary*, Washington, D.C.: Department of State

US Department of State, Bureau of International Narcotics and Law Enforcement Affairs (1996) *International Narcotics Control Strategy Report, Executive Summary*, Washington, D.C.: Department of State

US Department of the Treasury (1984) *Tax Havens in the Caribbean Basin*, Part 2, Washington, D.C.: GPO

Valencia Villa, A. (1992) *La humanización de la guerra: derecho internacional humanitario y conflicto armado en Colombia*, Bogotá: Tercer Mundo Editores

Van Der Vaeren, C. (1994) 'The International Drug Control Cooperation Policy of the European Community: A Personal View', *Bulletin on Narcotics*, Vol. XLVI, No. 2, pp. 1-7

Van Wert, J.M. (1988) 'The US State Department's Narcotics Control Policy in the Americas', *Journal of Interamerican Studies and World Affairs*, Vol. 30, Nos. 2 & 3 (Summer/Fall), pp. 5-18

Vargas, R. (ed.) (1994) *Drogas, poder y región en Colombia*, Bogotá: CINEP

Vargas Meza, R. (1995) *Políticas antidroga en Colombia 1986-1995: Prohibición, crisis institucional y ausencia de sociedad civil*, paper presented at CIIR seminar, London, 17 October (mimeo)

Wagstaff, A. and A. Maynard (1988) *Economic Aspects of the Illicit Drug Market and Drug Enforcement Policies in the United Kingdom*, London: HMSO

Walker III, W.O. (1989) *Drug Control in the Americas*, Albuquerque, N.M.: University of New Mexico Press

Walker III, W.O. (1991) *The Bush Administration's Andean Strategy in Historical Perspective*, paper presented at North/South Center, University of Miami, Florida conference, 13-15 June (mimeo)

Walker III, W.O. (1991) *US Drug Policy and Latin America*, paper presented at North/South Center, University of Miami, Florida conference, 13-15 June (mimeo)

Walker III, W.O. (1995) 'Drug Control and US Hegemony', in J.D. Martz (ed.), *United States Policy in Latin America: A Decade of Crisis and Challenge*, London: University of Nebraska, pp. 299-319

Walker III, W.O. (ed.) (1996) *Drugs in the Western Hemisphere: An Odyssey of Cultures in Conflict*, Wilmington, Del.: Scholarly Resources

Washington Office on Latin America (WOLA) (1991) *Clear and Present Dangers: The US Military and the War on Drugs in the Andes*, Washington, D.C.: WOLA

Washington Office on Latin America (WOLA) (1992) *Andean Initiative Legislative Update*, Washington, D.C.: WOLA

Washington Office on Latin America (WOLA) (1993) *Andean Initiative Legislative Update*, Washington, D.C.: WOLA

Williams, P. (1994) 'Transnational Criminal Organisations and International Security', *Survival*, Vol. 36, No. 1 (Spring), pp. 96-113

Williams, P. and C. Florez (1994) 'Transnational Criminal Organizations and Drug Trafficking', *Bulletin on Narcotics*, Vol. XLVI, No. 2, pp. 9-24

Williams, P. and E. Savona (eds.) (1996) *The United Nations and Transnational Organized Crime*, London: Frank Cass

Wish, E. (1990-91) 'US Drug Policy in the 1990s: Insights from New Data on Arrestees', *International Journal on Addictions*, Vol. 25, No. 3A, pp. 377-409

Zagaris, B. (1990) 'Developments in International Judicial Assistance and Related Matters', *Denver Journal of International Law*, Vol. 18, No. 3, pp. 339-86

INDEX